Creating and Delivering...

Totally
Awesome
Customer
Experiences©

The Art and Science of Customer Experience Mapping©

*"Discover the Secrets for Building a Powerful Revenue Architecture
to Increase Your Revenues and Create Lasting Customer Loyalty."*

Gary W. Millet
Blaine W. Millet

Library of Congress Cataloging-in-Publication Data

Millet, Gary W.
    Creating and delivering totally awesome customer experiences : the art and science of customer experience mapping / by Gary W. Millet and Blaine W. Millet. – 1st ed.
       p. cm.
    Includes index.
    Make a quantum leap beyond mere customer satisfaction using a powerful, proven, and measurable method that will delight your customers, ignite your associates and leave your competition far behind!
       ISBN: 1-881637-50-6
       1. Consumer satisfaction.   2. Customer services.   3. Customer loyalty.   I. Millet, Blaine W.
       II. Title.
HF5415.5.M55   2001   658.8'12
QBI01-201534

LCCN 2001099200

SAN 254-3222

First Edition

ATTENTION CORPORATIONS, COLLEGES, PROFESSIONAL ORGANIZATIONS AND ASSOCIATIONS:

Quantity discounts are available on bulk purchases of this book. For information, please contact Customer Experiences Inc. at 1-801-943-7342, 7810 South Prospector Drive, Salt Lake City, Utah 84121, **info@ceinc.info** or **http://www.customerexperiencesinc.com/**.

Dedication

While it goes without saying that this book is for Jessica, David, Alex, Jacque, Lorrie, Krystal, JB, Katrina, Joyce, Wayne and Iona, our immediate families...

Our extended families of Pete, Tula, Frank, Valerie, Lyn, Kelly, Dave, Marc, and Al count as well...

But this book is also dedicated to all the people who have gone to work day after day, believing they can make a difference in the world by how they treat, not just customers, but people...because it is the relationships we form in life that ultimately hold their value over any other possessions we ever seem to rent while we are here.

Acknowledgements

This is the hardest part of the book to write. A project this size requires the assistance and energy of many, many people. I hope I haven't accidentally left someone out. If so, please accept my apologies.

Let me begin by thanking my brother Blaine. It was his "think it all the way through" analytical mind that early-on helped to gel the concepts throughout this book. He then tested those concepts and tools for their practical application in organizations that he had studied and consulted. His editorial review comments were keen and sharp. He also has a great talent for pointing out holes and gaps that need to be filled and tied together. Blaine has forgotten more about the world of customer satisfaction surveying than most people have ever learned. His deep-rooted belief that merely satisfying a customer is simply an act of treading water and "hoping the competition doesn't out-do you" helped leverage the concepts behind understanding the empirical world of customer delight. Thanks, brother – wonderful to work with you!

A special thanks goes out to Robert Reid, whose complete dedication to delighting customers is overwhelming. He was very helpful in keeping our minds focused on helping the customer all the way through the entire process of writing the book and the chapter-by-chapter "reality check" he provided us. He was also instrumental and indispensable in getting this book ready for publishing. Robert, I can't thank you enough!

What can't I say about Lyn Johnson, the wonderful lady who not only wrote the Preface, but provided "spot on" critique, expanded ideas, and coordinated all the major graphics inside the book. She is simply one of the best friends a person could ever have. I appreciate the support and passion she develops for projects she believes have value. Thanks, Lyn, and thanks, Dave, for supporting Lyn's efforts!

I want to thank Brent Smith for lending us his restaurant for several weeks. I also need to thank him for the faith he showed by jumping feet-first into implementing the concepts and tools we showed him. (Thanks for the wonderful lunches, Brent, but you still owe me a Stout Kahalua Shake.) His comments in Chapter 7 were wonderful, and the readers will absolutely enjoy his tips in Chapter 10. Thanks, Brent!

We could not have done Chapter 8 without my friend Tim Harris. No matter what you ask this guy to do, he always had the same answer: "No problem." Thanks, Tim!

Sue Mackey's straightforward, honest comments and passion for reality are so refreshing that we now constantly need a "Sue fix" about every two weeks. Thank you so much for donating your great wisdom on the standards and performance measurement stuff in Chapter 10 – I appreciate you, Sue!

Drew Cherrington's excellent cover design makes this book exciting to pick up. We call him the "font king." Thanks, Drew!

Thanks to Jessica, the grammar queen, for always reminding me that "who" comes after someone and "that" comes after something. I must have been asleep in school during most of those sessions.

Wow, what a job Barbara, the "Editorial Empress." did getting the book ready for final reading. I absolutely love your keen eye, sense of perspective, and enthusiasm. I can't believe your "want to tell everyone in the world about the book" attitude. There is nothing like a true professional in your corner, especially when she is the "readers' advocate."

Kelly Clark, soon to be attorney-at-law Kelly Clark, spent hours editing the initial versions of this book, trying to help me write sentences everyone could read. I kept asking her, "What's wrong with 50-word sentences? They make sense to me." Thanks, Kelly!

Thanks so much to Jacque, Lyn, Thom, Sue, Joan, Ralph and Pam for doing a final read. We owe you all a new print cartridge.

Kudos to the hard-working, passionate staff at Buchanan Visual Communications – Shelly, Julie, Karry and David – who all made incredible contributions to a wonderfully finished book.

Sorry to my dog Saxon, the giant schnauzer who laid in my office continually for eight months wondering when I was going to get back to real life and start spending more time hiking.

I want to acknowledge all my friends and family who were positive in encouraging me to start this book and not demanding my time during the process. Thanks for your belief, encouragement and patience!

Finally, I want to thank all the people in the organizations we spoke with and wrote about in this book. They are the people who understand that customers are an organization's most valuable assets. Thanks for the inspiration and pioneering!

Gary

Foreword

As a result of September 11, 2001, our nation has been inspired by selfless acts of courage and unwavering humanitarianism and has experienced a resurgence of unprecedented national pride. This renewal of our best human attributes has triggered the emergence of a new national culture and business philosophy – a philosophy rich in humanism and caring. Already, simple terms like "customer service" are taking on new meaning. Anyone who was away from their home during this tragic time recognized the great human efforts made by everyone in the travel industry. The stories from countless travelers about the efforts of airlines, hotels, airports, cruise lines, and associated service personnel gives us a glimpse of the kind of customer experiences we are capable of delivering – when caring about a customer truly comes from the heart.

Integrating this new awesome level of customer experience delivery into our companies, however, can't ultimately rely on random acts of initiative and kindness. Truly great customer experiences must be both measurable and repeatable. Even if most of today's top executives believe that their company provides either good or even outstanding customer service and experiences, we all recognize that a "move heaven and earth for our customers" culture requires a solid road map everyone in the organization believes and can follow – a well-marked road map with numerous milestones to measure how far we have come and how far we have yet to travel.

Gary and Blaine have provided us with a way to create and deliver those road maps. *Creating and Delivering...Totally Awesome Customer Experiences* is insightful, timely and poignant. Their step-by-step analysis and customer experience mapping will guide you to providing the highest level of sustainable customer interactions and experiences possible.

The sooner you begin using the principles taught in this book to delight your customers, the sooner your work will become a much more delightful experience for you.

– Lyn Johnson
Executive Vice President
Marketing,
Buchanan Visual
Communications

Preface

Having 32 years of experience in serving the needs of Stakeholders (Associates, Customers, and Constituents), I have learned that there are two very basic principles that, if implemented well, almost guarantee the success and future of any organization whose objective is to serve the needs of Stakeholders.

The first principle demands that an organization focuses on the relationship it has with its Associates. When the Associates of an organization believe there is an environment of trust, openness, fairness and honesty and, when given the right tools, Associates will help create an environment where Stakeholders will have "…Totally Awesome Customer Experiences."

The second principle demands that all resources, in any organization, focus on the current needs, future needs and desires of the Customers. I have yet to meet any Executive Manager or any Associate within an organization who does not acknowledge that notionally their primary responsibility is to serve the needs of their Customers. Further, those same people realize that by effectively meeting the needs of their Customers, all Stakeholders will likewise be successful. I have, however, met Executive Managers and Associates who, in spite of their knowledge of knowing what they need to do and their desire to meet the needs of those they serve, did not either have the tools or the "know how" to implement and actualize such a Customer-focused culture within their organization.

Unfortunately, the grave reality is, it is extremely difficult to determine where to start in reshaping your organization towards a Customer-focused culture. Does one begin with Suppliers? Associates? Customers? Vision Statements? Mission Statements? Executives? It is a tough decision. Might I suggest that you begin with understanding the principles, analysis and, more importantly, the tools presented by Gary and Blaine Millet in, "Creating and Delivering Totally Awesome Customer Experiences." Gary and Blaine have compiled a most comprehensive guide with solid perspectives, principles and tools that actually work.

I would encourage you to take that first step on your personal Journey – read this book carefully. Then read it again. Then share this book with your Co-Workers and Support Managers. I quote Gary and Blaine, "All customers want delightful experiences, just as all organizations want loyal, satisfied and profitable customers, a strong brand and solid differentiation from their competition". It all begins with taking that first step on finding out how to get there.

Best wishes for much success in your Journey.

–Jack Schiefer
Sales Vice President –
Retired,
AT&T

Contents

Foreward

Preface

It's All About Experiences!

READING THIS BOOK...

You can read this book from two perspectives:

- To obtain a solid overview of the benefits, concepts, processes, and tools that create and deliver Totally Awesome Customer Experiences.

- As a daily reference guide on how to do it and how to implement it.

After you read the Awesome Customer Challenge, Chapters 1 and 2, our advice is to scan each subsequent chapter to see which sections best apply to your reading purpose. You can always come back and read for additional how-to detail.

Creating and Delivering...

Totally
Awesome
Customer
Experiences©

The Art and Science of Customer Experience Mapping©

It's All About Experiences!

At exactly 10:01 Saturday morning, Bob Williams entered Toys "R" Us. Bob was looking for a Barbie doll for his niece, Tawnya, who was turning nine years old that day. In fact, the birthday party was to begin at 12:30 p.m. sharp, and Bob had not yet purchased a present. Bob, like most men, knew very little about girls' dolls. This fact was never clearer to him than it was that Saturday morning at 10:10 a.m. as he stood in front of the immense doll section. It was overwhelming!

Bob immediately started his search by locating the Barbie dolls. He scrambled for the piece of paper his sister had given him with the name of the kind of Barbie doll Tawnya wanted. It was a *Cool Collecting Barbie Doll*®, but unknown to Bob, it happened to be a limited-edition, four-star, collectible Barbie doll. In plain English, these dolls sell like hotcakes and are often out of stock.

Bob was methodical in his search for the right Barbie. A third of the way through his search of the Barbie doll section, the unthinkable occurred. Bob encountered a big hole where the Cool Collecting Barbie Dolls should have been. He moved each doll aside, trying to find one that might have been misplaced. No luck.

A cold sweat ran down Bob's body as he checked his watch: 10:22. Did he have enough time to go to another store, find the Cool Collecting Barbie Doll, have it gift-wrapped, pick out a card, and make it to the birthday party (at least 40 minutes away) by 12:30? Then came the moment of mental gymnastics associated with the "favorite uncle" guilt trip. Maybe he should just pick out something else. Maybe Tawnya wouldn't notice. Maybe he could explain they didn't have any left. "What if I pick something she hates?" he thought. Then he remembered his sister telling him, "Whatever you do, make sure you get Tawnya the Cool Collecting Barbie Doll." He was stuck. He had to find that doll!

Rushing to the front to ask where the closest toy store was, he met Jeremy, a store clerk. "Do you know where the nearest toy store is?" Bob asked.

"In the South Towne Mall," replied Jeremy. "Is there something I can help you with?"

"No, I'm looking for this special Barbie doll called Cool Collecting Barbie

Doll, and you're all out. I desperately need to find this doll for my niece's birthday."

Jeremy quickly used his computer to check the in-store inventory. It showed they had one left. Jeremy came out from behind the counter. "Why don't we walk back to the Barbie section and see if we can find one that might have been misplaced?"

"I already did that," said Bob.

"This happens all the time," Jeremy said. "If you don't check the entire section, you can sometimes miss it."

Bob and Jeremy returned to the Barbie doll section. Jeremy carefully looked throughout the collection, trying to spot what Bob needed. "Sorry," said Jeremy, "I can't find it, either. Why don't you let me take a quick look in our storeroom in case someone just hasn't put it out or misplaced it?"

"Thanks," said Bob as he nervously paced, hoping Jeremy would be successful in his quest.

"None back there. Someone must not have recorded it in the computer," said Jeremy. "Let me call another one of our stores in the area. If they have it in stock, you can go pick it up."

"Here's the deal, Jeremy," Bob said. "I'm in a really big hurry, and I still have a 40-minute drive ahead of me once I find the doll."

"Where are you headed?"

"Centerville."

"Great. There are a couple of stores along the way. Let me take two minutes and see what I can do for you." Jeremy moved quickly to locate the phone numbers of the appropriate stores and give them a call.

It was now 10:45 as Bob once again looked nervously at his watch. "No luck," said Jeremy, "but let me call a couple of our competitors who specialize in collectible series of Barbie dolls. Maybe they have it." Jeremy took out what looked like a personal booklet and quickly started calling numbers.

On the third try, Jeremy looked at Bob with a big smile. "Found one!" he announced. It was 11:00 a.m. and Uncle Bob could not have been more relieved.

"Can you pay with a credit card?" asked Jeremy.

"Yes. Why do you ask?"

"If you give them your credit card number right now, they can have it waiting for you, all wrapped in a sack with the receipt, when you arrive. A

A customer experience crosses many aspects of an organization (some seen, some unseen). It's certain, however, that a customer sees his or her experience only in terms of a single event and judges the entire organization based on that single perception.

woman named Mary is helping us with this transaction from their end. I asked her to bring the gift outside. Give her a call on your cell phone just after you enter the parking lot. It will save you a lot of time if you don't have to get out of your car to pick up the gift. I also asked her to wrap the present for a 10-year-old girl. Is that about the right age?"

"She's nine," said Bob, "it will be perfect."

"Oh, by the way, here's 10 dollars of Toys "R" Us money, our birthday gift to your niece with our regrets that we didn't have the doll you wanted this morning." Jeremy then handed Uncle Bob a slip of paper with the directions to the competitor's toy store, along with Mary's number, and said, "Thanks so much for considering Toys "R" Us today for your niece's birthday present. I hope she has a delightful birthday – and you need to get out of here."

"Thank you very much, Jeremy. You've been a lifesaver!" Bob rushed out the door at 11:20 hurrying to pick up the Cool Collecting Barbie Doll, limited edition, so he could be a hero to his favorite niece on her ninth birthday.

We all relate to life through our experiences, whether business or personal. Uncle Bob's unique encounter with Toys "R" Us is just one example of thousands of Totally Awesome Customer Experiences delivered to customers every day. However, will Toys "R" Us repeatedly deliver the same Totally Awesome Customer Experience? Or was Uncle Bob's experience just one of those random acts of excellence he was fortunate enough to receive because he met up with Jeremy? The real question is, what will happen the next time Uncle Bob goes into Toys "R" Us?

One unique aspect of customer experiences is that they're rarely created and delivered by only one facet of an organization. The experience delivered to Uncle Bob by Jeremy in Customer Service came as a result of everyone's efforts at Toys "R" Us. Marketing produced the advertisements that got Uncle Bob into the store and provided him with the $10 of Toys "R" Us Dollars; merchandising helped Bob find his way back to the Barbie section; human resources facilitated Jeremy's hiring; training coached Jeremy in delivering the experience.

And so it goes. A customer experience crosses many aspects of an organization (some seen, some unseen). It's certain, however, that a customer sees his or her experience only in terms of a single event and judges the entire organization based on that single perception. For that reason, it is imperative for all departments in an organization to work together with a unified focus, that of concentrating on the customer.

This book will help your entire organization develop a solid process for creating and delivering consistent, repeatable Totally Awesome Customer

Once delighted customers form an emotional trust bond with your organization, they become proactive, passionate advocates who tell other potential customers how great you are.

Experiences, using a new and innovative tool called *Customer Experience Mapping*©. It also gives you a working framework and a common *customer experience language* base to assist you with your implementation. Warning: The customer experience language is purposefully overused in this book. We use it profusely and constantly to help reinforce its terms and their importance – but we promise that using this customer experience language inside your organization will greatly enhance your discussions, speed up your implementation, and make it easier for your employees to learn the process of creating and delivering Totally Awesome Customer Experiences.

This book will also help you deepen the relationships you have with your customers. It provides concepts, processes, and tools to strengthen your brand and build a hard-to-duplicate, lasting differentiation as you transform uninspired or merely satisfied customers into delighted customers. Once delighted customers form an emotional trust bond with your organization, they become proactive, passionate advocates who tell other potential customers how great you are.

AT THE END OF THE DAY...

Whether your organization is large or small; whether you primarily do business with other organizations or with individual customers; whether your business is brick and mortar or conducted via the Internet – the relationships you build and maintain with your customers are based on their experiences with you. All customers want delightful experiences, just as all organizations want loyal, profitable customers, a strong brand, and solid differentiation from their competition.

We wrote *Creating and Delivering...Totally Awesome Customer Experiences* to help you leverage your most valuable asset and your greatest investment opportunity – your customers. Our opportunity together is to make sure you have more delighted, loyal, profitable customers tomorrow than you have today – and more than your competitors.

Becoming an experience-based organization will help you consistently and repeatedly create and deliver the kind of customer experiences that will win the hearts, minds, and trust of your customers forever, providing the rewards customer-focused organizations justly deserve. Let's face it: if you don't, your competition eventually will.

We want to express our deepest and sincerest thanks for your trust and belief that we can help. We hope you will find reading and using this book a truly delightful experience, as well as helpful in providing the best in customer service to your customers.

The Awesome Customer Challenge

THE AWESOME CUSTOMER CHALLENGE

The most important assets of any organization are its customers. Without customers there are no revenues and no need to for any of its operations. The relationship an organization has with each of its customers greatly dictates the overall success of that organization in both the short and long term. With customers having more and more alternatives in the market place and hungry competitors just waiting for the chance for snatch up customers, it becomes more and more critical that every organization build itself a "Revenue Architecture" that leverages its customer focus, relationship, and brand into building customer experiences that translate into an emotional trust bond between the customer and the organization that translates directly into increased revenues and powerful customer loyalty.

American Express found that 43% customers having a positive experience with them use their credit card more often.

What is Revenue Architecture?

Revenue Architecture is the framework for consistently and continuously driving greater revenues while building strong customer loyalty. This framework should be utilized to launch and coordinate all the interactions or "customer experiences" an organization creates and delivers to its customers. Revenue Architecture specifically defines the paths by which an organization acquires and retains customers, increases customer response rates, and promotes deeper customer relationships – all while strengthening its brand. Revenue Architecture also provides the roadmap for investing and managing various operational and informational support systems that are necessary to deliver the ultimate experience to the customer. Our research shows that a failure to build an adequate Revenue Architecture leaves an organization's vulnerable to random acts of excellence and chaos, and rapid customer migration– both of which have very negative effects on profitability.

Customer experiences are the cornerstone of any Revenue Architecture. The more solid and predictable the customer experiences, the more solid and predictable the Revenue.

REVENUE ARCHITECTURE

You will notice, on the following page, the foundation of a Revenue Architecture is "being Customer Focused" and "having a Customer Trust Currency." It is upon this foundation that an organization can leverage its brand (Making Promises Customers Want and Delivering On Those Promises) into creating and delivering Totally Awesome Customer Experiences that form an

"Emotional Trust Bond," resulting in Delighted Customers that drive Increased Revenues and Greater Customer Loyalty. This of course begs the question...

How important is customer loyalty?

The advent of creating deeper customer relationships provides financial leverage and longevity. The true formation of an emotional trust bond with your customers provides the highest degree of differentiation and evokes the most powerful marketing program an organization can have, word-of-mouth.

In survey after survey, customer loyalty ranks as one of the top five concerns of CEOs and other top executives in an organization. Building and sustaining customer loyalty has long been one of the key strategic focuses of top organizations. From a relationship perspective, most people will agree that loyalty is an extremely important attribute. If an organization is going to manage its customer relationships and protect itself against raiding competitors, loyalty stands at the top of this very short list.

Unfortunately loyalty is not something an organization itself can acquire or create. Loyalty must be earned one customer at a time. In the purest sense, loyalty means being steadfast in your allegiance brought on by devotion, love, or vows to a person, an organization, a cause or principles. The creation of loyalty is an emotional event. It requires an emotional trust bond to be forged between the customer and the organization. The strength of loyalty's bonds comes with time and the experiences a customer has with the organization. Sometimes loyalty bonds don't outwardly appear logical.

Regardless, however, those emotional trust bonds represent the overall strength of those relationships.

From strategic perspective, why do organizations want or even care if they have loyal customers? What benefits does an organization derive from loyal customers?

For starters, loyal customers and expanded financials success are clearly linked. Consider. . .

- Research shows that organizations could increase their revenues by 85 percent if they could retain 5 percent more of their best customers.

- On the average, 60 percent to 70 percent of an organization's current customers will purchase goods and services during the year, while only 20 percent to 40 percent of lapsed customers will make purchases. Only 5 percent to 20 percent of new prospects will purchase anything from the organization.

- Most organizations realize that 80 percent of their business is generated by 20 percent of their customers. It's much more desirable to sell fewer loyal customers more products and services.

- On the average, it costs organizations fives times more (in just money) to acquire a new customer than to retain an existing one.

Loyal customers are also critical in the longevity of any organization. Consider. . .

- Delighted customers tell at least four other people about their experiences. Dissatisfied customers tell ten. Uninspired customers most likely tell no one.

In a health insurance study, it was determined that less than 13 percent of plan participants were loyal to their health plans, while less than 21 percent were considered loyal to their physicians. This means 87 percent and 79 percent of the plan participants weren't loyal to either their health plans or physicians! According to the study, of those plan participants who were loyal, their loyalty was a result of the personal relationships they had built with the health care centers and physicians. These people named trust as the single biggest factor at the center of those loyal relationships. Those plan participants who did express their loyalty said they were "very happy" with their overall experiences.

In short, the formation of loyalty requires the strength of emotional side of a relationship.

This brings up the next key question. . .

Satisfied customers are not loyal customers. Over 70% of all customers are in flux, just waiting for the next best deal...creating loyal customers can significantly reduces the number of your customers in flux as well as help you capture those in flux of your competitors.

Are satisfied customers loyal customers?

The word "satisfied" means desiring no more than what you have or ready to accept or acquiesce or being content. There's no passion in the word "satisfied." There's no emotional side creating the need to act or react – no reason to do anything except evaluate your contentment. In contrast to the word "satisfied" is the word "delight." It means giving or taking pleasure or joy. Delight carries with it passion, energy, and direction. So when we ask, "Are merely satisfied customers loyal customers?" The answer is "No!" Consider...

- Thomas O Jones and W Earl Sasser, Jr., in "Why Satisfied Customers Defect," agree that satisfied customers are not loyal customers. Jones and Sasser believe satisfied customers are neutral in their feelings towards an organization. Although they may like the product or service, they're just waiting for the next best deal to come along. These writers say that only totally satisfied customers (we call them delighted customers) are loyal because the relationship has progressed to the point where the customers believe the organizations really cares about them.

- A Xerox-sponsored research project on customer satisfaction concluded that delighted customers were six times more likely to continue purchasing products and services than customers who were merely satisfied. The study indicated that merely satisfying customers did not keep them loyal.

Billions of dollars are spent each year on customer satisfaction initiatives and loyalty programs, yet consider...

- The average organization loses 20 to 50 percent of its customers every year. In technology organizations, those figures are even higher. Customer turnover costs organizations billions of dollars each year.

- O'Brien and Jones, in "Do Rewards Really Create Loyalty?" indicate that most organizations today use loyalty programs and customer satisfaction incentives to promote or market their goods and services to new customers rather than designing their programs to create and sustain real loyalty. They believe that until this practice stops, there will be no ROI associated with loyalty program investments.

Are organizations at risk from not having loyal customers?

We have established that loyal customers are important, and that merely satisfied customers are not loyal. It stands to reason that if an organization's customer base is composed of impassionate, uninspired, merely satisfied customers, that organization is at risk of losing its most valuable asset to little more than a competitor who just comes along with a better deal. This lack of customer loyalty differentiation places an organization in fiscal danger and compromises its long-term profitability and viability.

What needs to happen?

An organization's objective should be to stop investing in efforts that will only satisfy their customers, and start investing in activities that will make them loyal. We know loyalty comes from building and maintaining emotionally binding relationships in which customers are consistently and repeatedly delighted in their experiences with the organization.

Those organizations that invest in delighting their customers to create and maintain an emotional trust bond with their customers will realize all of the true benefits only loyal customers can bring to an organization. These organizations will find it increases their revenues and lowers cost of building and maintaining customer relationships; compared to generating lower levels of revenues per customer while bearing the excessive cost of constantly having to acquire new customers in order to replace the impassionate, uninspired, merely satisfied customers who annually defect.

In our present society, the exciting reality is that the majority of customers are in flux. This means customers are either in some state of satisfaction or migration from one organization to another. This state brings tremendous opportunity to acquire large market share and hold onto that market share by creating loyal customers. The other key opportunity factor is one of control. Customers are now in more control of how they think, feel, and act than ever before. The norm has delightfully become the old Burger King tagline, "Have it your way." Customers will ultimately decide what they want and will buy. Customers will continue to gain increased access to greater numbers of offerings through different mediums over the next decade. This access will only accelerate customer influence and control over the offerings they wish to receive and accept.

Organizations that stand ready to respond to this challenge of delighting their customers will increase their market position, while those organizations trying to force their merely satisfying offerings onto customers will lose their market position. This repositioning is already taking place. Organizations are constantly exploring innovative ways to provide customers with unique experiences and offerings. Technology, linked with the human spirit, has ushered in what Patricia Seybold calls The Customer Revolution. Her book by the same name, along with Pine and Gilmore's book The Experience Economy, identifies and marks the beginning of a customer-centric era. This will be an era in which every customer will not only expect, but also demand that organizations present their offerings through customer experiences…tailored specifically to them.

Customers will expect organizations to understand their needs and desires and take them beyond being merely satisfied. Customers will want relevant and valuable offerings that not only fulfill their unique needs, desires, and dreams, but also delight them—quickly. Any organization not up to this task will struggle to differentiate itself from its competition and ultimately lose its most valuable assets: its customers.

People like Pine and Gillmore, Seybold, and others have identified this new customer or experience economy. They are right on target when they predict that an organization's success, in the future, will start and end with the customer. Customers are the most valuable assets within an organization. The customer is also the ultimate investment opportunity for any organization.

But recognizing that customers are an organization's most valuable assets and writing it on a mission statement plaque hanging in the reception area isn't enough. It's one thing to talk about the dream of a customer or experience economy, but it's another to create and deliver it from every department and employee within an organization. This leaves every organization with the need to meet the Awesome Customer Challenge to make its dream of a new customer economy come true…

*The Awesome Customer Challenge is to **stop merely satisfying** your customers and build a consistent and repeatable process to **start delighting** them. Delighting customers will fulfill the dream of creating a new customer or experience economy in which you can achieve customer loyalty, deepened customer relationships, stronger brand, and solid differentiation. Anything less will fall victim to your competitive forces.*

MEETING THE AWESOME CUSTOMER CHALLENGE

The only way to meet the Awesome Customer Challenge is by creating an experience-based organization. This means that an organization must have a foundation in which it believes that the customer is its most valuable asset and the organization must trust and be trusted by the customer.

What is the importance of becoming an experience-based organization?

Only experience-based organizations can consistently create and sustain delighted customers, a process which builds an effective Revenue

Architecture, which in turn builds greater revenues and loyal customers; only experience-based organizations let their customers tell them what is Acceptable, Relevant, and Valuable, and what promises they want the organization to make and keep; only an experience-based organization can effectively generate the kinds of customer experiences needed to form that all important emotional trust bond that leads to customer delight; and only experience-based organizations strategically place themselves in a position to use their operations and resources to support and leverage the customer experiences they create and deliver into increased revenues and customer loyalty.

This experience-based organizational behavior is in bold contrast to traditional operational-based organizations that believe a focus on improved operations will automatically generate the customer experiences necessary to create satisfied customers who somehow magically transform themselves into loyal customers.

Speaking of magic...when Walt Disney first designed Disneyland and the Magic Kingdom, his entire concept was experience-based. Anything operational that went into building Disneyland was a result of Disney's overwhelming drive to make families' and kids' experiences come alive. Disneyland's real product was to be its experiences. Disneyland even decided to call its employees "cast members."

Being experience-based is not always easy. Disney faced a lot of tough questions. How do you make believable wild animals? How do you make a Mississippi paddlewheel steamboat? How exactly do you go about building a big castle in the middle of Anaheim, California? The design of Disneyland-like theme parks had never been done before. By keeping his focus on customers' experiences, Disney finally came up with his brilliant idea of creating five unique experiences for customers. They would be the five uniquely different lands of Main Street, U.S.A, Adventureland, Frontierland, Fantasyland, and Tomorrowland.

Had Walt Disney listened to the operations people in terms of their perspective of what they considered possible, rather than keeping his organization and dream experience-based, Disneyland might never have turned out to be – well – Disneyland, having loyal Disneyland customers telling everyone on earth, "You can wish upon a star."

What is required to become an experience-based organization?

Becoming an experience-based organization takes vision, courage, enthusiasm, and two fundamental organizational foundation changes...

Experience-based organizations have the edge. They have built a Revenue Architecture that not only leverages increased revenues and greater customer loyalty, but acts as a guide to reduce unneeded operating costs that don't do anything to advance their success.

Fortune Magazine says that an 85% of dissatisfied customers tell 9 people, while 13% tell 20 people. However, a satisfied customer tells only 5 people. How many customers would a delighted customer tell?

Change #1 – Become and Enjoy Being Customer-Focused

There are two types of organizations: customer-focused and customer-manipulative. A customer-focused organization does everything in its power to provide its customers with the offerings and experiences they need to be delighted. A customer-manipulative organization tries to convince its customers they'll be satisfied in buying the products or services the organization wants to sell.

Change #2 – Develop and Use Customer Trust Currency

Customers are an organization's most valuable assets. The information an organization's knows about its customers and what it does with that knowledge in its relationship with the customer is its Customer Relationship Currency©. There are three levels of customer relationship currencies employed by organizations. They are: Customer Information Currency©, Customer Knowledge Currency©, and Customer Trust Currency©. Each type of currency has different purposes, powers and outcomes and is explained in detail in Chapter 2. Suffice it to say that each customer relationship currency also requires different levels of investment to develop.

Deeper and stronger individual customer relationships are the key benefits to any organization that progresses in its level of its customer relationship currency. Building customer relationships on the Customer Trust Currency level result in the formation of customer loyalty, strong brand equity, and the development of a unique type of differentiation that competitors have great difficulty in duplicating.

With those two changes in place, an organization can use this book's concepts, processes, and tools to build a very powerful Revenue Architecture. For it is only through translating customer-wanted promises into customer wanted realities using Totally Awesome Customer Experiences that a Revenue Architecture can ever deliver delighted customers that drive increased revenues and greater customer loyalty…creating the unique advocate who uses the most powerful marketing tool in the world, word-of-mouth on your behalf…this is what Meeting the Awesome Customer Challenge is all about. The Awesome Customer Challenge is now up to You!

One last comment. . .

This book focuses on the single biggest component to creating a solid Revenue Architecture, which is the creating and delivering of Totally Awesome Customer Experience Experiences. Failure to master the repeatability and consistency of your customer experiences will leave your

Revenue Architecture vulnerable to random acts of excellence and chaos by employees that cause customer confusion, brand erosion and loss of revenue and customer loyalty.

This book shows you how to master a very powerful, easy-to-use tool called Customer Experience Mapping©. Its mastery is fundamental to creating and delivering consistent and repeated Totally Awesome Customer Experiences, which are the cornerstone of any robust and effective Revenue Architecture.

Chapter 1

Are You Customer-Focused or Customer-Manipulative?

"An enterprise which wishes to endure over a long period of time and to remain in a healthy and growing state would certainly want a non-manipulative, trusting relationship with its customers rather than the relationship of the quick fleecing, never to see them again."

Abraham H. Maslow,
Maslow on Management

Trust, the cornerstone of any relationship, is the key word in Maslow's quote. Trust is integral to being customer-focused because it produces an organization that not only encourages the customer to participate in the control of the experience but also develops a product to delight the customer. For this reason, the Awesome Customer Challenge requires that you combine being customer-focused with developing a Customer Trust Currency. Once you combine these elements, trust will become a powerful differentiator and the cornerstone to your brand. Your organization's ability to consistently deliver on its promises will create what we call the Customer-Focused Reality.

BECOMING CUSTOMER-FOCUSED

To become customer-focused, trust must become a key part of the foundation of your organization. Dr. Peter Keen, in an article called "Are You Ready for the Trust Economy?", said:

> In a trust economy, partners must change the nature of their contractual relations with each other. Otherwise, the term is just an empty cliché. In conventional "ex-post" contracts, the parties lay out who is legally liable if something goes wrong, and how that is to be determined; the contract provides the base for a court to decide. Trust economies require "ex-ante" contracting, which accepts that things often will go wrong and aims at working together and ending the fault-liability mentality.
>
> Loyalty must work both ways in a trust economy...executives also need to understand there are two dimensions of trust: *trustworthiness* as a value and *trustability* as a skill. Trustworthiness is about sincerity and honesty. Trustability is about reliability, dependability, and competence. There are many concerns about trustworthiness in electronic relationships – deception on the

Executives need to understand there are two dimensions of trust: trustworthiness as a value and trustability as a skill.

Internet, hackers, viruses, authentication, digital signatures and the like. There are now far more concerns about trustability.

Although Keen is renowned in the Information Technology field, his comments seem to transcend every aspect of the organization's culture and being. Trustworthiness and trustability are a necessary basis for creating and delivering Totally Awesome Customer Experiences.

A customer-focused organization presents a sharp contrast to one that is customer-manipulative. Customer-manipulative organizations earn little trust from their customers. They want to maintain full control over their customers' experiences. They're basically trying to convince their customers they'll be satisfied with the experiences and product/services the organization has to offer them. Customer-manipulative organizations don't have loyal customers and never have trust as a key differentiator.

To be customer-focused you need to understand the process in which products and services are developed and delivered to the customer.

Another great way to understand what being *customer-focused* is all about is to understand the process in which products and services are developed and delivered to the customer.

The Traditional Operational Value Chain (Value Chain) depicts the process by which many organizations deliver their goods and services to their customers. It shows that an organization is a complete system, made up of inputs, processes, and outputs. The inputs, transformation processes, and outputs represent the acquisition and consumption of resources, such as money, labor, materials, equipment, buildings, land, administration, and management (basically anything your organization buys, uses, and ultimately delivers to the customer). How the organization performs the Value Chain activities determines the costs and profits of the organization.

An organization's traditional operational flow uses a Value Chain that looks like this…

Traditional Operational Value Chain
(Customer-Manipulative Value Chain)

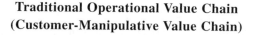

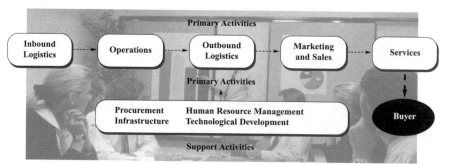

The Traditional Value Chain Model depicts organizations that are customer-manipulative.

Even the smallest organizations engage in hundreds of activities in the process of converting inputs (things they buy) into outputs (things they sell). These required activities could be divided into two groups called primary and support activities.

The primary activities are:

1. **Inbound Logistics** – The relationships with suppliers that include all the activities required to receive, store, and disseminate inputs.

2. **Operations** – Activities required to transform inputs into outputs (products and services delivered to the customer).

3. **Outbound Logistics** – Activities required to collect, store, and distribute the output (getting products and services to the customer).

The supporting activities are:

4. **Marketing and Sales** – Activities that inform buyers about products and services, induce buyers to purchase them, and facilitate their purchase (in this case convincing them the organization has what the customer should buy).

5. **Service** – Activities required to keep the product or service working effectively for the buyer after it's sold and delivered (customer service).

6. **Buyer** – The consumer of the goods and services at the end of the process.

The mere reference to the word "buyer" completely strips the humanity away from the true person at the end of the Value Chain – the "customer."

Customer-manipulative organizations take the position that they can better decide on the products and services a buyer wants or needs than the buyer. Their business model follows the traditional operational Value Chain by starting with engineering, moving to development, then to marketing, then to sales, and then to the buyer. In essence, a customer-manipulative organization desires all of the control and wants to dictate to buyers what they should want or need. Why? Because that's what they've decided to sell! The mere reference to the word "buyer" completely strips the humanity away from the true person at the end of the Value Chain – the "customer."

A great example of this operational Value Chain in action occurred when Coca-Cola initially released its New Coke product. It flopped, and it flopped big. New Coke was created and released as a counter-measure to the taste tests Pepsi was conducting with blindfolded customers. It was called the "Pepsi Challenge." Not understanding that the taste of Classic Coke had everything to do with the Coca-Cola experience, Coca-Cola released a new taste formula for the most revered brand in the history of carbonated beverages.

The consistency in the Coke experience was immediately lost! New Coke was a disaster. Customers who loved their Coca-Cola experience (which included the taste of Classic Coke) rebelled. The message many loyal Coca-Cola drinkers received was, "Oh, sorry, loyal Coca-Cola drinkers. You've been drinking an inferior-tasting soft drink for a 115 years. Thank heaven we finally fixed it for you."

We believe this incident was a failure of Coca-Cola to understand that the consistent taste of Classic Coke was one of the anchors of the Coca-Cola experience. Not only did the taste of Classic Coke represent Coca-Cola's brand, but it was also the taste customers had counted on for over a century. In the end, the customers voted for Classic Coke over New Coke, hands down.

In all the years of being a customer-focused company, Coca-Cola temporarily forgot their customers knew more about what they wanted in their Coca-Cola experience than the company did. They fell prey to the traditional Value Chain thinking – company-oriented versus customer-oriented. There are hundreds of examples of organizations that on occasion believe they know more about what the customer wants than the customer and become manipulative. What happened to Mac Pizza, Adidas cologne, and LifeSavers Gum?

Manipulation is a human trait and is highly dependent on motive.

Manipulation is a human trait. When we speak here of customer manipulation or being customer-manipulative, however, we refer to organizations that unduly influence, manage, arrange, or control the customer *without* the objective of creating customer delight. These organizations are primarily interested in selling their products or services by convincing customers they should buy them.

Manipulation is highly dependent on motive. When relationships are not anchored with trust, manipulation can easily take place. Manipulation places a wall between the vendor and the customer. When relationships are anchored with trust, customer-fucus means arranging, influencing and managing the resources of the organization to delight the customer – and there is no wall between the vendor and customer.

Customers may not always act logically or in accordance with all the textbooks on marketing, but one thing is certain: customers are the judges of what they want and what they don't want. Customers have the power to decide if an organization's offering will ever make it. Basically, customers are in control, and customer-focused organizations are excited about that fact.

In the Customer-Focused Value Chain, an organization begins with the customers (listening to their needs), proceeding through marketing (translating needs into desired offerings), then into product development (designing products and services for those offerings). Engineering comes next (producing the products and services the customer wants). Finally, the process goes back to marketing and sales and then to the customer. The key to an effective Customer-Focused Value Chain is listening and asking your customers relevant questions about what experiences and offerings they want. It's easy to get into the rut of simply thinking you know what the customer wants, thereby slipping into being customer-manipulative. That's a prime example of why customers don't trust organizations.

Customer-focused organizations use the power of the traditional operational Value Chain in reverse! We call it the Customer-Focused Value Chain.

Customer-Focused Value Chain

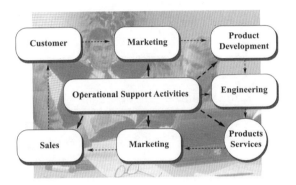

Is your organization customer-focused or customer-manipulative?

Question	Yes	No
1. If outsiders were to read your organization's strategic or business plan, would they say that the customer is the primary focus of that plan? Could they say that your plan is not based primarily on financial and operational objectives?		
2. Does your organization selectively decide its customer audiences (versus taking business from anyone)?		
3. Is your business plan built around selected customer audiences?		
4. Does your organization collect information about its selected customer audiences with the primary intent of using the information to create customer-focused products and service offerings, rather than using inside or consulting expertise to create products and offers?		
5. Does your organization present its offerings to its customers via customer experiences?		

(Continued on next page)

Question	Yes	No
6. Does your top management behave in a customer-focused way in their treatment of your customers?		
7. Does your organization periodically do a review of the experiences created and delivered by your competition?		
8. Has your organization diagrammed its customer experience process down through each department level?		
9. Does your organization separate experience transactions from operational transactions and treat them differently?		
10. Does your organization go through a formal process of building customer experiences?		
11. Does your organization audit the customer experiences it delivers for consistency and coordination among all departments?		
12. Can each employee in the organization describe the organization's customer vision and his or her role in that vision?		
13. Is employee performance measured and compensation directly tied to delighting or satisfying the customer?		
14. Has your organization defined the standards and measurements to determine what is delighting or satisfying the customer?		
15. Does every employee know the standards and the specific activities required to deliver an experience in accordance to the standards?		

Count the number of questions you were able to answer with a "yes." You can use the scale below to get a sense of how customer-focused your organization is today.

# Of Yes Answers	Customer-Focus Level
11–15	Your organization is customer-focused and has already made Change 1 happen. Congratulations! Your organization is ready to take full advantage of Customer Experience Mapping.

# Of Yes Answers	Customer-Focus Level
6–10	Areas of your organization are both customer-focused and customer-manipulative. Consistency is your challenge. Check your strategic planning process. You might find it to be more operationally- and organizationally-focused than customer-focused. A good indicator is to count up the number of times the word "customer" appears in your strategic plan. Do the same for your annual report. The good news is that you recognize the need to be more customer-focused. Customer Experience Mapping can help you progress more rapidly.
0–6	Your organization is most likely customer-manipulative. The organization probably behaves as if it knows what is best for the customer. It creates products and services it believes the customer will buy, but is not willing to give up control to the customer. Employees are most likely trained more on executing operations than on executing experiences. Management might say they're customer-focused, but their actions indicate otherwise. You should have management members read the Seybold, Pine and Gilmore books (see page 5) first.

Was the evaluation helpful? Did it help you isolate some of the areas in which your organization needs improving? How easy is it now to detect organizations that are customer-manipulative versus organizations that are customer focused?

DEVELOPING A CUSTOMER TRUST CURRENCY

Customer Relationship Currency is the overall knowledge you have and use in order to conduct business with your customers. There are three levels of Customer Relationship Currency: *Information*, *Knowledge*, and *Trust*. Each level carries with it certain benefits and costs. An organization needs to assess its present Customer Relationship Currency in order to develop a clear understanding of what it needs to develop **Customer Trust Currency**.

Today, most organizations operate at the Customer Information Currency level. They collect and use customer information for the purpose of delivering their product and services to the customer. The organization uses its own insight and assumptions to predict what will satisfy the customer.

Recently, more enlightened and aggressive organizations have discovered the power of Customer Knowledge Currency. They create Customer Knowledge Currency by transforming Customer Information Currency into Customer Knowledge Currency, using a path of systems and processes such as CRM (Customer Relationship Management), SFA (Sales Force Automation), data mining, and customer profiling. Customer Knowledge Currency delivers a far greater understanding of the customer's needs, enabling an

Customer Relationship Currency:

The level of knowledge you have about your customers in order to conduct business with them.

Customer Trust Currency:

The customer has formed an emotional trust bond with the organization so that the customer knows that the organization will use all the knowledge an organization has collected to consistently create and deliver Totally Awesome Customer Experiences.

organization to create and deliver more tailored product and service offerings that have higher acceptance rates and can predictably satisfy more customers and deepen relationships.

The Customer Trust Currency level is where a positive emotional trust bond forms between the customer and your organization.

You can create delighted customers only at the Customer Trust Currency level. This level of Customer Relationship Currency is a true "spendable currency" because it gives you the ability to directly ask your customers what they need and to get a truthful answer. When this emotional trust bond is formed, customers know that you'll use the knowledge your organization has collected about them to consistently create and deliver Totally Awesome Customer Experiences. They know their experiences will contain highly relevant and valuable offerings that will never jeopardize their privacy and trust.

Customer Knowledge Currency:

The business currency where an organization accumulates customer knowledge in order to create and deliver more tailored product and service offerings that have higher acceptance rates.

This level of Customer Relationship Currency is obtained through the transformation of **Customer Knowledge Currency** using a path of Customer Experience Mapping. This tool provides the consistency and repeatability required to attain this highest level of Customer Trust Currency.

The Customer Relationship Currency Model on the following page shows the three levels of Customer Relationship Currency, their purpose, outcomes, and means of progression from one level to the next.

Note that moving from one level of Customer Relationship Currency to another level requires two things:

- **First**, you must recognize that customer information and knowledge have value in more effectively interacting with customers and in building better offers and experiences that lead to greater levels of satisfaction and delight.

- **Second**, you must have the right path containing the proper tools to leverage that value.

Raising your Customer Relationship Currency level provides significant direct benefits: such as increased customer response rates, lower marketing and sales costs per customer, and deeper customer relationships.

Coupling a strong customer focus with Customer Trust Currency provides the formula to improve customer ROI while delighting customers. It also provides great motivation for operational-based organizations to raise their level of Customer Relationship Currency in order to become an experience-based organization.

Customer Focus + **Customer Trust Currency** = **Increased Customer ROI**

Customer Relationship Currency Model

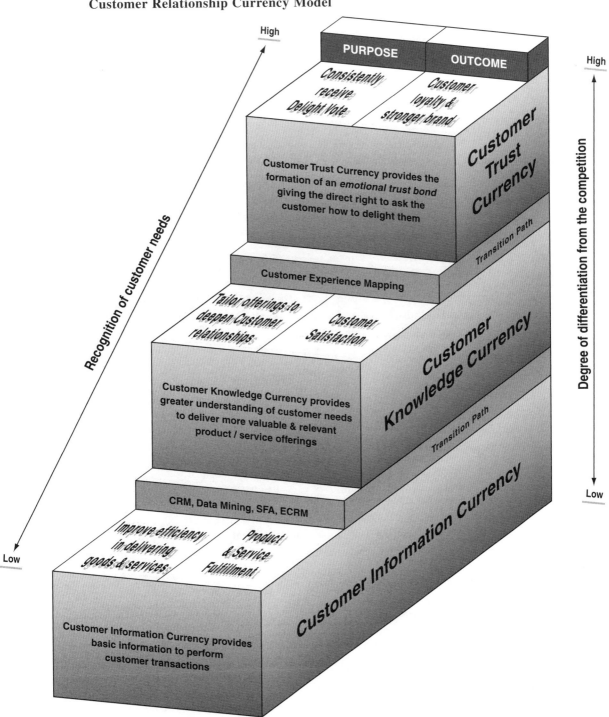

What is your organization's Customer Relationship Currency level?

Question	Yes	No
1. If we ask your customers to tell us the first word they think of when they think of your organization, would that first word be "trust"?		
2. Would you say your organization calls for the creation of trust as a key differentiator in your strategic planning?		
3. Would you say the word "trust" is a common word within your organization to the point of being strategic?		
4. Does your organization use trust as the true basis of its relationship with its customers?		
5. Does the relationship between your organization or your sales force and with the majority of its customers contain a strong emotional trust bond?		
6. Does your organization gather information about a customer to directly enhance the experience or offers to your customer, rather than merely for the purposes of transacting business?		
7. Does your organization have deep enough relationships with its customers that you have the moral authority to directly ask them about their needs and receive truthful answers under the belief those answers will be used for their benefit?		
8. Does your organization tie its brand promises directly to the brand experiences it delivers to your customers?		
9. Does your organization presently measure the outcome of each brand experience against its brand promises, and feed the information back to the respective departments for experience improvement?		
10. If we ask your customers to tell us how private they feel you keep the information they give you, would the majority of your customers tell us "it is perfectly safe and private?"		

Count the number of questions you were able to answer "Yes." Use the scale below to determine your Customer Relationship Currency level.

# Of Yes Answers	Customer Relationship Currency Level
8–10	Your organization is at the Customer Trust Currency Level. Coupled with being customer-focused, you should be able to easily use Customer Experience Mapping to consistently create and deliver Totally Awesome Customer Experiences and transition to an experience-based organization.
	This level delivers loyal customers and the greatest level of differentiation from your competition. Most likely your brand is strong and keeps getting stronger.

# Of Yes Answers	Customer Relationship Currency Level
4–7	Your organization is at the Customer Knowledge Currency Level. You now gather customer information through many different operational means, in many different areas of your organization. You might have even implemented systems like CRM, data mining, SFA, and ECRM to accelerate the process. Your company now views customer knowledge as an asset and a means to acquire, retain, and motivate customers. You place emphasis on making sure that brand experiences are matching up to brand promises. Your organization has taken a vital step in moving itself towards being experienced-based.
	This is a big step up from Customer Information Currency, but you still have much to do to integrate the emotional side with the knowledge side to transition to the Customer Trust Currency level. The Customer Experience Mapping process will help seamlessly integrate those two sides together.
0–3	Your organization is at the Customer Information Currency Level. You use customer information primarily to transact business with your customers. Most of the products and services you render are created by people inside your organization or by outside professional help. You may use customer survey cards, but the information isn't very helpful; it serves more as a barometer on how your employees are doing than as a measure of customer delight. Most likely, your organization is operational-based.
	You should give serious thought to how to give more control to your customers in letting them help with the products and services they want and in improving your organization.

Was the evaluation helpful? Did it help you isolate some of the areas in which your organization needs improving? Is it easier to think of organizations that have a Customer Trust Currency in operation? How easy is it now to detect organizations that do not?

MERGING CUSTOMER-FOCUS WITH CUSTOMER TRUST CURRENCY

"Trust" is one of those words that require further explanation. As with most words that are emotional in nature, its definition and context tend to be rooted in people's personal experiences. This fact makes defining such words a bit difficult.

For our purposes, we define "trust" as "two or more people engaged in a transaction or experience whereby outcomes are highly likely and very predictable." Let us also make the point that trust is not gained by any one-time event. Trust is built through a relationship between people who are always testing the veracity and durability of that relationship. Customers come to

Leveraging the new customer economy will come easily for customer-focused organizations using Customer Trust Currency to share control of the customer experience with their customers.

trust an organization when the actions and behaviors of that organization become consistent with their promises. Likewise, the trust between an organization and a customer increases as that organization continues to prove their loyalty.

There are three methods by which people enter into trust relationships.

- The **first** occurs when one party gives trust, as they define trust, without necessarily knowing the rules of trust held by the other party. They are generally seeking a match to their definition of trust while validating the trust over time. (The majority of these relationships end up in disappointment.)

- The **second** method involves going into a relationship distrusting each other while trying to understand the definition of trust in that relationship and proving that trust is warranted. (The majority of these relationships never work, for they never overcome the distrust.)

- The **third** and most productive method is entering into a relationship with neutral feelings, mutual respect, and a basic understanding of the promises made. Each party carefully measures their experiences to substantiate the promises and validate the trust. (This solid method is somewhat slow, but most often yields the best long-term results.)

Organizations show respect for the customer by sharing control of their experiences and by keeping their promises. By meeting these expectations, the organization builds mutual trust with the customer.

The market is made up of existing customers and potential customers. No matter how minor a contributor a customer is at the present time, each is a member of your overall organization. They deserve respect simply because they participate in your organization. When your organization reaches out to existing customers and makes them feel important, customers quickly and positively respond.

Once the customer feels valued as an important part of your organization, he or she will contribute to the growth of your organization. This contribution cements the customer's resolve because it validates his or her decision. This customer validation becomes a strong, driving, passionate force. They subsequently pass their passion and drive to other potential customers. In doing so, each customer once again becomes even more important and further resolved in thinking that he or she made the right decision. This customer validation cycle works powerfully in acquiring, retaining, and motivating customers.

As we mentioned earlier, the customers who loved the Classic Coke experience weren't interested in the New Coke product. They had trust in their association with Coca-Cola and knew what it meant and how it felt to be a Coke drinker. They trusted that a Coke would taste like a Coke all the time, every time. They could trust the taste, they could trust the organization, and they could trust the experience. They voted their experience over the promise of the taste of a new product. Coca-Cola had temporarily lost its customer focus!

George MacDonald once said, "To be trusted is a greater compliment than to be loved."

The bottom line is that customers are real, feeling people, each with an identity by which he or she wants to be recognized. The late Mary Kay Ash, founder of Mary Kay Cosmetics, once said, "Everyone has an invisible sign hanging from their neck saying, 'Make me feel important.' Never forget this message when working with people."

A customer-manipulative organization uses its customers' identities to devise gimmicks, tricking them into thinking the organization cares. Sooner or later customers discover that the organization has no real respect for them. Eventually their relationship with that organization collapses as customers move to another organization in hopes of finding a more trusting relationship. If they can't find one, then they simply use price and availability as determining factors until they do find one.

TRUST IS THE DIFFERENTIATOR

Dr. Keen says, "Trust relates to a complex mix of forces: reliability of operations, keeping promises, always considering each case and customer situation on its own merits and not as an anonymous statistic, and treating customers as people and not transactions. Trust is both a differentiator, when all providers have good quality and convenience, and the very foundation of relationships – personal and business."

The key to coupling Customer Trust Currency with being customer-focused is genuinely doing everything in your power to recognize each customer's individual identity and to build their emotional trust bond with your organization. This is the point at which your organization becomes experience-based.

We would add price to the mix. Trust is a bigger differentiator than price. Why would people pay $15 to ship a package overnight with FedEx when they could pay $9 to ship the same package overnight with the US Postal Service? Simple. They *trust* FedEx to get that package there overnight, but they can only *hope* the US Postal Service will.

June 19, 2001, marked the day Colleen Barrett, Executive Vice President of Customers (don't you just love that title?), became Southwest Airlines' President and Chief Operating Officer. In an article entitled "Corner on Customer Service," Colleen says:

> June 18, 2001, marks Southwest Airlines' 30th Anniversary.
> Frankly, I don't know of many relationships that began in 1971

that can celebrate this milestone. What an accomplishment. Way to go, Team! When I say Team, I include Employees and Customers – for surely we could not have reached our 30th without the magnificent kinship between our employees and customers...I bet not many airlines get calls like I do, telling me that "Sally Jones, 'my' gate agent in San Antonio, hasn't been around for the last two weeks – is something wrong?" Our employees call me to say that their best customer is ill or is retiring, and we need to send a gift. When we know each other this way, as real people with actual names and familiar faces, we tend to forgive human foibles and we treat each other with respect, trust, and understanding of the frustrations and stresses of the day.

Thanks, Colleen – we couldn't have said it any better! Trust has become a strong differentiator for Southwest. A number of other low-fare airlines have entered the market, but they have failed to capture the customer loyalty or market share Southwest enjoys. They don't understand that low fares are not the key differentiator of Southwest – it's the trust people have for them. What happens to strong differentiators? Well...they usually become the cornerstone of your brand. Wouldn't trust be a great brand cornerstone for your organization?

MAKE TRUST THE CORNERSTONE OF YOUR BRAND

We believe the promises you make and the experiences you deliver to your customers *really represent your brand*. Each time your organization projects its brand image through its offerings, it sets forth promises. Each customer experience delivered is matched against those promises and represents the opportunity for the customer to vote. When customers find consistency between your promises and their subsequently delivered experiences, you build trust and brand. "Because when you absolutely, positively have to have it there overnight...you don't call the US Postal Service...Do you?"

What happened when one of Value Jet Airlines' planes crashed in Florida? The organization's reputation for safety dropped immediately. Their ridership and stock price also dropped like stones. Investigations and negative accusations prompted the organization to change its name.

Why didn't the same thing happen when a Delta Airlines jet crashed in Dallas? We believe it had everything to do with trust being part of Delta's brand. Delta had been flying for years. People thought of it as a premier airline with safety as a strong part of its brand experience and brand image. Customers perceived Delta as a trusted carrier of people. People said the Delta crash was just an unlucky, random accident.

Unlike Value Jet, Delta did not suffer through a phenomenon called **brand word association.** This phenomenon caused the phrase "lack of safety" to associate itself directly with the words "discount airline." Trust can prevent a lot of negative brand word associations from forming. Unfortunately in the case of Value Jet, the words "discount airline" quickly became associated with "we knew you weren't safe." This association eroded Value Jet's brand almost overnight.

Brand Word Association:

The attributes of a word or phrase that associates itself directly to the brand of an organization, whether negatively or positively.

Trust in a brand also plays a crucial role when an organization tries to introduce new products and services into new markets. Educating customers is a very time-consuming and expensive task. In fact, in Geoffrey Moore's book *Inside the Tornado*, he writes specifically about the extreme difficulties new technology has moving from innovation to mass adoption – a phenomenon he calls "crossing the chasm." We believe that crossing the chasm has a lot to do with the trust and power the brand has to make customers feel comfortable in new product adoption.

The trust that customers develop for your products, services, management, technology, and image becomes the brand experience customers really want. Your brand equity is built over time as brand experiences consistently match brand images (promises).

One mark of a customer-focused organization is a strong brand. It provides both the promises and experiences the customer wants. A customer-manipulative organization can only provide the promises and experiences it wants to provide the customer. One of the single biggest business challenges facing all organizations today is building a strong brand; one of the biggest struggles in building a strong brand is consistently delivering customer experiences that support the customer promises made by the brand. Harnessing the power of trust helps to strengthen and solidify your brand by helping you repeatedly deliver on those desired promises.

In the short term, a customer-manipulative organization can appear to be customer-focused. It does so by projecting a solid brand image implying that they can deliver what their target audiences want. This facade, however, unravels when the organization can't deliver a brand experience that supports those promises. The failure to match your brand image (promises) with your delivered brand experiences is **brand erosion**.

Brand Erosion:

The decrease in an organization's brand equity as a result of conflicting brand promises, deliveries, or both to a customer.

Customer-focused organizations create differentiation within their markets by providing desired experiences and offerings that match their brand image. They understand that by continuing to deliver consistent experiences, they reinforce their brand image. The building of brand equity then becomes a self-perpetuating process.

There are literally thousands of trust stories and trust brands. Some organizations already create and deliver Totally Awesome Customer Experiences resulting in trust. They know it strengthens their relationships with their customers. McDonald's and Wendy's are trusted over the local hamburger joint by a visitor from out of town (even if the hamburger at the local joint is twice as good). People trust FedEx over the US Postal Service. They trust Bayer aspirin over Smith's Food King aspirin.

A pithy slogan making a clear promise works well only if the organization delivers on it. Examples of this include: Volvo's "Safety First"; Dominos' "30 minutes or it's free"; Michelin's "the only thing between you and the road"; Budweiser's "born on date" (the trusted guarantee of freshness); Dell's "service security blanket"; Crest's "the cavity fighter", etc. Trust is the most powerful differentiator an organization can have with its customers. Trust sets forth an emotional promise in the mind of the customer that the organization's products, services, and experiences will deliver on their promise. This builds very strong relationships. Trust is a key to being customer-focused.

The failure to match your brand image (promises) with your delivered brand experiences spells brand erosion.

Trust helped Southwest Airlines break the "discount airline" mold. Southwest has demonstrated over and over to their customers that they aren't a "discount airline." Their customers know them as a "low-fare airline" whose safety and service takes a back seat to no one. Southwest has created a powerful brand. It's built on the idea that Southwest is a symbol of "Freedom to Move About the Country" for a reasonable fare. Southwest consistently matches its brand image to the brand experiences they deliver to its customers. Southwest customers can trust that they will not only arrive at their destination safely and on time, but that the experience will also be affordable and enjoyable. If you've never flown on Southwest, you should try it. Some of the flight attendants and pilots are very humorous, and it's obvious that their CEO, Herb Kelleher, wants traveling to be fun. He and his team want to delight customers. Southwest is consistently rated as one of the top two airlines for customer satisfaction (customer delight) and on-time arrivals. It's a great success story – and a great brand trust story.

CONSISTENTLY DELIVERING ON YOUR PROMISES

Did you know that organizations that produce both good and bad customer experiences are actually worse off than those organizations that consistently produce only average customer experiences? The answer, once again, is trust. People apparently perceive consistently average experiences more positively than a mixture of really good customer experiences and really poor customer experiences. When you confuse the customer, you erode your trust and your brand.

For instance, we've eaten in some pretty incredible barbeque joints in Dallas (we call them joints because of their unique ambiance) where the quality of the food is consistent, but the service is inconsistent and sometimes quite pathetic. One particular place we like to go is a bit different. The service is consistently pathetic. In fact, the service is so pathetic that it has transformed itself into entertainment.

The rudeness of the servers has become part of the experience. If however, their pathetically rude service ceases to be consistent, then customers will no longer perceive the rudeness as part of the experience. They'll perceive the rudeness as lack of caring or poor management. This inconsistency will result in a loss of customers. Inconsistency erodes trust and ultimately leads to failed experiences, creating dissatisfied customers.

In the case of our favorite barbeque joint, if we couldn't trust that their pathetic service would take place each and every time, we'd stop going. The last time we were leaving it, we overheard a guy say, "This place always has the most pathetic service you could ever find. You'll love it! It's a great laugh." Trust becomes a part of all your products. It's fundamental to creating and delivering Totally Awesome Customer Experiences, even if part of the product being delivered in your customer experience is an element as unusual as rudeness.

Those organizations that adjust to being experience-based will enjoy the benefits of customer loyalty, hard-to-duplicate differentiation, a strong brand, and will ultimately be the organizations that win the hearts of the customers.

THE CUSTOMER-FOCUSED REALITY

Being customer-focused means that you start with your customers' wants and needs and a genuine desire to create and deliver Totally Awesome Customer Experiences around the fulfillment of those wants and needs. Being customer-manipulative means that you start with what you think you can sell to customers. Then you try to build experiences around what you think will get the customer to buy. "We have every color of car you want, as long as it's black. We're sure you'll love black, because everybody who buys from us picks black."

Peter Drucker once said:

> Quality in a product or service is not what the supplier puts in. It is what the customer gets out and is willing to pay. A product is not quality because it is hard to make and costs a lot of money, as manufacturers typically believe. This is incompetence. Customers pay only for what is of use to them and gives them value. Nothing else constitutes quality.

Do you know the single biggest reason why it's important for organizations to be experienced-based and customer-focused with a robust Customer Trust Currency?

Customer-Focused Reality:

The consistent creation and delivery of Totally Awesome Customer Experiences for the purpose of delighting customers.

Customer-focused reality is where organizations consistently create and deliver Totally Awesome Customer Experiences for the purpose of delighting their customers.

Customers Vote

"You Don't Need a PhD; You Just Need a Pulse..."

Robert Reid,
Former VP Global Services,
Twelve Horses, Inc.

Chapter 2 is definitely a reality check of who is really in charge! It begins with the power of customers to vote about their experiences. The chapter then proceeds to the Customer Satisfaction Continuum and the importance of receiving the Delight Vote. We then examine the value of the customer vote, along with why it's crucial to take your organization beyond customer satisfaction all the way to customer delight. We explore why customer satisfaction initiatives have failed to deliver customer loyalty, and we show you how to use customer satisfaction initiatives to leverage customer delight. The chapter concludes with customer delight as a strong differentiator and prepares you to learn the process of creating and delivering Totally Awesome Customer Experiences.

FROM BEGINNING TO END, THE EXPERIENCE COUNTS.

I was in a major department store in New York City a few months ago purchasing a wool scarf...

Two gentlemen were in front of me at the cash register, checking out. The checkout clerk appeared to be friendly and was handling the transaction in an uneventful manner. They completed their checkout and were almost out the door when the clerk suddenly shouted, "You didn't sign the charge card receipt!"

Although I was next in line, I'm positive I didn't hear the clerk say to me anything like, "Excuse me sir, it will just be a moment. We forgot to take care of something here. Thanks for your patience." Nor did I hear an apology offered to the other two gentlemen for screaming at them. I let it pass, for I was much more interested in what was happening with the gentleman who allegedly didn't sign his charge card receipt. I distinctly remembered that he did sign a receipt.

When the gentlemen returned to the counter, the clerk said bluntly, "You didn't sign the charge card receipt." She clearly implied that the mistake was the customer's, and that he needed to correct it immediately. I don't recall hearing anything like, "I'm so sorry for the inconvenience, but I failed to get your signature on the right receipt. My mistake."

The men were confused and slightly upset. The accused man said, "I already signed the charge card receipt." He told his friend and the clerk that he didn't want to sign another receipt for fear he would be double-charged and have the hassle of getting the wrong charges reversed. She said, "You won't be double-charged, since you never signed the receipt in the first place."

This little verbal foray just increased the intensity of the conversation. By then the accused gentleman was completely insistent that he had signed the charge card receipt and was searching for the copy of the signed receipt in the depths of his coat pockets. Meanwhile, the checkout supervisor entered the game. I was certain the supervisor would resolve the situation quickly and amicably, to save us all from a potentially explosive and embarrassing situation.

To my complete surprise, the situation escalated. The supervisor, without taking a moment to even assess the situation, looked at the clerk's unsigned receipt, pushed it in front of the poor man who was still looking for his receipt, and asked him to sign it, pointing his finger directly at the blank line on the receipt. Now the fight was on! The customer started shouting at the clerk and supervisor, insisting he had already signed the receipt and that he resented being treated like a liar. It was getting really ugly, really fast.

The gentleman finally produced the paper he had signed. He uncrumpled it and shoved it in front of the clerk and supervisor with a "so there" attitude. It was indeed a signed copy of something, but only a copy of the list of items showing the customer the charges for his review. Mistakenly, the customer had thought it was the credit charge receipt and signed it. It had a signature line and it looked a lot like a receipt. It was an easy mistake for anyone to make.

The customer presented his copy of the signed receipt to the clerk and supervisor, fully expecting an apology – or at least recognition he wasn't a common shoplifter. To my total and utter amazement, the supervisor said, "You can clearly see that this is not the charge card receipt. You should carefully read things before you sign them. If you had carefully read this slip, you would have recognized that it was an itemization of your purchases."

I couldn't believe what I was hearing. The supervisor might as well have said, "Hey, stupid, you must be a remedial reader. This situation is your fault. You're lucky we even let you shop in our store."

You can guess the rest. The man was furious. He scribbled his name on the real receipt, threw the pen down on the counter, gave the clerk and supervisor an incredibly dirty look, and vowed never to return to this @#!$% store *ever* again. Both men stormed out the door. Did I forget to mention how loud this whole incident was?

This is what we call an Experience Touch Point, and one that didn't go very well. What would be the pulse of any of the customers who viewed this scene?

There's one final caveat to this story. As I plopped down my purchase on the counter to check out, I overheard the supervisor telling the clerk, "You have to stand up to customers like that in this store. They're the ones who give you a bad day. We just don't need those types!" I can only assume that he was referring to the "well-dressed, well-spoken, good-paying customers" whom they just berated and the "will-never-be-back" type of customers.

I now looked straight into the eyes of the clerk. She smiled one of those "I can't believe you saw and heard that whole thing" smiles and said, "Sorry for the delay. Can I check you out?"

All I could say was, "I hope it goes better for me than those last guys. Should I be taking a class or something first?" You can bet I made sure I followed *all* the store instructions.

I used my voting power to write the CEO a letter with my thoughts (never heard back). I likewise voted never to return to that store. How would you have voted? How do you think the eight to ten people right behind me voted? What's your pulse on this one?

Preventable? Absolutely! Correctable? Absolutely! Tragic? Absolutely! Will it happen again? Absolutely! The event was cultural and will not change without new customer-focused leadership intervention.

When all is said and done, the vote that customers cast at the end of their customer experiences is what really counts.

When all is said and done, the vote that customers cast at the end of their customer experiences is what really counts. This vote will dictate their loyalty, their emotional trust bond, and their willingness to spread the good word about your organization. When customers are delighted with their customer experiences, they give you the Delight Vote. Any other votes they cast simply range from a satisfied vote to a dissatisfied vote. Consider these straightforward thoughts in putting customer voting and customer delight into perspective...

- Customers are the experts and they are in control of their votes.

- Customers vote all the time and tell others how they voted.

- The objective of a delivering a customer experience is to create delighted customers and receive their Delight Vote.

- You can place a value on a customer's vote.

- A vote from a delighted customer counts more than any other customer vote.

- Customer satisfaction initiatives will not create the Delight Vote or customer loyalty.

- Your organization is in danger of losing its customers if you don't get the Delight Vote.

- Delighted customers who cast the Delight Vote in your favor create true differentiation for your organization.

- It's very important to leverage your operational activities into your experience-based efforts to delight your customers.

CUSTOMERS CONTROL THE VOTE

Customers have all the control. No organization knows more about their customers' experiences than their customers!

To think otherwise is dangerous.

Customers have all the control. No organization knows more about their customers' experiences than their customers! To think otherwise is dangerous. Regardless of background, education, tastes, and viewpoint, we all have customer experiences on a daily basis. In fact, we're all self-declared experts. We recognize good experiences from bad ones and we know the promises kept versus the "hot air." And we certainly don't keep those experiences to ourselves. What would a good party be without experiences as our main topic of conversation? When we have a good experience, we tell four others; when we have a bad experience, we tell ten. We know and tell exactly what we would do to improve those bad experiences. We love organizations to focus on us, but we hate being manipulated.

Since customers are experts on customer experiences, tapping into that knowledge is a great opportunity. As Reid says, "You don't need a PhD; you just need a pulse in order to understand the difference between a good customer experience, a bad customer experience, and a Totally Awesome Customer Experience." Isn't it funny that as customers we don't understand why organizations can't get those experiences right, but when we try creating and delivering them, we seem to suffer from a change in perspective?

Another thing we do as customers is *vote*. We vote with our checkbooks, our recommendations, our actions, and our silence. Regardless of what an organization believes, customers are in control because they're the only ones that have a vote – and that vote is valuable. Customer-focused organizations are always looking to garner the prized Delight Vote from their customers. They know that without the Delight Vote, they can't create loyal customers and true differentiation; all the customer satisfaction initiatives in the world won't help. It's the process of creating and delivering Totally Awesome Customer Experiences that will help you delight your customers and set your organization apart from your competition.

CUSTOMERS VOTE ALL THE TIME…AND TELL OTHERS HOW THEY VOTED

As customers, we get plenty of practice voting on customer experiences. There are thousands of examples of bad customer experiences, similar to the experience in the New York City department store. You probably have an even better one to tell. There are also thousands of examples of really good customer experiences. It isn't luck that separates the bad customer experiences from the good customer experiences or from the Totally Awesome Customer Experiences. Superior planning and the desire to consistently delight your customers makes the difference. Remember Uncle Bob at Toys "R" Us? How do you think he voted?

There are thousands of examples of customers telling and voting about their experiences. We easily captured a few examples directly off the Internet. Please note that we didn't select these examples because of their experience "wow" factor. On the contrary, we chose these experiences because they're so incredibly unspectacular, incredibly common, and available in the public domain. These are just great examples of the everyday experiences customers are having, voting on, and telling others about.

Customer Vote:

The vote cast by a customer during a Touch Point Experience as to whether to continue interacting with the organization.

These examples represent what is happening to customers everywhere, in every market and in every industry. It doesn't matter if the environment is business or personal. It doesn't matter if the customer is acting on behalf of a business or himself. It doesn't even matter if the customer is an employee.

These two examples are from the business-to-consumer computer market. In reality, we could have selected any industry. As you read them, remember how important every single customer vote is to an organization, and how often a customer shares an experience and opinion with other customers.

"Oh No, My Computer is Broken!"…Scott Greenspan's Apple Customer Experience

After using the Duo, I decided to go portable for my main system and ordered a Bronze G3 in the 400 MHz. flavor. I was very pleased when it arrived about 2 weeks after I ordered it in late May, soon after the introduction. The machine met and often exceeded my expectations in all areas but one – the amount of heat it produced. I was concerned after using it in the car dealer's service waiting room and my legs got rather warm. It tended to crash on a fairly regular basis once it got warm. I

Customers know a ton about customer experiences.

used the XLR8 Processor Info control panel to keep track of the processor temperature, and found that it often exceeded 185°F or 85°C before crashing. This seemed excessive, and I had never heard or seen the fan come on. I called Apple to ask at what temperature the fan was supposed to come on, and after being assigned a case number, I was given a bit of the old run around. No satisfaction at that point. This was in early June of 1999.

Now, in the meantime, I had attended a graphics show, New Media 99, in early May, 1999. While there, I filled out a card for some type of contest at the Apple booth, knowing full well that the main point of the cards was gathering customer and potential customer names. After some research on the net, I found that the maximum operating temperature of the disk drive, a Toshiba, was 60°C. The drive is located right next to the processor (everything in a PowerBook is right next to the processor), so the temperature inside is obviously too high for the drive. This info was to prove crucial later.

I called Apple Service again, gave them my case number, and gave them the info about the drive operating temperature. Yawns from the Apple end. Here I was with a $5000 CDN lap warmer, and I can't even find out how hot it has to be before the fan will come on. (It did have a fan; I lifted the keyboard to check.) I got Red Tag involved but they couldn't get any further than I could. I was getting very frustrated, until an Apple sales rep called, to see if I needed any further information on the items I had seen at the New Media show.

In the meantime I had also purchased OS X Server, but that's another story (anyone want it cheap?). Well, I complained about these two issues, and gave all the information I had kept about the internal temperature, the disk operating environment and the case number. I was asked for the dealer's name and told to await a call. The next day, Jim King called and I was asked to bring my computer in, along with all the packaging and get my replacement. This was at the time when folks all over were complaining about delays in receiving their new machines, and my brand new replacement arrived the next day. We transferred the files, and I took my new computer with me in less than an hour.

The Apple rep called back to check that everything worked out, and I was pleased to report that everything had, and to thank

him for his efforts. This new PowerBook has been my work-
horse since then and I've been very pleased with it. I recently
left it on all weekend to collect my e-mail and on Sunday night,
after close to 70 hours of continuous operation the XLR8
Processor Info control panel reported a temperature of 68°C, a
difference of over 15% from the first computer. I've had very
few problems with this computer, and am glad I went portable.
The moral? Fill out those warranty cards, or sign up online.
Apple keeps track of when a computer was delivered to the
dealer, so they've got a good idea of when you purchased it. If
you have any issues in this regard, a good relationship with the
dealer is a great bit of help. Filling out surveys at trade shows
also seems to have been a bonus in this regard. You may end up
with a lot of "junk" mail, but the one time you need it, the help
can be invaluable!"

Scott has become an Apple customer experience expert. He knows what he
likes and what he doesn't like. He knows what Apple needs to fix and how
to fix it. Scott is both a customer experience voter and an expert. He can
help Apple. Scott had amazing resilience in keeping himself from just voting
"*I'm out of here*" to Apple. How many people would have gone as far as Scott
before they voted to end the customer experience? Yet, Scott still voted for
Apple. Apple should talk to Scott, one customer experience expert with a very
strong pulse for Apple. Scott has already told thousands, including all of us.

"Won't Anyone Just Listen to Me?"...An ABC Computer Customer Experience (company identity is masked)

Dear Al:

I've been reading your article on your experience in 1996 with
ABC. I could have sworn I wrote it. We bought an ABC computer in Feb. 1998. After 7 months of crashing and freezing, we
were referred to our local ABC service depot. We were first told
it needed a Dimm, motherboard and an on/off switch. When the
service depot had the machine for two weeks without working
on it we began calling ABC, first asking for a replacement and
finally for a full refund. Our experience has been the same as
yours: many apologies at first, but when we refused to accept
their apologies and demanded they stand behind their product
and service we got the silent treatment. I have been searching

the net looking for complaints about ABC products and service and only after reading your article do I understand why they are hard to find (I assume they have all signed release forms).

I am glad you refused to do so as it renews our hope of a positive outcome for us. We continue to send e-mails to ABC weekly and have already done the BBB complaint, which we have not heard back from. We have also posted a complaint at an Internet site. Like you, we figure our last resort will be small claims court. I do hope we make out as well as you. Many thanks for posting your story. It's reassuring to know we are not alone...I look forward to hearing back from you.

Trudy & Ron

Trudy and Ron are also customer experience experts with a pulse. How do you think they voted?

In the process of selecting these two scenarios, we spent an entire day searching for as many documented customer experiences as we could find on the Internet. The search was eye-opening. There were hundreds. We were tempted to read them all. We saved a number of them. The point is that there are all kinds of experts on having both good and bad customer experiences. They were not PhDs; they were just people with a pulse who were willing to share their experiences and how they voted on those experiences with other people.

Voters tell others how they voted. It's human nature to do so. Customer-focused organizations actually look forward to the opportunity of receiving the Delight Vote from their customers and leveraging the customer's word-of-mouth power.

THE DELIGHT VOTE IS YOUR NUMBER ONE OBJECTIVE

Every organization wants to receive the **Delight Vote** from its customer. Fredrick Hertzberg, an organizational psychologist, often spoke of a satisfaction continuum in which people would vote on their feelings of an experience.

Hertzberg's theory states that there are various mental and emotional points on the satisfaction continuum at which a person can be dissatisfied, not satisfied, or satisfied. He maintained that a person with dissatisfaction would immediately seek new offers in order to move from being dissatisfied. Customers with no satisfaction respond best to offers they believe will provide them satisfaction. The person having satisfaction will continue in that state until he or she recognizes another satisfactory offer having more perceived value or lower risk. This satisfaction continuum applies equally to customers.

Delight Vote:

The vote cast at the end of a customer's experience that goes beyond mere satisfaction to build a customer's loyalty, emotional trust bond, and willingness to spread the "good word" about your organization to others.

Experience Voting Point:

An area of potential conflict of Experience Touch Points with a customer's acceptability filters, triggering a conscious or unconscious vote to either stay engaged with or reject an Experience. These conflicts can be in the form of questions, doubts, or feelings of combativeness within your customer. An Experience Voting Point can come as a result of interacting with single or multiple Experience Touch Points.

We assigned customer satisfaction attributes beneath each of the satisfaction continuum points for what a customer "feels, does, wants, and is."

Customer Satisfaction Continuum

	Dissatisfaction	No Satisfaction	Satisfaction
Feels	Antagonistic	No feelings	Satisfied
Does	Complains openly	Never complains	States satisfaction when asked
Wants cost	Offers to move from being dissatisfied	Offers to move to satisfaction	Offers of higher value/lower
Is	An enemy	A prospect for a competitor	A satisfied customer

We believe there is another point on the Customer Satisfaction Continuum called Delight.

Customer Delight Continuum

	Dissatisfaction	No Satisfaction	Satisfaction	Delight
Feels	Antagonistic	No feelings	Satisfied	Passion
Does	Complains openly	Never complains	States satisfaction when asked	Raves to others
Wants	Offers to move from being dissatisfied	Offers to move to satisfaction	Offers of higher value/lower cost	Asks for additional experiences and offers
Is	An enemy	A prospect for a competitor	A satisfied customer	A loyal customer

Satisfied customers readily migrate from one satisfying offer to another. How many times have you or your friends changed your long-distance carrier based on the latest and greatest offer? This migration is generally based on either a higher-value or lower-price offer. The speed of migration depends on the risk involved. Satisfied customers have not become loyal because they haven't formed the emotional trust bond it takes to get them to Delight. How many times have you been only satisfied with a product and service and felt that driving passion to phone everyone you know? "Not many!" How many times have you been overwhelmingly delighted by an experience and told everyone you meet? "Lots!"

Customers move from being satisfied to being delighted when they receive experiences and offers that create an emotional trust bond between them and your organization. This bond evokes the feelings of passion and trust and drives your customers to rave about their experience with others.

*A customer-focused
organization does not just
want the Satisfied Vote;
they want the passion and
loyalty that comes from
the Delight Vote. This vote
represents a step beyond
customer satisfaction and
is the essence of the
Awesome Customer
Challenge.*

THE VALUE OF A CUSTOMER'S VOTE

What do you believe is the value of a customer's vote? How would your organization quantify it? The more you believe customers are in control, the more value you place on their votes. If organizations feel that the customer has very little control (customer-manipulative), the value of the customer's vote is perceived to be low. On the other hand, if organizations feel that the customer has a lot of control (customer-focused), the value of the customer vote is high. It all depends on your belief. The value of a customer's vote is what drives most customer-focused organizations to invest millions in trying to get the customer's vote. They realize that a customer's vote contains all of their future potential revenue.

The other important aspect of the value of a customer's vote is the "word-of-mouth" factor. When customers tell others how they voted on their experiences, their stories influence the decisions of prospective customers. If a customer tells four other people that he voted positively, and two of those people subsequently become your customers, what is the real value of the original customer vote? One or three? If a customer tells ten other people that she voted negatively, and four of them choose not to become customers because of that vote, is the value of the original customer vote (-1) or (-5)? Assessing the value of the customer vote can be tricky. One thing is for sure: a vote is rarely isolated to a single customer.

THE DELIGHT VOTE IS WORTH MORE

Organizations spend millions to collect and use customer feedback information for the purpose of trying to increase customer loyalty. That's the primary objective of customer satisfaction surveys and initiatives.

*Customer Delight:
Customer delight is
the realization a customer
has when stepping beyond
being merely satisfied, to
mentally and emotionally
bonding with an organiza-
tion. It includes developing trust and passion in
the process, because both
physical and emotional
expectations have been
exceeded.*

One key premise of customer satisfaction theory is, "Satisfied customers increase customer loyalty, market share, and brand equity." We don't think so. Satisfied customers are not loyal customers. Customer satisfaction is not **customer delight**. Customer delight only comes from a customer experience that has the power to step customers beyond being merely satisfied to a place where they mentally and emotionally bond to your organization and develop trust and passion.

You can measure the difference between a Satisfied Customer and a Delighted Customer in terms of customer loyalty and the "telling factor" that raving fans muster. Loyal customers have a strong desire to continue building their relationship with you because they trust you. This desire goes beyond just being satisfied with your products and services. Delighted customers promote you. They're out spreading the word of your greatness and how smart they were in selecting your organization as theirs.

We asked Robert Reid for a personal experience with moving from being a satisfied customer to a delighted customer. It took him less than a minute to start telling us about Cheri, the dental receptionist. Here's Robert's experience with something as enjoyable as a root canal...

What a painful beginning to the morning! I woke up with an excruciating toothache. Straightway, I called my regular dentist, only to find out that he couldn't fit me in for a couple of weeks! So like anyone else, when I got to work, I started asking my co-workers about recommendations for a good dentist from the approved insurance list.

One co-worker gave me a rave review of her dentist, so I quickly gave him a call. Cheri answered the phone with a very warm greeting and asked how she could help me. I told her of my painful predicament and she empathized with my situation. Then she offered to have me come in right away to have my tooth looked at. I was already impressed!

When I arrived at the dentist's office, Cheri readily recognized me, got my insurance card, and led me back to the dentist's chair, offering me a magazine. She said that the dentist would be right with me. Shortly thereafter, the dental assistant came in, introduced herself, and took a few x-rays. A few minutes later, the dentist came in, calling me by name and introducing himself. After examining the tooth – the one that made me jump when he blew air on it – he said that based on the x-ray and exam, I would need a root canal. He then went through a thorough explanation of what a root canal procedure is, the reasons they are needed, and the steps from right now to a happy smile again. Finally, he asked if I would need any pain medication and gave suggestions how to reduce the pain until I met with the root-canal specialist. Then he said to step out to the desk and Cheri would assist me. And assist me she did!

Cheri must have heard that I was going to need to get a root canal because she had already called my insurance to find out coverage and local providers on the approved list. From the list, she recommended a few, and after I selected one close to home, she called that office to get me an appointment. The doctor had no openings for several days, so she scheduled a tentative date and said she'd confirm later in the day. Then she suggested I pick another one on the list to see if that doctor had an earlier time available.

Loyal customers have a strong desire to continue building their relationship with you because they trust you. This desire goes beyond just being satisfied with your products and services. Delighted customers promote you.

The Delight Vote is worth more! Consistently delighted customers become loyal customers. Their trust and passion help you build your brand. Delighted customers never hesitate to go out of their way to tell others about their experiences and how they voted. They also have a strong desire to see your organization grow so that they feel important and excited that they made the right decision.

We went through three endodontists in this same fashion until she finally found an opening. She scheduled the appointment and wrote down all the logistical info for their office. She explained that after the root canal, it would take a few days for the tooth to settle before I could return to have the crown work completed. I left the dental office still in pain but fully educated, game plan in hand, and oddly enough, feeling good. After I left, Cheri called the other endodontists and cancelled the tentative appointments.

Later that day, with a few pain killers in my blood stream, I left for my appointment to have the root canal. When I got back to work, I thanked my co-worker for the great dentist and told everyone else to stop seeing their dentists and get hooked up with this one!

PS. Cheri even scheduled me for my next regular cleaning six months down the road.

As I reflect on this event, it still amazes me. When I went back for my crown work, I was remembered and treated just like family. They even sent me a thank-you card after the visit. Also, a few weeks before my cleaning appointment, Cheri called to remind me. What's even more interesting is how easily I moved from what I would call a satisfied customer with my old dentist to a delighted customer of Eddie's. I can't remember the name of the endodontist or his staff. But this I do know: if you're ever in Pleasant Grove, Utah, and looking for a great dentist, look up Eddie Faddis' Family Dental Practice and say, "Hi" to Cheri for me.

An organization delivers customer delight through consistent and repeatable Totally Awesome Customer Experiences. These experiences have the capability to link the physical, intellectual, emotional, and spiritual components together in a feeling that's greater than the sum of the parts of the experience. It's a feeling that you can't analyze by asking your customer a million typical customer satisfaction survey questions in order to find out how to duplicate that feeling. Much like fine wine-making, it's the perfect combination of both art and science in which both are important to the outcome.

CUSTOMER SATISFACTION INITIATIVES FAIL TO CREATE CUSTOMER LOYALTY AND PRODUCE THE DELIGHT VOTE

Why have customer satisfaction initiatives failed to increase customer loyalty? Because they follow a flawed theory. Their premise is that improving operational efficiency will in turn lead to increased customer loyalty. Unfortunately, this notion could not be farther from the truth. Customer loyalty can thrive only in an experience-based environment. This means that the organization's primary focus should be to create and deliver good customer experiences, using operational activities to support those experiences.

Organizations spend millions of dollars and thousands of executive hours to design and deploy various flavors of customer satisfaction surveys and customer loyalty programs. Typically, we see a lot of data gathered, a lot of analysis performed, and a lot of reports written – but we still don't see loyal and delighted customers emerge. When results are weak, the management generally ends up blaming the customers or employees.

How many of your own organization's customer satisfaction initiatives over the past five years have yielded a substantial and sustainable return? Ask yourself if all those customer satisfaction programs, surveys, seminars, and classes have really put your organization any closer to finding the solution to increasing customer loyalty, brand equity, or competitive differentiation. Does your organization have significantly more delighted customers today than last year or in previous years because of your customer satisfaction initiatives?

Customer satisfaction surveys are notorious for measuring how well an organization is performing its operational processes, back office procedures, and tasks for the customer. However, the questions asked and information gathered from most customer satisfaction surveys have little to do with the essence of delivering or measuring a customer's experience. Seeing is believing. Pay attention to the next few customer satisfaction surveys you read. Notice how many questions are oriented to the organization's operations as opposed to the customers' experiences.

Here are just a few samples of operational-oriented questions we took directly from our file of customer satisfaction surveys:

- Did your question to our organization get answered in less than five minutes?

- Were our customer service people courteous and friendly?

- Were you treated with respect and professionalism?

- What was the most serious problem you have had with our company?

- How many times did you contact us before your most serious problem was resolved?

- How would you rate the quality of our communication?

Customer satisfaction surveys are notorious for measuring how well an organization is performing its operational processes, back office procedures, and tasks for the customer. However, the questions asked and information gathered from most customer satisfaction surveys have little to do with the essence of delivering or measuring a customer's experience.

- How do you use our products and services?

- How would you rate what other customers think about our products?

- How would you rate our financial stability?

- How many times a year do you contact us?

- How would you rate your present sales representative?

- How would you compare our products to the competition?

- Do our representatives refrain from using high-pressure sales tactics?

- How easy is it to carry on transactions with us?

Few companies who ask their customer to rate the fulfillment of their expectations – ever ask the customer what their expectations were for the quality of the products, the level of service, or how they wanted to be treated by their personnel.

Here are a few questions we find rather absurd. All of these questions ask the customer to judge the organization's performance based on their own expectations – expectations which happen to be completely unknown to the organization doing the survey...go figure.

- Considering what you think it should be, please rate the overall quality of service you received. The answers are: Much better than expected, better than expected, or much worse than expected.

- Thinking about your expectations for XYZ, including its products, services, and personnel, how would you rate your overall satisfaction with the company?

- How well did we meet your expectations?

Keep in mind that not a single company asking the customer to rate the fulfillment of their expectations ever asked the customer what their expectations were for the quality of the products, the level of service, or how they wanted to be treated by their personnel.

The other concept that strikes you when reading through a customer satisfaction survey is that there is no emotion, no passion that they really want to know, no reason they need the information (other than to improve their performance). Some even offer monetary gift donations to charities if you'll fill out the horrible thing!

Customers don't care about your operations. They care only about their experiences!

For example, do you think the customer cares if your organization has perfected the transaction of transferring an order between your call center and your distribution center? No! The customer just wants to get the order on time. A month later, do you think the customer remembers or cares how long it took to speak with a representative? Again, the customer doesn't care. The customer cares and votes about his or her experience with your organization as a whole. While operational survey information might be helpful in clarifying and evaluating operational transactions, it doesn't measure the delight of the customer, and most certainly isn't the basis behind customer voting.

No wonder fewer than five percent of customer satisfaction surveys are ever returned. Customers find customer satisfaction surveys irrelevant and confusing. They believe nothing will change even if they fill them out. Customers don't break their experiences down into twenty-seven different operational-based processes, analyze the execution of each process, and tabulate and average the results to determine whether they've had a great customer experience. They just care about being delighted.

In our opening story, Uncle Bob might not remember if Jeremy, the Toys "R" Us clerk, was properly attired, or if he spoke clearly, or helped him within three to five minutes. He most likely won't remember if the location where the Cool Collecting Barbie Dolls should have been was properly labeled, or if the store was crystal clean, or the merchandise was arranged properly by specific toy category.

But what Uncle Bob, who was desperately looking for that special Cool Collecting Barbie Doll for Tawnya, will remember is the experience he had when he needed help. He will remember that Jeremy...

- took the time to physically check if they had any more special Barbie dolls in the back storage room.

- called two other Toys "R" Us stores to find out they were also out of the doll

- called their competition until he found one who had the doll.

- had Bob buy the doll over the phone from their competition so he could complete the transaction right there to save him time.

- asked the competition to gift-wrap the doll and to wait outside the store for Bob to pick it up without having to go into the store.

- wrote out the street directions so that Uncle Bob could get there quickly.

- gave the uncle a birthday greetings card from Toys "R" Us with a complimentary Toys "R" Us coupon for $10 of Toys "R" Us dollars.

- and told him, "Thanks for being a Toys "R" Us customer."

If Toys "R" Us can consistently repeat Uncle Bob's experience each and every time Bob goes into a Toys "R" Us, Bob will become an impassioned customer of Toys "R" Us forever and so will his friends and associates. We wonder with how many people Uncle Bob shared this Totally Awesome Customer Experience? What would it take for a competitor to wrestle Uncle Bob away from Toys "R" Us?

Does this mean that customer satisfaction initiatives aren't useful in obtaining information about how well you're doing operationally? Does it means it isn't important to improve your processes and create better efficiencies inside your organization to help support the experiences you deliver? Not at all! It means that traditional customer satisfaction activities are better at improving the operational aspects of an organization than they are at supporting customer experiences and leading to customer delight.

Creating customer delight is not about operational efficiency. It's about having a defined process that consistently and repeatedly creates and delivers Totally Awesome Customer Experiences.

In Chapter 6, we will talk about Experience Touch Points. Experience Touch Points are the points at which your organization interacts with your customers. The ideal creation of Experience Touch Points requires the most effective and efficient use of people, process, and technology. Customer satisfaction information can help. Our recommendation is to not use the operational information from customer satisfaction surveys for more than its intended use. If you need to gather operational information, let your customers know why you need their help. You'll be amazed how powerful honesty is in getting customers to help you.

The realization that traditional customer satisfaction initiatives don't obtain the desired results has led some organizations to search for alternative ways to increase customer loyalty. For instance, Ruby Tuesday's, a national restaurant chain, has strategically moved away from traditional customer satisfaction initiatives. They now invest their time, money, and energy in training higher-quality personnel with the hopes that an increase in the quality of personnel will result in better service and customer satisfaction. American Airlines invested in a major customer service training initiative for their flight attendants with the same motive in mind. Organizations are constantly spending millions of dollars searching for the magic formula that will improve their "customer loyalty" quotient. That formula includes an experience-based orientation.

THE DANGER IN NOT GETTING THE DELIGHT VOTE

The simple reality is that merely satisfied customers can easily be dragged away by your competition. One of the most well known examples of satisfied customers being dragged away was the market-share battle between Amazon.com and Barnes & Noble. When Barnes & Noble looked at the competition, they looked at both the large booksellers (such as Borders and Tower), and the small local bookstores like Sam Weller and Peterson books. They didn't realize that their biggest competitor would start out as a "virtual competitor" and would later take away their number-one position in the book selling market.

This story seems obvious to all of us today, but what really happened is that Amazon.com challenged the loyalty of Barnes & Noble customers and won. The reason they won is that Barnes and Noble customers weren't loyal. Barnes and Noble only had satisfied customers. Their differentiation was only at the product service level, not the relationship level. Barnes and Noble regrouped, realizing that their brick-and-mortar strategy needed strengthening.

They discovered the need to create and deliver a better overall customer experience. They needed to create a differentiation on a relationship level and move away from just a simple product/service level in order to build those emotional bonds with themselves and their customers. Barnes and Noble is now creating and delivering a full brick-and-click experience they hope will move improve their relationships with their customers, creating more of an emotional bond helping them move beyond merely satisfied customers to creating delighted customers. Time will only tell who will eventually win, but we can tell you who will be the voters – the customers.

Customer satisfaction initiatives have delivered sporadic results in improving customer loyalty. This is because these initiatives primarily focus on improving operational processes and activities, not on creating or delivering delightful customer experiences.

The danger in not getting the Delight Vote is that it leaves your organization vulnerable to competitor raids on your customers. The issue here is that traditional customer satisfaction initiatives lack lasting differentiation. It's very difficult to continually find ways to create lasting differentiation on the product/service level. Left to feature/pricing battles, differentiation becomes very easy to duplicate or improve upon by the competition. Where is the customer while this is going on, jumping back and forth with the "next best deal." This "leap-frogging" is very common in industries where differentia-

The danger in not getting the Delight Vote is that it leaves your organization vulnerable to competitive raids on your customers.

Emotional Trust Bond:

The bond in a relationship whose primary strength is derived from the knowledge and feelings of trust and security.

tion is primarily product/service (how many times have you changed long-distance providers with your phone service) and much less common in industries where differentiation is achieved through customer relationships.

In our present electronically switched-on economy, creating and delivering product/service offerings is much easier, much broader, and much less expensive than it was yesterday. Technology has attempted to eliminate a significant amount of either geographic or relationship differentiation, which were the main protection for many organizations. In the absence of strong relationship differentiation, the product/service differentiation level leaves the customer in a very dispassionate position. It places their acceptance decision based on "thinking" not "feeling." The winner is simply the company with the latest and greatest product or service. The loser is the company wanting to build band loyalty and repeat customer business. Unarmed with ways to build emotional relationships with their customers, many organizations fall by the way side seeing both their customers and profit margins evaporate.

Perceivable differentiation is the only protection organizations have against failing prey to the lowest level of differentiation, which is price. On the flip side however, the opportunity is to build relationship differentiation through providing consistent and continuous experience offerings that create an emotional trust bond with a customer. This is where customer delight and loyalty are formed. This type of differentiation is very tough to break or duplicate. When a customer is delighted and loyal, price becomes much less of a differentiating factor because differentiation is now being produced at the relationship level rather than the product/service or commodity levels.

CUSTOMER DELIGHT CREATES RELATIONSHIP DIFFERENTIATION

Customer delight is the point on the satisfaction continuum where the description of how a customer feels towards his or her experiences with an organization cannot be described in terms of the experience components themselves. Customer Delight is much more than the sum of the parts of an experience.

The difference between a satisfied customer and a delighted customer is the emotional trust bond that forms between the customer and the organization. This bond takes a customer beyond meeting his or her expected needs of a product or service. Customer delight is the point on the satisfaction continuum where the description of how a customer feels towards his or her experiences with an organization cannot be described in terms of the products, service, price components themselves. This is because the offering has become an experience for the customer in which the customer can only describe it in both emotional and thinking terms. It's at this point on the satisfaction continuum where a significant point of differentiation between Satisfaction and Delight occurs. This point of differentiation is a result of forming of the emotional trust bond between the customer and the organization that has evoked both delighted thoughts and delighted feelings within the customer. This is the point on the satisfaction continuum where the value of the customer's experience itself is greater than the value of the entire specific components within their experience and evokes the Delight Vote.

This type of relationship differentiation is very difficult for competitors to match because it forms an emotional barrier rather than an economic barrier to entry. It has nothing to do with making your physical products better or cheaper or more available. It has to do with trying to compete against a feeling a customer has about doing business with one organization versus another. The emotional feeling conjures up attributes that are extremely difficult to identify and duplicate.

Until your customer moves from Satisfaction to Delight, you're vulnerable to competitive raids. We can't tell you how many times have we seen situations where an organization believes they are safe because they have satisfied customers, only to see "the next best deal" steal their customers away. The Internet has significantly heightened the frequency of these situations. It's phenomenal in the fact that so much information and so many product/service offerings have now become instantly available. It was a medium that allowed product/service level differentiation to be created rapidly and test from traditional brick-and-mortar businesses by merely challenging the strength of the customer relationship itself, as in our Amazon.com versus Barnes & Noble example.

Customers found themselves suddenly being offered product/services with the incredible speed. Customers had the instant ability to accept or reject those offerings. This was something they had never experienced from traditional brick-and-mortar organizations relationships. In pre-Internet days, most organizations assumed they had solid relationship differentiation and it was easy to identify your competition. They all had physical addresses, they offered the same kinds of basic products and services, and they usually went through the same channels of distribution. Today, your competitors may not be very well-known, but many of them can quickly find out who your customers are and rapidly and easily present them with offerings...and if that relationship differentiation is not strong, Internet competitors can suddenly enter your market and take away customers you thought were as loyal as they come – only to find out that they were merely satisfied customers, not particularly loyal, and just waiting for the next best deal to move.

On the other hand, those customer that had solid relationships between themselves and an organization, found the Internet offerings to be impersonal and confusing. There is no doubt the Internet has voraciously tested the traditional relationship between the customer and vendor. In fact, some relationships have been changed so radically that it has left many customers

The Awesome Customer Challenge is to "stop merely satisfying your customers and start delighting them.

wondering what is trustable, trustworthy, and safe. The Internet has also left many vendors wondering what is effective and profitable.

The Internet has in many ways has helped to define what a true relationship needs to be in order to build true relationship differentiation. Today, many organizations continue to struggle in understanding that the Internet is only a tool and they must find their own balance between what can be done and what ought to be done in building the proper relationship with their customers.

What we do know is that merely satisfied customers are looking for the next best offer. They're not raving fans and they do not constitute any significant level of relationship differentiation. We also know that delighted customers become invested mentally and emotionally into making your organization better because you make them feel important. They've come to expect relevant and valuable offerings delivered through consistent and repeated awesome experiences. The bottom line is that when customers have put their trust in you and you in them, you've reached a point of relationship differentiation. This type of emotional trust bond creates a strong relationship differentiation and makes it very hard for competitors to steal your customers.

LEVERAGING CUSTOMER SATISFACTION INTO CUSTOMER DELIGHT

We started this book with stating that the Awesome Customer Challenge is to "stop merely satisfying your customers and start delighting them. Delighting customers will fulfill the dream of creating a new customer or experience economy in which customer loyalty, longevity, brand equity, and solid differentiation can be achieved."

To move from customer satisfaction to customer delight requires you to identify and separate all of your experience-based transactions from your operational-based transactions. (We show you how to do this in Chapter 7.) It requires your organization to become experience-based instead of operational-based. It also requires you to create and deliver memorable, impacting and emotionally bonding customer experiences where all of your operational transactions are linked into supporting those experiences. Only when you realize the value operational information has in supporting your customer experiences can you leverage your customer satisfaction efforts into customer delight efforts.

Chapter 3

A Delightful Experience at Rivers...A Customer Experience Mapping Case Study

*"Try to imagine your business from a customer's point of view
rather than from a business management point of view."*

Brent Smith,
Owner of Rivers Effortless Dining

Chapter 7 is simply delicious! Together we take a step-by-step guided tour through a case study conducted at Rivers Effortless Dining, an upscale, progressive restaurant, using the process of creating and delivering a Totally Awesome Customer Experience and Customer Experience Mapping. Why a restaurant, you ask? Because all of us are "dining experience experts." Almost everyone knows what a delightful dining experience should be – so let's see if Brent and his crew were up to the task.

AN EVENING AT RIVERS

As you approach a well-lit, crowded parking lot on a rainy Friday night, you notice a young man standing under a jumbo umbrella motioning for you to pull up to the curb. He opens the passenger doors, takes the passengers under his jumbo umbrella, and in a very respectful voice says, "Hi! My name is Trent. Welcome to Rivers. Rivers doesn't have valet parking, so please take this umbrella so you can make it back here dry after you park your car." He closes the car door and escorts your guests to the front door, safe and dry. He comments to your guests as they enter, "Thanks for coming to Rivers tonight. I hope we can make this a delightful experience."

Just inside the door, your guests see a fire in a huge rock fireplace at one end of a lobby full of natural colors and warmth. They feel comfortable and immediately at home. Off to their right are the brewing towers where Rivers brews their award-winning microbrews. Even before your guests have taken in all the restaurant décor and ambiance, they're greeted with a big smile from Andrea, one of the hosts. She asks them if they've been to Rivers before (unless, of course, she recognizes them from a past dining experience). They tell Andrea this is their first time at Rivers and they're waiting for you to park the car. "No problem. While you're waiting, let me just hand you the Rivers Story. The card will tell you a little bit about Rivers and shows you the location of our restrooms, our 'experience wall,' our private party rooms, the bar, and our patio."

You make it from the parking lot dry and thankful. You hand the umbrella back to Trent, who opens the door for you. You meet up with your guests just in time to meet Andrea. She shakes your hand, asks your name, and inquires whether this evening is a special event for someone. You tell her your name is Terry and you're celebrating "getting together with old friends for dinner on a Friday night."

Andrea then hands you a Rivers Story card, repeats quickly the usefulness of the card, and hands you a pager. She tells you the wait will be about 35 minutes and escorts you and your guests to the waiting area, where she mentions you can get a cocktail or beverage while you wait.

In less than two or three minutes a cocktail waiter greets you in the waiting area. "Welcome to Rivers! My name is Andy. May I get you a cocktail or beverage?"

As the four of you finish ordering your drinks, an hors d'oeuvres server asks if you would enjoy a complementary hors d'oeuvre from Mike, the head chef. As you talk, eat, and read the story of Rivers, your cocktails arrive. The next thing you know, it's twenty minutes later. You decide to take a quick look at the experience wall before they buzz you. The experience wall is past the bar on the way to the restrooms. The wall is lined with framed letters from customers talking about their delightful experiences at Rivers. You notice they aren't dated 1999 or earlier; they're all very recent. You read a few and return to your friends, telling them about the experience wall.

Right behind you in the waiting area are the awards for their beer brewing. There are also some handouts describing their beer-making process and their different beers. Suddenly your buzzer goes off, indicating it's time to be seated.

As you hand your buzzer to Brittany, the table runner, she says, "Thanks, Terry. I certainly hope your wait was pleasant." You appreciate being called by name and think that the wait not only went by fast, but was also quite pleasant.

You respond to Brittany by saying, "Thank you – we didn't even notice; the time flew by."

"That's wonderful. Please permit me to escort you to your table." All of you follow Brittany to your table. Before anyone sits down, Brittany asks, "Does this table meet with your approval?"

You collectively answer, "Yes," and everyone sits down. Brittany puts a credit card jacket down on the table and says, "I'll just leave this for Aaron. He will be your server tonight. Thanks again for trying Rivers for the first time, and I hope you have a delightful experience with us tonight. I'll let Aaron know you've arrived."

Within minutes Aaron arrives, picks up the credit card jacket, and welcomes all of you to Rivers for the first time. He looks at you and says, "Terry, it looks like you and your guests are celebrating a Friday night out with old friends. I don't mean you're old, I mean you've known each other a long time." All of you smile at Aaron's innocent comment. "Let me introduce myself. I'm Aaron – and you are?" Within a few seconds Aaron has introduced himself and found out everyone's first name. You still wonder how he knew your name, that it was your first time to Rivers, and that you were celebrating with old friends on a Friday night. It doesn't really matter, because you're having such a wonderful time so far.

Aaron asks, "Can I refresh your beverages? Or perhaps tell you about our microbrews?"

You listen as Aaron describes a few of the very unique microbrews, but decide to stick with what you were drinking. "Okay. I'll be back shortly with some ice water and wonderful homemade bread."

As Aaron returns with another round of beverages, ice water, and bread, he says, "I just want to mention that my job tonight is to make your dining experience at Rivers truly delightful. I would very much appreciate your help in letting me know what I can do to accomplish that for you."

You pause for a moment, thinking about what Aaron just said and thinking to yourself, "What would be a truly delightful dining experience?" Now you're trying to conjure up both the physical images and emotional feelings of what have been truly delightful dining experiences.

Aaron then asks, "Can I interest anyone in one of our fresh appetizers?" Aaron proceeds to describe his two favorites and why. He then tells you the head chef Mike's and the owner Brent's favorites, but you can tell Aaron is quite convinced his choices are better.

You and your guests choose one of Aaron's favorites and an order of calamari, which is one of Sarah's favorites. After he takes your appetizer order, he proceeds to introduce you to the chef's specials, but not in the standard "spit them out with their one hundred different ingredients so fast that no can remember a single thing they just heard except maybe chicken, or fish of some kind." Aaron speaks slowly and deliberately. He describes each special with passion.

You notice that every special has a story behind it. Although the stories are short, they're memorable. The stories are about the thoughts and history behind why Mike created it. Aaron tells you about the Ahi Tuna special. "Mike prepares the Ahi extra spicy and rare because one day Brent, the owner, asked him to prepare something with a kick to it that he could take camping. He wanted something that would keep well in the cooler and cook reasonably quickly. Brent loved it." Aaron finishes the stories, which certainly make all the specials easy to remember.

Aaron says, "Let me get your appetizer order into the kitchen. Then I'll be back to take your main course orders...oh, by the way, I'm not sure how you would like to pace your dining tonight. What is your pleasure?"

You're looking at your other guests when Nancy says, "Since we haven't seen each other for over a year, we're not in a big hurry, except for those appetizers." You all laugh because everyone is getting a bit hungry and the appetizers sounded so good. "But we'd like to wait a bit for the main course to be served."

"Wonderful. I'll speed up the appetizer order, come back to get your main course order, and get those menus out of your way so you can relax, and enjoy each other's company. Does that sound all right with everyone?" Everyone nods.

As Aaron leaves the table, Kim can't help mentioning how pleasant Aaron is and how special he seems to make people feel.

The appetizer is on the table in about ten minutes!

"If it's all right with everyone, I can take your main course orders now and let you relax." In less than two minutes, Aaron takes all four orders and goes off, letting you talk, eat, relax, and enjoy your time together. As you think about your main course order, you're not sure whether you ordered it because it was what you wanted to eat or because of the great story behind it.

Aaron occasionally checks back to see if your beverage containers are full. He says nothing that interrupts your conversation, and all of you appreciate his courtesy. When you finish your appetizers, he reappears and asks, "Would it be all right if I place your main course orders into the kitchen now?" You all say yes and go on with your conversation.

Twenty minutes later, your main courses arrive. Aaron says, "Kim, the Ahi looks wonderful – one of my favorites. Terry, Mike would love to know what you think about the rack of lamb tonight. Sarah, that swordfish looks to kill for, and Annette, you're absolutely going to be delighted with the lobster salad; the dressing is phenomenal. Please enjoy. Is there anything else I can get for anyone right now?"

Aaron makes sure your wine and water glasses are filled. Just before he leaves, he says, "You might want to think about leaving some room for dessert. We can always box what you don't finish, because Rivers is absolutely famous for its desserts. When I return I'll tell you about a unique dessert called a Stout Kahalua Shake – it's truly unbelievable."

You immediately think, "Beer and ice cream? How can that taste good? But maybe there's something I'm missing."

The food is undeniably excellent and hot. You continue your conversation as though you're the only people in the restaurant. Aaron only checks back to see if everything is okay, leaving you to your conversation.

When you finish, Aaron appears once more, asking, "Are you ready to see what we have for dessert? Can I have anything boxed up for anyone?"

"I'd like to hear more about the Stout Kahalua Shake," Annette says.

"The Stout Kahalua Shake is a combination of vanilla ice cream, our famous Stout Lager, and Kahalua, all made into a thick shake. If you don't like it, you don't pay for it – but I get to drink the rest. All of our desserts are made here at Rivers. Our dessert chef is very particular about what ends up on the menu. My favorites are, of course, the Stout Kahalua Shake and the bread pudding with whiskey sauce. Before you order, however, I'd like to buy the table one of our Crème Brule's as my way of thanking you for coming to Rivers for your first time. Now what else would you like to try?"

Aaron takes the dessert order and asks if you would like an after-dinner drink, espresso, cappuccino, or coffee, then once again makes sure everything is properly taken care of at your table before he departs.

Five minutes later, dessert arrives with your after-dinner drinks. You can't believe how good the Stout Kahalua Shake tastes! Aaron was right. It's unbelievable.

The desserts are shared and conversation resumes, but some of your conversation is about how wonderful the evening has been. Aaron then asks, "Is there anything else I can get anyone?"

Everyone says no and Kim tells Aaron, "This was just delightful, and you have been marvelous."

Aaron graciously thanks her and asks, "Is it all right if I bring the check? You can pay it at your leisure, but I wouldn't want to hold anyone up just in case." You tell him yes.

Before Aaron returns, Nick, one of the floor managers, approaches your table and says, "I just wanted to stop by to say hello and welcome you to Rivers. I understand this is your first time here. How is your dining experience going with us tonight?"

To create a Totally Awesome Customer Experience it takes the desire to go beyond satisfying your customers to wanting to delight them.

You notice that everyone is trying to talk to Nick at the same time. You're hearing comments like "wonderful," "superb," "delightful," "can't wait to come back," from all around the table.

"I hope you'll return so we can repeat this experience for you many times. Thanks so much for coming in. I believe Aaron will be right back with your check. Have a wonderful evening and please have one of our people help you to your car if it's still raining outside."

Aaron returns with the check, simply setting it in the middle of the table and leaving you alone to finish the last few words of your hour-long, non-stop conversation. Aaron collects the check. When he returns, he says, "It has been my pleasure serving you tonight. I hope I did my job in making this a delightful dining experience. I would love it if you ask for me again when you return. Did Nick remind you to have someone help you to your car if it's still raining out? Splendid. Thank you so much, and I look forward to being of service again on your next visit to Rivers."

Andrea engages you on the way out, thanking you for coming to Rivers for the first time and hoping that your Friday night "long overdue" conversation was wonderful. She also reminds you of the rain and gets the door. Trent has you back in the car, safe and dry, and you can't help thinking, "That was a delightful experience."

It took Rivers six complete Customer Experience Maps, all coordinated and executed beautifully from start to finish, to receive Terry's, Kim's, Annette's, and Sarah's Delight Vote without a single Experience Voting Point. This Totally Awesome Customer Experience did not take place by chance. It took place because each experience-based transaction was carefully mapped, trained, and executed. Everyone read the audience and passed the information to each other as a team. Therefore, Aaron knew how to engage the table, how formal he needed to be, how involved, and so on. This kind of planning takes commitment, imagination, knowledge, and discipline.

Just so you know, we had no idea how complex running a large restaurant could be! Restaurants are not simply a service business. They're a just-in-time manufacturing business as well. They often deal in both business-to-consumer (dining at the restaurant) and business-to-business (catering) activities. They're constantly challenged with issues such as inventory obsolescence, employee turnover and training, predicting customer volume, brand presence, customer awareness, customer loyalty, competition, and even the weather. They have all the issues.

We found out that running a successful restaurant requires an incredible amount of time and effort. It's really a passion business. We had a totally awesome experience working with Brent Smith, the managing owner of Rivers Effortless Dining. His enthusiasm, his quick thinking, and his passion for his business made Customer Experience Mapping and producing a Totally Awesome Customer Experiences at Rivers enjoyable and exciting.

By the way, the Totally Awesome Customer Experience you just read came as a result of using the concepts, processes, and tools in the first six chapters of this book. It's the translation of Rivers' Customer Experience Vision put into practice. We wrote out the experience soon after we reviewed Rivers' Customer Experience Maps. We also attended their "experience kick-off meeting" with all of the employees and saw the maps in action. That made it quite easy.

WELCOME TO RIVERS EFFORTLESS DINING

Rivers Effortless Dining is an upscale restaurant with a very nice microbrewery and an excellent wine list. Its location at the base of the beautiful Wasatch Mountains in Salt Lake City near four of Utah's finest ski resorts makes an ideal place for visitors and residents alike to share the ambiance and cuisine of this wonderful restaurant. We have eaten there many times.

Rivers is large. Including its beautiful patio and two large party rooms, Rivers can seat over 350 customers. Its size, over 14,000 square feet, presents its own set of challenges in keeping a dining experience highly personal and intimate.

The owners of Rivers Effortless Dining are Brent Smith and Steve Urry. The vision for Rivers is Brent's. Prior to Rivers, Brent started, partially-owned, and managed a company called Redrock Brewery, a successful microbrewery and pub eatery in downtown Salt Lake City. Before Redrock, Brent was in the construction business.

Brent is a very imaginative businessman. His sense of humor and quick wit made it fun to work with him. We also noticed that Brent has the unique ability to move quickly back and forth between his right brain and left brain. This ability worked extremely well when he needed to concentrate on both the art and science of Customer Experience Mapping. We asked Brent to provide you with as much of his insight and commentary as possible throughout this case study. We're sure you'll find Brent's comments invaluable when you begin your journey.

Gary first met Brent on the Fourth of July (Rivers is always open). During their first meeting, Brent told Gary the story of Rivers. This story, presented on the following page, reflects Brent's vision and mission for the restaurant.

The Story Behind Rivers...

There are three elements of a restaurant with which all customers come into personal contact: the physical elements (commonly called the ambiance), the staff (the people who work at the restaurant), and the food. We built Rivers with the mission to bring all three of those elements together for our customers as a single delightful experience.

We began fulfilling our mission by creating an environment that closely resembles nature. We wanted the ambiance of Rivers to have a relaxing effect on people by surrounding them with natural elements. Our wall colors, window frames, floor colors, rocks on the fireplace, wood floors, and walls all reflect the colors of the surrounding mountains and fauna. All of these elements work together to bring about a feeling of peacefulness.

Our staff at Rivers is hired and trained in a way to instill a feeling of family. They are encouraged to socialize together after work and invited to dine and taste all the food at Rivers. This fosters a great cooperative working environment, creating relaxed feelings and caring. We believe that a relaxed and friendly atmosphere for employees to work in will promote a relaxed and friendly atmosphere for our customers.

Rivers' menu was designed with familiarity in mind. We pride ourselves in giving our customers foods they feel comfortable ordering and eating. In many ways the Rivers' menu resembles the way our customers might eat at home, with the exception of our preparation and presentation methods. Our head chef strives to serve standard American foods, creatively prepared and presented.

Rivers is open almost every day of the year. We want our customers to know we will be there for them whenever they want to feel special and want to relax and enjoy a wonderful meal in a great environment served by friendly, caring people.

Brent Smith

GETTING DOWN TO BUSINESS – THE EXPERIENCE BUSINESS

In our first official session, called our Awareness and Briefing session, we spent several hours with Brent discussing the objectives and potential benefits of doing the case study for Rivers. We talked about the concepts and principles behind creating and delivering Totally Awesome Customer Experiences. We also described some of the tools, such as Customer Experience Mapping and the Initial Transaction Assessment, we developed to help create and deliver Totally Awesome Customer Experiences.

We then talked in depth about the Awesome Customer Challenge to stop merely satisfying customers and start delighting them. It was interesting to watch Brent go through the thought process behind the Awesome Customer Challenge. His comments:

> The Awesome Customer Challenge is absolutely right. Who rushes home to call up their best friend and tell them about a satisfying experience? No one. I wouldn't. On the other hand, I can see our customers immediately getting in their cars, grabbing their cell phones, and calling their best friends and telling them they just had the most delightful experience at Rivers. This is where we must be, every day, at every table.

Brent mentioned that his general manager had just resigned and the timing could not have been better. He also mentioned that until he found the right replacement, he was going to assume the general manager's role. He looked forward to learning and using the new processes and tools himself before introducing them to the Rivers staff. He thought the entire idea was too important to delegate. We provided Brent with a manuscript of this book and scheduled the first working session.

Here are some of Brent's comments after our Awareness and Briefing session:

> Prior to discussing customer experiences with Gary, I had not realized my restaurant was such an operational-based business. We worked hard at making operations the sole focus of our efforts. We thought by making the business efficient and effective from an operational perspective – that is, everything works smoothly, customers are being seated, food is being delivered, bills are being paid – the customer will leave totally satisfied and become a loyal customer. However, as we have discovered, mere customer satisfaction does not create the desired "word-of-mouth" activity necessary to create a really successful restaurant. You need customer experience-based techniques to create delightful customer experiences, which will fuel the dis-

cussion your customers have with their friends. This is how to create the business you really want to have, and this is what we will be doing from now on at Rivers.

Our next session was our first working session. It marked the actual beginning of the engagement. We took some time to discuss in detail Customer Experience Mapping. We discussed our approach to the engagement, starting with Chapter 6 (implementation) and moving to Chapter 3 (the process of creating and delivering Totally Awesome Customer Experiences). Chapters 4 and 5 contain the detailed tools we will use.

We started out by giving Brent the Customer Focus and Customer Trust Currency questionnaires (Chapter 1) to fill out. The responses would give us a starting point.

Rivers originally scored a "6" on the customer focus questionnaire and a "6" on the Customer Trust Currency questionnaire.

The initial customer focus questionnaire showed Rivers as being customer-manipulative. Their complete focus was on perfecting their operations, in addition to training their employees on those operations. They assumed that great operations would lead to loyal customers. They also assumed that they knew more about what the customers wanted in a dining experience than the customers themselves. After all, Rivers, not the customer, was in the restaurant business. What could a customer know that Rivers didn't know about having a Totally Awesome Dining Experience? The answer, of course, always turns out to be "a lot."

When we first asked Brent if Rivers was customer-focused, he said, "Absolutely. We work very hard at performing all of the operations necessary to be as efficient and effective as we can be in taking care of the customer."

As we look back on the engagement, we still marvel at the rapid change Rivers has made in converting from an operational-based to an experience-based organization and from being customer-manipulative to being customer-focused. Brent says:

> Now that we see what an enormous difference being experience-based makes, we'll never go back to being operationally focused. It will still take some time for everyone to adjust because of all of our previous habits, but we're getting there fast. What is truly amazing, however, is that our new perspective allows all of us to see new opportunities much quicker and implement them much faster.

The score on the Customer Relationship Currency questionnaire surprised us. Rivers scored at the Customer Knowledge Currency level. We expected them to be at the lower Customer Information Currency level. When we took a closer look, we finally understood why. It was Brent's rigorous insistence that Rivers always makes good on the promises it makes to their customers. This policy builds trust.

Although Rivers has no formal customer data-gathering system (CRM or the like), they track all information about the meals, the times, the servers, the tips, and so on. They use this information in predicting customer behavior. In addition, Brent had used a survey service called the "Secret Shopper." This service sends a professional dining person, posing as a customer, to rate the performance of your restaurant during his or her visit. We reviewed the Secret Shopper report in some detail. We noticed that the vast majority of the performance categories were operational in nature, but some segments did provide some customer insight. Because the Secret Shopper was only a single data point, however, Brent did not fully rely on the results in the report to make decisions.

Last but not least, Rivers did some customer satisfaction surveying. We examined Rivers' customer satisfaction cards over lunch (the blackened halibut salad and cold shrimp soup were out of this world). Brent stated that the results of the survey were inconclusive as well. They didn't lead him to any specific course of action. He wasn't convinced the information was accurate, and it didn't have a "pulse," as Brent put it.

Most customer satisfaction surveys are company and operationally oriented, not customer experience focused. If you want to improve the customer experience, that should be the focus of the survey.

To finish up our Customer Trust Currency discussion, we talked about knowing customer audiences. We discovered that Brent had a pretty good grasp of Rivers' top four audiences and was presently targeting his advertising to those audiences.

Phase One

After lunch we began Phase One, the Initial Transaction Assessment (Chapter 6). We spent the rest of the afternoon learning Brent's vision and mission objectives and doing the assessment. We laid out all the experience-based transactions along with their associated operational-based transactions and compared them to Rivers' vision and mission objectives.

Experience-based Transactions

This exercise was very helpful to Brent. For the first time, Brent was able to see his business from the perspective of the customer rather than from the perspective of an operations manager.

Here is a recap of Rivers' mission objectives...

- Create an ambiance that provides the look and feel of nature to help customers relax.

- Treat employees as extended family, training them with the skills necessary to deliver experiences to and evoke special feelings from the customer.

- Prepare excellent food that the customer easily recognizes and enjoys time after time.

- Be available any time our customers want to feel special.

In the interim, we met Mike, the head chef, and we briefly discussed the engagement objectives with him. He was delighted about the direction. We let Brent do most of the explaining. We were impressed by how much Brent already understood about meeting the Awesome Customer Challenge.

Brent was gracious enough to let us show you some of the results they created by using our tools in transitioning Rivers from an operational-based organization to an experience-based organization. In the next few pages, we show you those results.

Here's the completed Initial Transaction Assessment for River's experience-based transactions.

Experience-based Transactions – Rivers

Transaction Title	Transaction Purpose
Calling for Reservations	Allows the customer to make a reservation within the guidelines of the restaurant. Since there are guidelines, extra care must be taken to handle guests who want reservations but don't qualify, making sure they're still excited about coming to Rivers. This is also the first contact a customer might have with Rivers. We must appear enthusiastic and professional.
Getting to and from the Entrance Safely, Easily and Dry	We don't want soggy customers. This doesn't start their dining experience out on a positive note. We need to get them from the parking lot into our restaurant in a great mood and ready to enjoy the rest of their dining experience.
Hosting	To make guests feel welcome as they begin their dining experience. It's the first and last human contact our guests have, so it's very important. It's a primary point of acquiring information to create the continuous experience. Hosting covers both the welcome and farewell to restaurant guests.
Waiting for the Beeper to Go Off	On busy nights guests must wait. We need to make waiting just as delightful as enjoying their meal. Waiting can never be allowed to dominate the customer's experience.
Getting to the Table	We want our guests to have a continuous experience in getting from the waiting area to their table.
Serving Food and Drink	The point of a dining experience is dining. Most of the time our guests spend with us will be with our servers. There will be five different segments we must consider. They are: selection and callout of food and drink, waiting for food and drink, eating and drinking, manager introduction, and paying the bill. The guests must also be passed from the host or runner to the server, and back to the host when finished.
Calling for Private Party Reservations	Private parties are worth a lot of money and goodwill. Callers are looking for a person to immediately help them through the process. It must be fast, competent, and well-organized.
Hosting a Private Party	Private parties must delight the sponsor and their guests. Delighting guests encourages them to return to dine on their own and to tell others about the party.
Delivery to the Marriott Residence Inn Guests	Provide Marriott guests the ability to order room service from Rivers. This helps the Marriott extend their customer value.
Catered Events	Extend Rivers' reach beyond its present walls to include a larger audience.
Beer-Tasting and Wine-Tasting Events	Provide an awareness of the fine beer brewed at Rivers and the extensive wine list.
Event Sponsorship	Gain exposure to audiences of Rivers' food and beverage at special events like Gallivan Center Concerts

Operational-based Transactions

Since Brent is already a master at operational-based transactions, he didn't want to spend the time we had together to assess operational transactions. He mentioned that they've documented all their operational transactions and used them in training their employees. Everyone in the restaurant understood the operational transactions. We did, however, convince Brent to spend some time and effort performing an operational transaction assessment at a later date, since it would provide him three distinct advantages:

- Help eliminate time-consuming and costly operational transactions that don't support experience-based transactions.

- Help increase server face time with customers by shifting unnecessary operational transactions away from the server.

- Help demonstrate to servers the direct impact that perceived unnecessary operational transactions can have on the quality of the experience of their customers and amount of tips they receive.

Here are Brent's comments after doing the Initial Transaction Assessment. You'll find them quite insightful.

> Most companies have a mindset that begins and ends with the operations of their business. This makes their businesses operationally based. Rivers was no exception. But once your organization has mastered these operational procedures, you must move on to the more important aspects of your business – the customer experiences. You will initially struggle to change your collective mindset from being operationally based to experience-based. This is because everything we are taught or read comes from an operational management approach. Even the great management books that I've read concentrate on operations. It's hard to believe how much I've learned about my business in just a couple of sessions by simply changing my mindset to an experience-based orientation. My managers are also working very hard to re-orient themselves.

> The power of the Initial Transaction Assessment is that it lays out everything right in front of your eyes. It allows you to walk yourself through the customers' experience...trying to feel their expectations, and learn what it will take to delight them. It's really a different thought process, but once you do it you will never go back to operationally based thinking again.

Phase Two

Once we completed our Initial Transaction Assessment, we went into Phase Two, where Brent decided which Totally Awesome Customer Experiences he wanted to tackle initially. He selected two:

- A Totally Awesome Customer Experience for the casual customer who comes to Rivers to feel special and to enjoy a great meal.

- A Totally Awesome Customer Experience for private parties.

Brent did not want to do Phase Three, a pilot, so we moved directly into Phase Four for doing a rollout. In this particular case, Brent was the only voter, so we had the luxury of moving forward quickly with the process of creating and delivering for the two selected Totally Awesome Customer Experiences on a rollout basis.

We recalled a conversation during this session in which we asked Brent how applicable he felt the principles and tools were to different types and sizes of organizations. Brent responded:

> I don't think business type matters. What matters is whether your organization is concerned enough to want to create and deliver delightful experiences to your customers. That's it in a nutshell. Just look at the horrible experiences you get at your doctor's office, or with your attorney, or any professional or governmental organization, for that matter. Look at grocery stores, mutual funds companies, or the claims department in insurance companies. They can all use everything we're doing here at Rivers, maybe even more. At least we knew going into this process that our job was to satisfy the customer. I wonder if they even know that? Now we know that our job is to delight the customer.

> As for the size of the organization, that doesn't matter, either. A one-person office can use this as well as General Motors. The key is to make these concepts and tools work for you in your environment. What matters is your commitment to making great experiences happen for your customers. You have to come to the full realization that you no longer want to just satisfy your customers, but instead you want to delight them. If you get that simple idea and make it your goal, these concepts and tools will deliver the results you're looking for. If you

don't get that idea and it isn't your goal, you might as well just carry on with trying to improve your operations, believing, as we once did, that being great at operations will someday give you loyal customers.

I can imagine that larger organizations with a more political environment won't be able to implement as quickly as we can. But they can implement if they want to do it. There's no doubt that smaller to mid-size businesses will have the edge when it comes to implementing quickly.

RIVERS' CUSTOMER EXPERIENCE MAPPING

We began our third session by starting on the selected experiences. We were now fully enveloped in the process of creating and delivering Totally Awesome Customer Experiences (Chapter 3) using Customer Experience Mapping (Chapter 4).The first step was to visualize the two selected Totally Awesome Customer Experiences. Here are their visions:

For the casual dining experience...

> We want to make our customers as comfortable at Rivers as they are in their homes by always making them feel special with a delightful dining experience. We want our customers to tell their friends about their delightful experience and come back many times to relive those experiences. We want our customers to feel in control of their delightful experience and to understand the story behind Rivers and our passion for making each visit a totally awesome dining experience.

For the private party experience...

> We need to recognize that we have two different customers to delight at a private party: the party host and the party guests. We want the party host and the party guests to feel that Rivers was the best possible place to hold their celebration or event. A party host must feel that hosting a party at Rivers is a no-hassle process and that we've helped them meet all their party objectives. We want everyone telling everybody about his or her awesome experience.

After developing the visions, we addressed the basic customer audiences. We would do specific profiling later during the Customer Experience Mapping phase.

Customer Audience Chart – Rivers

Description of the Audience	Audience # and Rank
The corporate diner ordering wine, beer, spirits	1
The corporate diner ordering non-alcoholic beverages	2
Meetings with corporate diners extending through dinner	3
Meetings with corporate diners extending through lunch	4
Corporate lunches	5
Women's/Men's and professional clubs	6
Seniors	7
Non-corporate diner ordering wine, beer, spirits	8
Non-corporate non-drinkers ordering non-alcoholic beverages	9
Families	10

We next established the Customer Experience Maps we needed to create our Customer Experience Map Pool for both Totally Awesome Customer Experiences.

Here are the Customer Experience Maps we needed to build:

Customer Experience Map Chart – Rivers

Customer Experience Map (CEM)	Map Number
Calling for Table Reservations	CEM 1
Getting from the Parking Lot Safe and Dry	CEM 2
Hosting	CEM 3
Waiting for the Buzzer to Go Off	CEM 4
Getting to the Table	CEM 5
Serving Food and Drink	CEM 6
Calling for Party Reservations	CEM 7
Managing a Private Party	CEM 8

Then we simply created the Customer Experience Map Pool.

Customer Experience Map Pool – Rivers

CEM	Audience Number									
	1	**2**	**3**	**4**	**5**	**6**	**7**	**8**	**9**	**10**
	PI 2	PI 3	PI 4	PI 2	PI 3	PI 3	PI 4	PI 5	PI 5	PI 4
CEM 1 Table Res	X	X	X	X	X	X	X	X	X	X
CEM 2 Safe/Dry	X	X	X	X	X	X	X	X	X	X
CEM 3 Hosting	X	X	X	X	X	X	X	X	X	X
CEM 4 Waiting	X	X	X	X	X	X	X	X	X	X
CEM 5 Table	X	X	X	X	X	X	X	X	X	X
CEM 6 Serving	X	X	X	X	X	X	X	X	X	X
CEM 7 Party Res	X	X	X	X	X	X	X	X	X	X
CEM 8 Manage	X	X	X	X	X	X	X	X	X	X

Does everybody now see Brent's challenge as a restaurateur? Every customer audience he encounters can use any of the Customer Experience Maps. It's not until Brent brings in more specialized events such as beer-tasting or Marriott dinner delivery service that specific Customer Experience Maps are required. Rivers personnel must have a complete understanding and be thoroughly trained on all Customer Experience Maps at all times.

We finished the session with matching the appropriate Customer Experience Maps to the two selected Totally Awesome Customer Experiences.

Experience	CEM 1	CEM 2	CEM 3	CEM 4	CEM 5	CEM 6	CEM 7	CEM 8
Table Dining	X	X	X	X	X	X		
Private parties		X	X			X	X	X

As we were finishing our third session together, Brent made a comment about using customer experience language that really hit home. It reinforced the attempt we've been making in the book to punctuate the use of customer experience language...

> To discuss delighting customers requires a new language. It isn't good enough to continue with your same old operational language with a few experience interjections. When you start using the customer experience language, employees begin to take you seriously. They begin to feel what customer expectations are and take the proper actions to meet those expectations, rather than simply wanting to manipulate your customers into the experience they feel like delivering. We thought the use of the language was a bit overdone when we first started this process. We now realize that if we had not started to overuse the language a bit ourselves, especially with our employees, they would have seen this entire process in the perspective of "business as usual" or "Brent's idea de jour." It's my experience that employees tend to take a wait-and-see attitude, so you need something that keeps the process flowing. The customer experience language helped us to overcome a lot of issues right at the beginning of the process.

The fourth, fifth, sixth, and seventh sessions were all dedicated to building the required Customer Experience Maps using Customer Experience Mapping. We initially helped Brent build the first four Customer Experience Maps, but after that Brent built them without our assistance. We started with building the Customer Experience Maps for the Casual Customer experience – the customer who simply comes to Rivers to feel special and enjoy a great meal. The following pages contain a sample collection of three Customer Experience Maps that Brent has been kind enough to share. They are for the "casual dining experience" customer.

Rivers' Customer Experience Map #3

Map Title: *Hosting*

Customer Audiences: Casual Diners

Experience Response Point:

We want our guests to feel welcomed in a friendly, organized environment where they are immediately recognized, made to feel very special, and appreciated for coming to Rivers.

Experience Touch Points:

1 **Greeting the guests** and getting them prepared to be seated or enter the waiting area.

This is what the host will do at this Experience Touch Point.
   A. Greet the guests with a positive attitude and big smile.
   B. Have them introduces themselves, using their first names.
   C. Ask the guests if they have ever been to Rivers before. If this is the guests' first time, hand them a Rivers Story card and explain the points of interest in the restaurant.
   D. Ask how many people are in their party, and where they would like to dine (inside or outside).
      a. If there is no wait, the host escorts them to their table. If this is their first time to Rivers, the host uses the map on the back of the Rivers Story card to point out the locations of the restrooms, phones, bar, brewing towers, experience wall, and private dining rooms. The host seats the guests and either introduces them to their server or tells the guests that he or she will notify their server they are seated and waiting.
      b. If there is a wait, the host explains the waiting procedures (the buzzer system, the waiting areas, and so forth). If this is their first time here, escort them to the waiting areas, and seat them in the best possible relaxing place. Host tells the guests there is a cocktail person who will be around shortly to take their drink orders.

(continued)

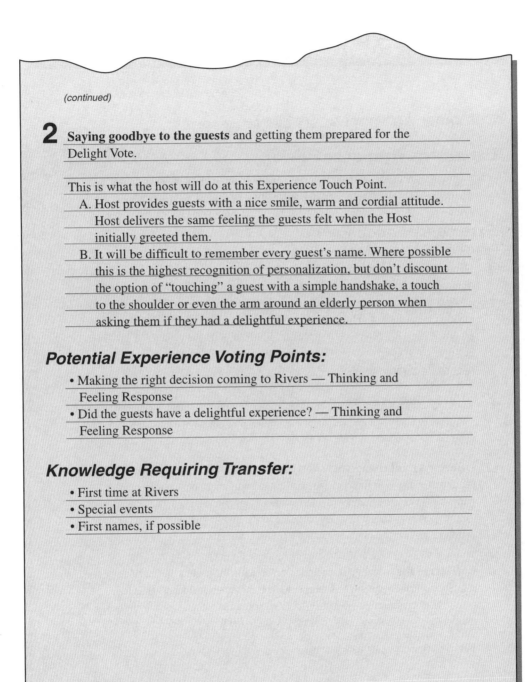

(continued)

2 **Saying goodbye to the guests** and getting them prepared for the Delight Vote.

This is what the host will do at this Experience Touch Point.
   A. Host provides guests with a nice smile, warm and cordial attitude. Host delivers the same feeling the guests felt when the Host initially greeted them.
   B. It will be difficult to remember every guest's name. Where possible this is the highest recognition of personalization, but don't discount the option of "touching" a guest with a simple handshake, a touch to the shoulder or even the arm around an elderly person when asking them if they had a delightful experience.

Potential Experience Voting Points:
- Making the right decision coming to Rivers — Thinking and Feeling Response
- Did the guests have a delightful experience? — Thinking and Feeling Response

Knowledge Requiring Transfer:
- First time at Rivers
- Special events
- First names, if possible

Rivers' Customer Experience Map #4

Map Title: *Waiting for the Buzzer to Go Off*

Customer Audiences: Casual Diners

Experience Response Point:

We want our guests to feel that the wait was what they were told and the waiting experience was not only enjoyable, but went by quickly.

Experience Touch Points:

1 **Offering a beverage or appetizer**. The cocktail person (CP) greets guests in a timely manner and warmly welcomes them to Rivers. CP asks if they can get the guests a beverage or an appetizer while they are waiting for their table to be prepared. The order must be filled quickly. CP casually asks the guests if they are having a delightful experience. If the answer is anything but a yes, CP asks why and immediately communicates any concerns to the host or floor manager.

2 **Offering hors d'oeuvres**. The hors d'oeuvres person moves through the crowd at busy times, offering guests hors d'oeuvres with an engaging smile and thanking them for coming to Rivers.

3 **Offering visual engagement**. The media around Rivers (including the art, the awards, the delighted customer letters, and perhaps some published pamphlets on the brewery or the restaurant) will all be coordinated in the map of Rivers. This will allow a guest to do a self-guided tour, or engage in reading.

2 **Retrieving the buzzer**. The runner or host will initiate contact as they see a guest approaching the host stand with the buzzer blinking. If at all possible, the runner or host should have some information on the guests, especially their names, whether this is their first visit to Rivers, and any

(continued)

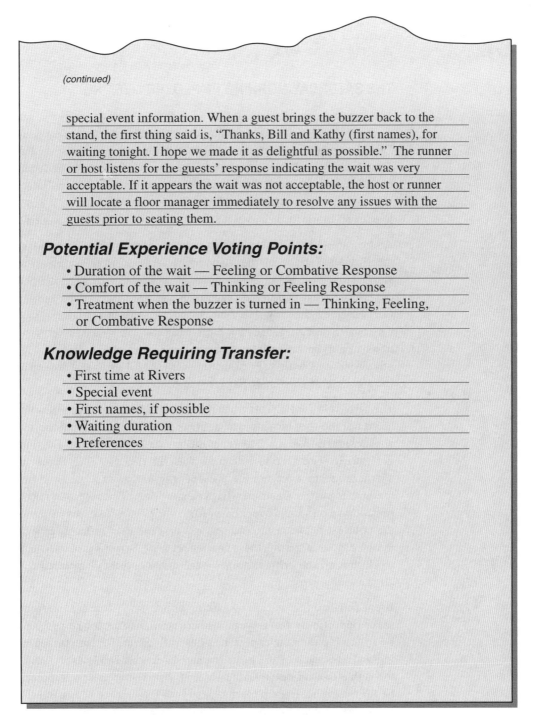

(continued)

special event information. When a guest brings the buzzer back to the stand, the first thing said is, "Thanks, Bill and Kathy (first names), for waiting tonight. I hope we made it as delightful as possible." The runner or host listens for the guests' response indicating the wait was very acceptable. If it appears the wait was not acceptable, the host or runner will locate a floor manager immediately to resolve any issues with the guests prior to seating them.

Potential Experience Voting Points:

- Duration of the wait — Feeling or Combative Response
- Comfort of the wait — Thinking or Feeling Response
- Treatment when the buzzer is turned in — Thinking, Feeling, or Combative Response

Knowledge Requiring Transfer:

- First time at Rivers
- Special event
- First names, if possible
- Waiting duration
- Preferences

Brent arranged some role-playing for a couple of Customer Experience Maps we had built.

Once the eight Customer Experience Maps were completed, Brent was ready to begin training his staff and putting them into action. Brent started this process by calling a company meeting. Brent invited us to the Saturday meeting as observers.

THE SATURDAY MORNING EMPLOYEE MEETING

You can imagine all the talk that went through the 65 employees as we were meeting with Brent and his management staff during this case study process. Everyone knew something was up, but no one was sure what it entailed. They had noticed that Brent's language was different. He had started to talk more about customer experiences and Experience Touch Points and this strange new term, Customer Experience Mapping. No one was quite sure how everything fit. It was time for Brent to share his new vision.

Andrea started the meeting with announcements and the regular employee meeting stuff. Each of the managers took a turn talking about operational stuff. This took about 30 minutes to complete. Brent got up and began explaining what had taken place over the past four weeks and what he had learned along the way. He did a wonderful job in explaining the Awesome Customer Challenge. He accomplished this task by asking employees questions about being satisfied versus being delighted. Brent made it quite humorous, but with very high impact. He had arranged some role-playing for a couple of Customer Experience Maps we had built.

The first role-play involved the map for "Hosting." The role-playing team acted out the way hosting was at present and then acted out the way the map was designed to work. The team did great! It was a lot of fun and everyone got into it. The second role-play was for the "Serving Food" map. Once again, the team acted out the present way food was served and then the new method from the Customer Experience Map. The role-playing had a high impact on every employee. Even from our perspective, it was amazing to see the contrast between the old process and the new process, especially when you see people acting the experiences out. Scripting needed a little more work, but all the critical points were made and they appeared to stick with all the employees.

Brent finished the session by talking about the vision and the future, and the sheer opportunity for servers to increase their tips by 20 to 30 percent just by following the new experience-based formula. He then talked about training and how each of the hosts, runners, servers, and bussers would be going through a one-on-one training session. Brent shared how important it would be for everyone to learn all the Customer Experience Maps and their linkage in the creation and delivery of Totally Awesome Customer Experiences. He also mentioned that becoming experience-based would eliminate a lot of stress in the non-tip-related areas such as hosting, cooking, and dishwashing. He also indicated that as the restaurant increases its profits, the salaries in the non-tip-related areas would increase as well.

Brent's enthusiasm made the meeting stand out and become something greater than just another regular employee meeting. You felt a new energy. It was clear he had set a new direction and standard for Rivers during that meeting.

The hardest part is keeping focused on Experiences and not getting dragged back down into the operations.

BRENT'S FINAL COMMENTS

We couldn't have asked for a better case study opportunity. Brent's passion, energy, and ability to implement quickly made this a delightful experience for us. We want to end this case study by leaving you with Brent's final comments.

> The process of creating awesome customer experiences at Rivers has only just begun. Coming up with your vision and building your Customer Experience Maps only marks the starting point of what will end up being a long-term commitment to delighting our customers. We've not yet mastered the subtleties of using the different Experience Touch Points in our experiences, but we'll get there. We also need to extend this process beyond our physical restaurant to our website, our catering, our advertising, and all points of contact with our customers.

> We have a lot of training and retraining to do. This will be a major key to our success. Your maps are only as good as your ability to train your employees to use them and they must use them with passion.

> One of the major benefits of this process is that I now understand the type of employees I want to hire in the future, whether management or staff. This process focused me immediately on the individuals I want in my company. I always thought hiring great operational people was the key. I now know that hiring people with a passion for delighting others is the first criteria.

> From a business perspective, this knowledge will make us more competitive. We will be out to win over the customers of our competitors. Once we do, it will be nearly impossible for them to win them back. I am only guessing how much additional revenue becoming experience-based will generate, but my preliminary estimates are about 20 to 30 percent from where we are today. Since we have a lot of fixed costs, I imagine the profit growth will be even greater.

Rivers' Customer Experience Map #6

Map Title: *Serving Food*

Customer Audiences: Casual Diners

Experience Response Point:

We want our guests to have a delightful meal and feel good about paying their bill while anticipating what they want to order next time they come in.

Experience Touch Points:

1 **Introduction of the server.** This takes a moment as the server scans the table packet left by the runner. The information card needs to contain as much information as possible. The key pieces of information are: name, first time, special event, and waiting time. Other information is optional, but helpful. The information will be in the form of color-coded icons. The table packets will be color-coded themselves to let the server know if the customer is a "first timer" or returning customer. The servers introduce themselves to the guests and tell the guests the purpose of their job. If it's the guests' first time at Rivers, "My job is to make this a delightful dining experience." If this is not their first visit, "As you probably know, the purpose of my job is to…" The server tries to get everyone's name and make some notes. The server will make deserved compliments to the guests. The server will ask some "high criteria" questions to increase trust and build rapport rapidly. The server establishes the amount of time the guests have to dine and the experience the guests are hoping to achieve.

2 "**Can I get anybody a cocktail or beverage?**" The server takes the order and returns to the table with the drinks. "Can I interest anyone in an appetizer? We have some wonderful appetizers. Let me tell you a couple of my favorites. What is your pleasure?" If they don't order an appetizer, the server will ask the guests if they want to enjoy their cocktail or beverage, or move directly to the specials. The specials will all have a short story behind them from Mike, the chef. The server asks if there are

(continued)

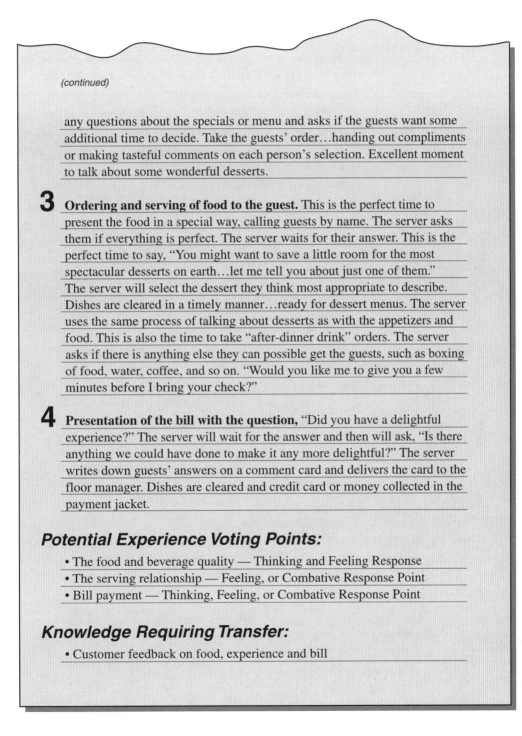

(continued)

any questions about the specials or menu and asks if the guests want some additional time to decide. Take the guests' order...handing out compliments or making tasteful comments on each person's selection. Excellent moment to talk about some wonderful desserts.

3 **Ordering and serving of food to the guest.** This is the perfect time to present the food in a special way, calling guests by name. The server asks them if everything is perfect. The server waits for their answer. This is the perfect time to say, "You might want to save a little room for the most spectacular desserts on earth...let me tell you about just one of them." The server will select the dessert they think most appropriate to describe. Dishes are cleared in a timely manner...ready for dessert menus. The server uses the same process of talking about desserts as with the appetizers and food. This is also the time to take "after-dinner drink" orders. The server asks if there is anything else they can possible get the guests, such as boxing of food, water, coffee, and so on. "Would you like me to give you a few minutes before I bring your check?"

4 **Presentation of the bill with the question,** "Did you have a delightful experience?" The server will wait for the answer and then will ask, "Is there anything we could have done to make it any more delightful?" The server writes down guests' answers on a comment card and delivers the card to the floor manager. Dishes are cleared and credit card or money collected in the payment jacket.

Potential Experience Voting Points:

- The food and beverage quality — Thinking and Feeling Response
- The serving relationship — Feeling, or Combative Response Point
- Bill payment — Thinking, Feeling, or Combative Response Point

Knowledge Requiring Transfer:

- Customer feedback on food, experience and bill

The hardest part so far is keeping focused on experiences and not getting dragged back down into the operations. I keep reminding myself that operations are only there to serve the experiences. This relearning will take us a while, but we're getting better at it every day. We're using the customer experience language more and more. I really listen hard to hear if my staff is using it, and our servers are catching on.

Let me throw in a couple of cautions. If you think you know everything about your customers, you're wrong. If you think your operations will deliver experiences that create loyal customers, you're in danger.

Good luck going through the process. It's worth your time and energy. The rewards are absolutely huge. I do know one thing; you will never go back to the way you thought about your business before.

Customer Experiences Drive Your Organization's Revenue

In the Awesome Customer Challenge we talked about the need to build effective Revenue Architecture. A Revenue Architecture specifically defines the paths by which an organization acquires, retains, and motivates its customers; increases customer response rates; and promotes deeper customer relationships—all while strengthening its brand.

Your Revenue Architecture is the framework for consistently and continuously driving greater revenues and building strong customer loyalty. This framework is the vehicle for consistently creating, coordinating and delivering all customer interactions or "customer experiences" an organization needs to be successful...and an organization's success is dependent on the ability of those customer experiences to acquire more customers, create greater customer response rates, lower customer turnover and improve sales to existing customers.

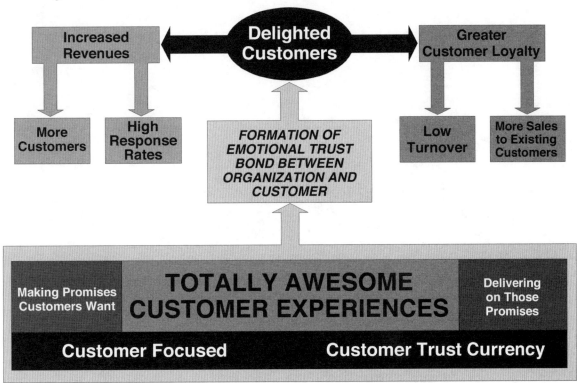

Because creating and delivering Totally Awesome Customer Experiences is the cornerstone to building effective Revenue Architecture, the remaining chapters of this book are dedicated to helping you master the concepts, processes and tools of creating and delivering Totally Awesome Customer Experiences.

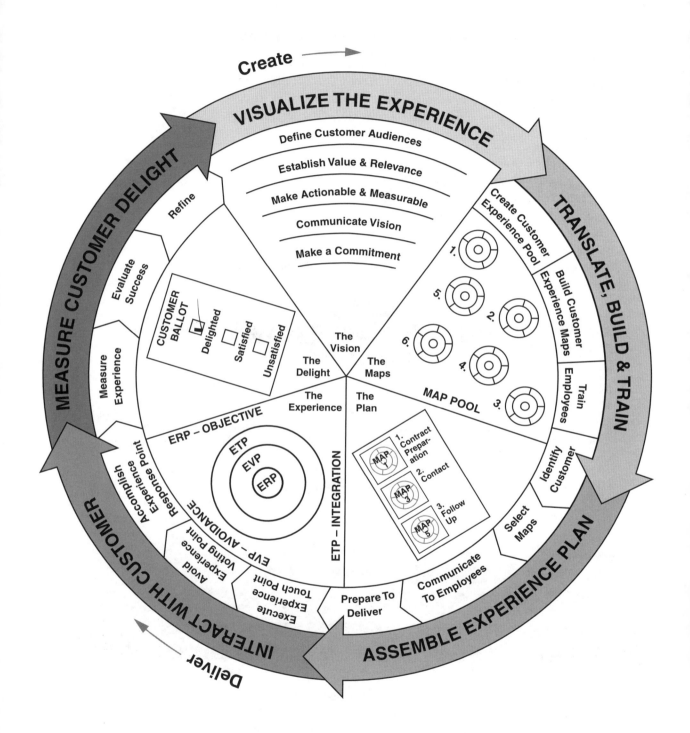

The Totally Awesome Customer Experience... What it Takes to Create and Deliver One

*"A mission could be defined as an image of a desired state
that you want to get to. Once fully seen, it will inspire you to act,
fuel your motivation and determine your behavior."*

Charles Garfield,
Author of Peak Performers

This chapter will help you fulfill the dream of creating delighted customers and becoming an experienced-based organization. This happens when you create and deliver Totally Awesome Customer Experiences. You produce a Totally Awesome Customer Experience when you execute the right Customer Experience Maps for the right customer audience. The result? Delighted customers!

The remainder of this book is dedicated to helping you make your dream come true...

CREATING AND DELIVERING

When you first read Charles Garfield's quote above, in a business context, you can't help but think it as oriented towards management. However, in looking at his statement in a non-management orientation, it begs the question, what will inspire and motivate non-management employees to change their behavior in helping the organization accomplish its mission?

Here is what we found out...

First, behavior modification is fundamental to change and change is fundamental to organizations with missions requiring growth.

Second, new strategies should incorporate the inspiration, motivation and tools needed to help employees think, feel, and act, in a way that insures the proper execution of those strategies.

Third, if training is to be effective in inspiring, motivating, and modifying employee behavior, then tools and measurement systems in which new behavior can be monitored and improved must be readily available and used.

To this point, two months ago we were talking with an organization about their needs for improving the experiences they deliver to their customers. They told us they were putting together an RFP (Request For Proposal) for customer service training and would like us to be one of the three companies to submit a proposal. A week later we received the RFP. The training RFP called for a one-time, "blanket" approach aimed at making their employees more aware of the need to be customer-focused. When we inquired about their plans to support the training and measure the impact of the training on employee behavior, they indicated they didn't have any money in their budget to include those aspects into their RFP.

We respectfully sent back a rejection letter declining their offer to bid. Our rejection letter suggested they withdraw their RFP until they did have the budget to make their training investment valuable. The letter stressed that when training is done without a proper customer experience foundation in which experiences can be visualized, built, assembled, delivered and measured, the training by itself, will have very little impact on changing employee behavior and ultimately little or no impact on improving customer experiences. A copy of our rejection letter was also sent to the CEO. About two weeks ago, we received a call from the CEO asking us to discuss what would be necessary to set up a strong customer experience foundation in which a training investment would have a long lasting impact toward changing behavior and accomplishing their mission going forward.

A bank executive in Denver put it best when she said, "Everyone on our management team really buys into the need to become experience-based, but what we want to know is how we can insure that every one of our tellers and other 'front line' personnel can actually assemble and deliver a consistent and repeatable customer experience in every branch location in our system. We feel the training we have done in the past gives us a temporary shot in the arm, but after a while we see the same erratic behavior we had before the training."

Our answer to her was, "Change rarely happens with training alone, no matter how much training you do. The bottom line is...if you want to stop the random acts of excellence and chaos your customers are experiencing now...then you must find a way to mobilize your employees into an inspired and motivated group of people who have been given the tools and training to consistently and repeatedly deliver totally awesome customer experiences. The tools and training will only come through the implementation of a process that will first CREATE an experience, and then help you DELIVER that experience to your customers."

Creating a totally awesome customer experience means you develop a solid foundation in which the experiences you want to deliver to your customers are visualized, built, trained and assembled into an experience plan in which each and every employee understands their role in delivering that experience to the customer.

Delivering a totally awesome customer experience means that employees have been trained to execute, measure and evaluate specific activities within their customer experience role that will assure the accomplishment of the experience plan and result in a delighted customer.

Creating and delivering a totally awesome customer experience requires a process in order to turn your employees' random acts of excellence or chaos into a well-orchestrated symphony of planned and measured activities that ultimately result in delighted customers, higher revenues and improved customer loyalty...an experience-based organization. This process is called the Five-Step Process of Creating and Delivering a Totally Awesome Customer Experience.

THE FIVE-STEP PROCESS

Creating and delivering a Totally Awesome Customer Experience is actually a process that lets you define how you want to consistently interact with your customers. When you do it correctly, you create delighted customers. You create and deliver a Totally Awesome Customer Experience by performing the following five basic steps:

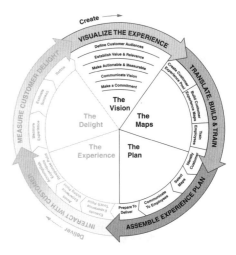

Step One – *Visualize the Experience*
> Define your customer audience, make it simple, valuable, actionable, measurable, and easy to communicate. Make the commitment to make it happen.

Step Two – *Translate the Vision, Build the Maps, and Train Employees*
> Translate your Customer Experience Vision into your Customer Experience Map Pool, build your Customer Experience Maps, and train your employees on how to use them.

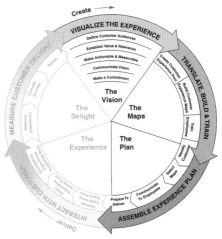

Step Three – *Assemble the Experience Plan*
> Identify the customer, select the appropriate Customer Experience Maps, communicate information to employees and prepare for delivery.

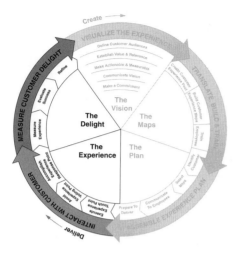

Step Four – *Interact with the Customer*

    Touch your customers, avoid triggering any voting points and accomplish your response goals.

Step Five – *Measure Customer Delight*

    Track, evaluate and refine customer delight.

An Overview of Customer Experience Maps and Customer Experience Mapping

Customer Experience Maps are the building blocks of a Totally Awesome Customer Experience. Their purpose is to provide all of the customer interaction necessary to generate a delighted customer response. Customer Experience Maps are simple strategic plans with a single objective and supporting activities we call Experience Touch Points. Complete details on Customer Experience Maps and Customer Experience Mapping (the tool that creates them) appear in Chapter 4. A complete glossary of **Customer Experience Language** terms appear in the back of the book. Please look over this glossary now. It can help you become familiar with the language from this point forward.

A **Customer Experience Map**...

- Documents your strategic decisions on interacting with customers for both implementation and change.

- Acts as a strategic and tactical reference guide for deploying your Experience Touch Points.

- Acts as part of the training manual for your employees.

- Provides the moral authority for employees to act on behalf of the customers without fear or reservation.

- Focuses the whole organization's attention on the customer.

- Maximizes the effect of customer interactions while minimizing the costs.

Customer Experience Language:

A specific framework of language used inside your organization to describe the terms and measurements surrounding customer experiences. You use it to enhance your discussions, speed up your implementation, and make it easier for your employees to learn the process of creating and delivering Totally Awesome Customer Experiences.

- Provides insight into what operational transactions are required to support the accomplishment of an Experience Response Point.

- Directs the acquisition of resources required for your Experience Touch Points.

- Places the organization on alert as to the potential areas (Experience Voting Points) where customers will most likely make decisions on their experiences.

Customer Experience Map Diagram

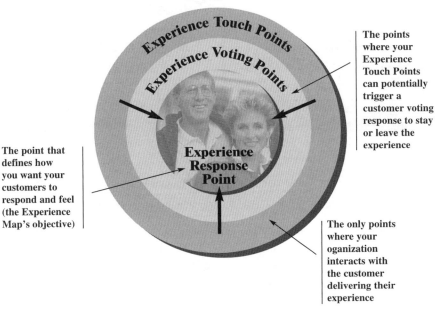

Customer Experience Map:

The strategic plan for identifying the Experience Touch Points that will lead to positive votes at Experience Voting Points, resulting in the accomplishment of the Experience Response Point

Experience Plan

The creation of plan to deliver a customer experience based on the appropriate assembly of Customer Experience Maps specific to the right customer audiences.

The science of Customer Experience Mapping is all about the creation and delivery of an executable Customer Experience Map. The art of Customer Experience Mapping has to do with the imagination and creativity of the Experience Touch Points within the maps themselves.

As you can see from the illustration, the Customer Experience Map consists of three interactive components: an Experience Response Point, Experience Touch Points, and Experience Voting Points.

Customer Experience Maps give you the power of consistency and repeatability in the creation and delivery of your Totally Awesome Customer Experience. The science of Customer Experience Mapping is all about the creation and delivery of an executable Customer Experience Map. The art of Customer Experience Mapping has to do with the imagination and creativity of the Experience Touch Points within the maps themselves.

On the inside ring, you find the **Experience Response Point** – the objective of a Customer Experience Map. The Experience Response Point defines how you want the customer to respond and feel at the end of this experience.

The outer ring contains the **Experience Touch Points**. These are the only points where you interact with your customer; they are the vehicles you use to achieve your Experience Response Point. Because of the importance of Experience Touch Points, we've dedicated Chapter 5 entirely to them.

Experience Response Point:

Defines the desired response expectations or actions from a customer as a result of delivering the appropriate Experience Touch Points for a Customer Experience Map. The key measurement indicator as to the success or failure of that Customer Experience Map.

Experience Touch Point:

Any point of interaction between the customer and the organization. An Experience Touch Point is where the organization tactically delivers the experience to the customer.

The middle ring represents Experience Voting Points. Experience Voting Points lie between the Experience Touch Points and the Experience Response Point. These are points along your path where a customer can decide continue to terminate his or her experience.

Totally Awesome Customer Experience

Create   **Deliver**

Determine Experience **Response** Points	Execute Experience **Touch** Points
Build Experience **Touch** Points	Avoid Experience **Voting** Points
Identify Experience **Voting** Points	Accomplish Experience **Response** Points

=

Workflow for **Creating** and **Delivering**
Totally Awesome Customer Experiences

Every Customer Experience Map contains these potential Experience Voting Points. Depending on the conflict or acceptability of your Experience Touch Points, Experience Voting Points can sometimes be triggered. A triggered Experience Voting Point exhibits itself in the form of questions, doubts, or combative responses by the customer. These questions, doubts, and combative responses are reactions to the acceptability of an Experience Touch Point. Depending on the reaction, they can severely damage your chances of accomplishing your Experience Response Point. The severity of conflict created by the Experience Touch Point ultimately determines whether customers vote to stay engaged in their experiences or leave. The trick is to be creative enough in the design and execution of your Experience Touch Points to avoid triggering negative responses.

Chapter 4 walks you through the science of Customer Experience Mapping in much greater detail, demonstrating the use of all of a Customer Experience Map's components. The chapter also includes an illustration of the creation of a Customer Experience Map.

Here's a sample on the next page of a Customer Experience Map from our website planning case study in Chapter 8. Please pay particular attention its format and structure rather than to its content.

Creating a Totally Awesome Customer Experience comes from the first three steps of visualizing, translating/building/training, and assembling Customer Experience Maps. Delivering a Totally Awesome Customer Experience comes from the interaction with the customer and measurement of customer delight. The Experience Touch Points contained within all the Customer Experience Maps assembled for a customer's experience represent the entire interaction your entire organization has with that customer during their entire experience. The Delight Vote is the vote customers make at the end of their customer experience (Chapter 2) as to whether or not they were delighted with their overall experience.

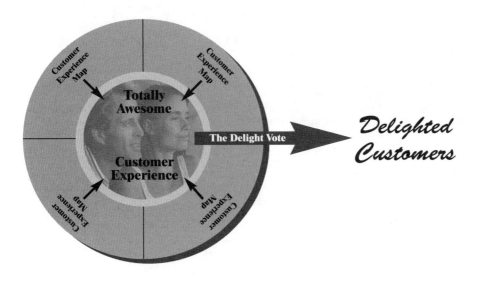

Sample Customer Experience Map #1

Map Title: *Sample transaction*

Customer Audiences: 1, 2, 3, 4, 5, 6, 7, 11

Experience Response Point:

We want Trusted Site Members to find it easy to receive valuable help with their experience problems. We want our Trusted Site Members who submit answers to help solve problems to feel special and appreciated.

Experience Touch Points:

1 **The Posting of a Problem.** Posting a problem is handled by an easy-to-follow wizard. This Experience Touch Point is direct, uncontrolled, and informational. The most critical elements we need to know for posting the problem are:

    A. The category of the problem
    B. When the problem needs to be solved
    C. The e-mail address if different than the registered one
    D. The problem itself expressed in terms of customer experience language

We will send e-message acknowledgements to problem-givers, telling them we received their problems and posted them. Answers to problems will be sent via e-message with our problem-solving sponsor's web wrapper, along with active links and summary synopsis, but no offerings unless authorized. This approach gives our sponsor branding opportunities without infringing on our Trusted Site Members' privacy. Another notice will go out when a Trusted Site Member's problem has been removed from the system due to their posted deadline or ours.

2 **How To Help Solve a Problem.** Providing help must be intuitive and fast. This Experience Touch Point is direct, uncontrolled, and informational. The most critical elements for helping our trusted members solve problems are:

(continued)

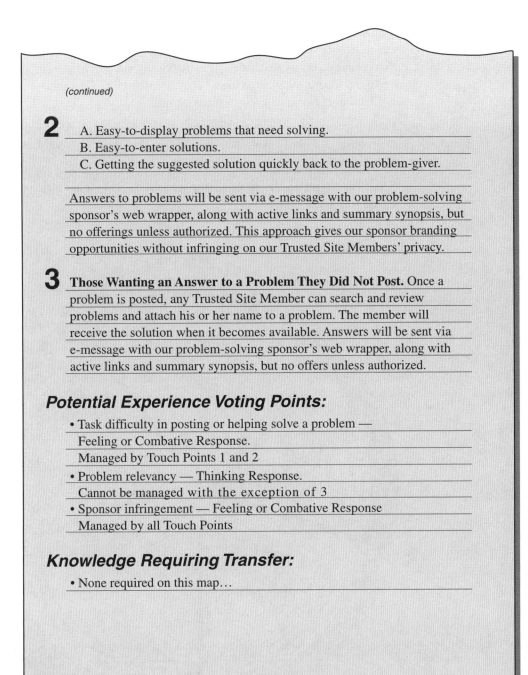

(continued)

2 A. Easy-to-display problems that need solving.
 B. Easy-to-enter solutions.
 C. Getting the suggested solution quickly back to the problem-giver.

Answers to problems will be sent via e-message with our problem-solving sponsor's web wrapper, along with active links and summary synopsis, but no offerings unless authorized. This approach gives our sponsor branding opportunities without infringing on our Trusted Site Members' privacy.

3 **Those Wanting an Answer to a Problem They Did Not Post.** Once a problem is posted, any Trusted Site Member can search and review problems and attach his or her name to a problem. The member will receive the solution when it becomes available. Answers will be sent via e-message with our problem-solving sponsor's web wrapper, along with active links and summary synopsis, but no offers unless authorized.

Potential Experience Voting Points:

- Task difficulty in posting or helping solve a problem —
  Feeling or Combative Response.
  Managed by Touch Points 1 and 2
- Problem relevancy — Thinking Response.
  Cannot be managed with the exception of 3
- Sponsor infringement — Feeling or Combative Response
  Managed by all Touch Points

Knowledge Requiring Transfer:

- None required on this map…

Totally Awesome Customer Experiences don't just happen. They aren't just a series of random events that customers sometimes enjoy because they happened to encounter a great, customer-focused employee. And these customer experiences don't just come from marketing or customer service or well-executed operational activities. Totally Awesome Customer Experiences need support from the entire organization.

Let's proceed in dissecting the basic Five-Step Process of Creating and Delivering a Totally Awesome Customer Experience as shown below in the diagram.

The Five-Step Process of Creating and Delivering a Totally Awesome Customer Experience

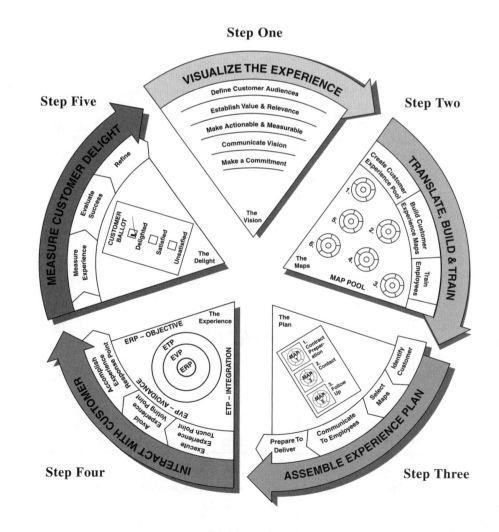

CREATING A TOTALLY AWESOME CUSTOMER EXPERIENCE

Step One – Visualize the Experience

- Define Your Customer Audiences

- Establish Value and Relevance

- Make It Actionable and Measurable

- Communicate Vision Effectively

- Make a Commitment

Step Two – Translate the Vision, Build the Maps, and Train Employees

- Translate Your Customer Experience Vision to Create Your Customer Experience Map Pool

- Build Your Customer Experience Maps

- Train Your Employees to Use the Maps

Step Three – Assemble the Experience Plan

- Identify the customer

- Select the Appropriate Customer Experience Maps

- Communicate Information to Employees

- Prepare to Deliver

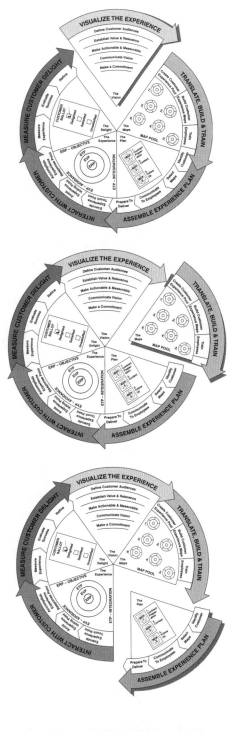

CREATING A TOTALLY AWESOME CUSTOMER EXPERIENCE
STEP ONE – VISUALIZE THE EXPERIENCE

"None of us is as good as all of us" –Ken Blanchard

Collectively, your organization can build a bigger Customer Experience Vision than you can alone. Get as many people involved as you can. Remember, without a solid vision there will be no experience, just random Experience Touch Points that may or may not help you accomplish your dream. They certainly will not lead to customer delight. Here is the path of "musts" to creating an effective Customer Experience Vision.

- Must have defined customer audiences.

- Must be simple, with both perceived and real value for your customer and your organization. The customer must be delighted.

- Must be actionable and measurable. This means the vision can be translated into easy-to-implement Customer Experience Maps and be measurable in terms of customer delight and receiving the Delight Vote.

- Must be written in simple, straightforward language so it can be communicated effectively to team members and customers.

- Must have the commitment of the entire organization to make it happen.

A. Define Your Customer Audiences

The more you know your customer audiences, the better experiences you can deliver. Maslow's concept about the different stages of human needs is brilliant. It's important to identify the level of need you're trying to fulfill.

The levels begin with physiological needs and proceed to safety needs, social needs, esteem needs, and finally, self-actualization needs. In a perfect world, people love and are loved, understand and are understood, and give and receive. Ideally, you'd like to deliver highly relevant offers and experiences to each individual customer based on his or her specific needs. Usually, it doesn't always happen. Clearly defining your customer audiences will, however, maximize your investment in those customer audiences. To do this, you must determine the **fit** and **priority** of your audiences.

**Needs
per Maslow**

Maslow's Hierarchy of Needs

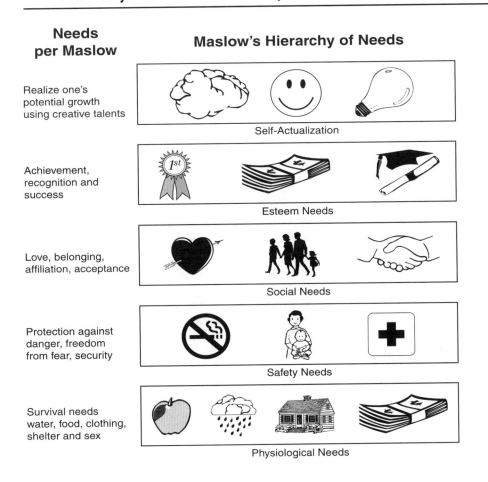

Realize one's
potential growth
using creative talents

Self-Actualization

Achievement,
recognition and
success

Esteem Needs

Love, belonging,
affiliation, acceptance

Social Needs

Protection against
danger, freedom
from fear, security

Safety Needs

Survival needs
water, food, clothing,
shelter and sex

Physiological Needs

Finding the fit...

Unfortunately, one size doesn't fit all! It's human nature to think your products and services apply to everyone. Not everyone wants McDonald's two all-beef patties, special sauce, lettuce, cheese, pickles, and onions on a sesame-seed bun, because some may want it their way at Burger King or served by Dave at the drive-up window at 2:00 am.

Research has shown that customers respond much better to relevant, personalized product or service offers than they do to mass population offers. Finding the fit means identifying your audiences' special needs. The science of gathering knowledge about customer needs and behavior (CRM, data mining, profiling, and so on) focuses on identifying those unique attributes that increase customer response rates. The more precisely you can identify the *right* customer audience, the more precisely you can create the *right* Totally Awesome Customer Experience to deliver to that audience.

If you've identified your customer audience as vegetarian, for example, it doesn't make much sense to create and deliver a customer experience for delighting beefeaters.

We were at a financial institution discussing Customer Experience Mapping with the Chief Operating Officer (COO.) We discussed how much they knew about their customers and their needs. We asked what kind of customer profiling they used (collection of demographic, psychographic, and feeling information) and what they did with the information once they collected it.

The COO told us they did very little customer profiling. Other than having a customer's age, social security information, customer contact information, amount and frequency of deposits, loan balances, years they'd been a member, number of loans, and status as an Internet banking customer, they didn't actually know much about their individual customers' needs. Up to this point, they hadn't budgeted monies to invest in the tools or processes to collect and mine that information.

The COO told us, "So far, we've had to rely on our good perceptions and outside professionals in designing programs we hoped would fit our customers' needs." He also admitted that they've been researching the use of customer profiling tools and databases to enrich their collection of customer information. He's going to include the costs in this year's budget. He firmly believes in the power of customer knowledge in helping them do a better job in identifying their most profitable customers. We can't disagree.

Chapter 5 introduces you to a tool called "The Audience Audit." This tool helps you detail audiences by demographics, psychographics, and feelings in creating effective and delightful Experience Touch Points. Experience Touch Points are where you need the real precision to create greater acceptability and perceived value by your customer.

When you deliver a customer experience to a more segmented audience, the probability of achieving your Experience Response Points greatly increases. This is, in essence, the thinking behind one-to-one marketing. You might find it helpful to read a book by Don Pepper and Martha Rogers called *The One to One Future: Building Relationships One Customer at a Time*. In theory, the more you can personalize a customer's experience, the more likely you are to create a positive customer response. The real trick is being able to economically create and deliver a one-to-one experience without either causing an invasion of the customer's privacy or missing the mark and looking silly. Creating one-to-one experiences is a very challenging art.

CRM, data mining, and customer profiling are tools to help organizations find the audience fit. They help an organization determine a customer's most important needs, along with trying to identify the customer's behavior habits. These tools help to transform Customer Information Currency to Customer Knowledge Currency. Customer Experience Mapping is another tool to help you determine audience fit. It combines the use of customer knowledge with a customer-focused discipline to prepare an experience offering that customers will perceive as, not only exceeding their most important needs, but also helping them to form an emotional trust bond with your organization.

This is how Customer Experience Mapping helps to transform Customer Knowledge Currency to Customer Trust Currency (one of the key changes required to becoming an experience-based organization). It's also the basis for helping you to move customers from being merely satisfied to being delighted. The greater your customer knowledge and the more trust your customers have in your organization, the better you can define which audiences you can best delight with your experiences and offers. This ability leads to higher acceptability, better customer response rates, and greater profitability.

Chapter 9 discusses the use of CRM, database mining, and one-to-one tools in leveraging customer knowledge in creating and delivering Totally Awesome Customer Experiences. We'll also discuss the hot topic of customer privacy and how critical Customer Trust Currency is in understanding the roles customer knowledge and customer privacy play in a customer's experience.

Prioritizing your audiences...

A great example of prioritizing customer audiences is Zions National Bank's "Gold Service Club" for their valued clients. The Gold Service Club provides you a membership card that entitles you to valuable services over and above their regular array of bank services. Scott Anderson, their president and CEO, has established a hotline that any gold service member can call if not completely satisfied. (We would change "completely satisfied" to "completely delighted.") We like Scott's idea of the Gold Service Club because it prioritizes Zions' investment in selected audiences. It also provides a natural and non-intrusive conduit for gathering more information about a specific customer. This program allows Zions to provide more personalized offers and experiences in the future.

Take your time in deciding who your customers should be before you decide what you want them to do or what experience you want them to have. Make sure you can delight them, and they will be profitable for your organization.

Invest in your most profitable customers. Invest in those audiences for whom you can best fulfill their needs and delight them. They'll be your most profitable customers over time. This is all part of the economics behind Totally Awesome Customer Experiences.

Select and prioritize your customer audiences based on your belief in your ability to deliver relevant and valuable offers and experiences that will delight your customer and be profitable for your organization.

B. Must be Simple and Valuable to Your Customers and Organization

This is an exciting and enjoyable part of the process. Simplicity and value are the key words in creating your vision. Simplicity means that your vision is easy to perceive and understand. Valuable means that you're focused on customer delight as the outcome. Whoever invented the vision of the "Happy Meal" is a genius.

A vision focused on customer delight means that you're prepared to deliver relevant offerings to your customers that fulfill their physical, emotional, and psychological needs beyond the point of making them merely satisfied.

You want your vision to be customer-focused. You also want to use Customer Trust Currency in its creation. By combining customer knowledge and emotional fulfillment that meets or exceeds expectations the customer really cares about, you can create customer delight. This is the real value for your customer.

The real value to your organization comes from increased customer loyalty, brand equity, and differentiation. A side benefit will be lower costs of marketing and sales because Customer Trust Currency removes customer acceptability barriers while increasing customer response rates. You'll also find that customer delight creates deep differentiation from your competition and forms a significantly greater barrier to customer defection.

Here's an example of a vision with some objectives we received from a financial services organization:

> We want to create a great customer experience for our 300 Retirement Plan Sponsors in which we can take the traditional, periodic "information update" transaction and transform that transaction into a "We Empower You" transaction (the VISION). The new transaction will provide the sponsors with easy-to-read, easy-to-understand, already synthesized recommendations that are easy to convey to their employees. We want to delight the Plan Sponsors by drastically cutting their information absorption time, minimizing questions they must answer from their employees, and decreasing calls they have to place to our call centers or visits to our website. We also want to change our call center and website to orient them towards solutions and recommendations, not just information, while being directed and meaningful. We want to decrease the amount of information sent and upgrade this information to reduce our costs of the printed material and the labor to organize and send it. We want to deliver our customer experience in the way the

customer wants it and to see how many transactions that are currently paper-based (being sent to the masses and slow in their delivery) can be converted to electronic, personalized, fast documents. We want our customers to help us by giving continuous feedback on their experiences, not on our segmented operational tasks, and we want to measure their feedback against how delighted we believe they should be. We think we will save money, pick up additional plans, and be invited to provide additional services to our Plan Sponsors.

C. Must be Actionable and Measurable

Actionable means your vision can be accomplished and translated into Customer Experience Maps. Measurable means you can establish measurements that will tell you whether you've accomplished your vision. As Edwards Deming once wrote, "If you cannot measure it, you cannot manage it." Your vision must be capable of measuring the Delight Vote.

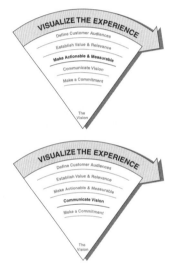

D. Must Communicate Your Vision

The lack of communication in presenting your vision to both employees and customers can be deadly. Here is the basic rule: if no one understands your vision, it's not a vision. A lack of understanding in your communication results in confusion, incorrect assumptions, and misguided efforts, leading to an unsuccessful implementation. Take the time to craft a vision that people can understand.

Here are five effective guidelines to help you communicate your vision to your customers and team members.

1. Seek understanding...

Communication requires understanding, not agreement. It's more important that people understand you than agree with you. Asking for agreement before understanding will undermine your communication efforts. When people think they must agree with you rather than just understand you, they tune you out and keep you at arm's length. First seek their understanding. Then move to gain their agreement or acceptance.

2. Select your communication approach...

Carefully pick the approach you plan to use. It doesn't matter whether the communication is verbal, written, visual, or whatever. It matters whether it's effective. A good communicator always understands the best way to present to an audience.

3. Profile of your audience...

Understand how they best relate to you and you to them.

4. Select your means of communicating...

Select the most efficient and effective way to reach your audience: in small groups, individually, or whatever. Don't confuse this with the method of communicating.

5. Confirm audience understanding...

Confirm that your audience understands the vision. In the case of customers, this means communicating the expectations of what you're promising to deliver.

E. Must be Committed To Making It Happen

Creating and delivering Totally Awesome Customer Experiences takes teamwork. You can't do it alone. Once everyone understands your vision, you'll need motivated team members throughout your organization to make it work. There are scores of good books on this subject alone. Keep in mind that people respond differently to different methods of motivation. One size does not fit all! You may need several different techniques to be effective. Here are two axioms to keep in mind:

1. Transfer your belief to their belief...

You must transfer your belief to their belief. If your belief doesn't transfer, you still own it and they're still observers, not participants or owners themselves. Merely satisfied customers have generally not accepted your beliefs. That's why they don't feel motivated to tell you their experiences or promote your organization. Delighted customers have felt the transfer of belief in the emotional trust bond they've formed with your organization. That's why they tell everyone and become loyal to your organization.

2. Committing to a call-to-action...

People must commit to a call-to-action. For employees, ask them to accept a call-to-action. The best way is to talk to them directly and personally. Avoid large groups whenever possible. Asking for commitment in a large group allows someone to invisibly abstain. Asking for personal commitment places the responsibility on each person to either commit or abstain. If he or she accepts, that gives you the moral authority to question that person's commitment from then on. Personally asking also heightens the level of commitment.

Asking for a commitment pushes any disagreement to the surface in a positive and direct way and lets you deal with it at the beginning. Without direct commitment, disagreement will eventually rear its ugly head behind your back and poison the opportunity for all. A call to action on the customer's part is when they tell others. The greater level of importance your customers feel will determine their level of participation in the belief transfer to others. They all want to wear your John Deere baseball cap wherever they go, because "Nothing runs like a Deere."

CREATING A TOTALLY AWESOME CUSTOMER EXPERIENCE STEP TWO – TRANSLATE, BUILD, AND TRAIN

Part of creating your Totally Awesome Customer Experience requires you to translate your Customer Experience Vision into Customer Experience Maps, build those maps, and train your employees to select and execute them. Translate means that you completely lay out all the Customer Experience Maps that could be used in a customer experience (Customer Experience Map Pool). Build means you create each segment of a customer experience (Customer Experience Maps) that will be delivered to your customer audiences, while train means that your employees must become intimately familiar with how each map works and how all maps work together in delivering the customer experience.

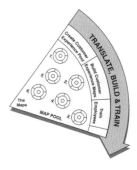

A. Translating Your Customer Experience Vision into Your Customer Experience Map Pool

A Totally Awesome Customer Experience is created from Customer Experience Maps. It could be one map or it could be many." The entire collection of Customer Experience Maps required for you to deliver a customer experience to any of your customer audiences is called a **Customer Experience Map Pool**." All Customer Experience Maps within your Customer Experience Map Pool must be relevant and valuable to the overall experience.

For instance, a Lexus car dealership wouldn't build Customer Experience Maps that cater to teenagers. A Lexus dealership would build Customer Experience Maps for adults and perhaps for the "teenager" in adults. In this case, a teenage Customer Experience Map would not be relevant or valuable.

Your Customer Experience Maps must support and contribute to your **Customer Experience Vision**. During the building of your vision, you'll outline all the audiences whom that experience will affect. Some of these audiences might be selective audiences to which only certain Customer Experience Maps apply during an experience. For example, our Lexus deal-

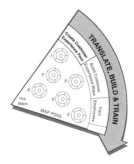

Customer Experience Map Pool:

The entire collection of Customer Experience Maps required for a Totally Awesome Customer Experience

Customer Experience Mapping is the tool that turns your vision into a Totally Awesome Customer Experience.

Customer Experience Vision:

A vision focused on customer delight. It is prepared to deliver relevant offerings to your customers that fulfill their physical, emotional, and psychological needs beyond the point of making them merely satisfied.

Initial Transaction Assessment:

A tool for identifying all of the organization's transactions in relationship to their value to the customer and the organization.

ership might want to build its Customer Experience Map Pool to contain two sets of Customer Experience Maps. One might be for the experience you deliver to a customer audience between the ages of 30 and 40 with a mean income over $120,000 and who have two or fewer children. The other set might be for an experience you deliver to a customer audience over the age of 60, with a mean income of $90,000 and no children still living at home.

Translating your customer experience vision into your Customer Experience Map Pool creates a solid basis of documentation for your experience path, as well as a wonderful guide to use in training your employees and determining your resource requirements. Your Customer Experience Map Pool makes certain that your Totally Awesome Customer Experiences will be both consistent and repeatable for all your defined customer audiences.

There are three essential elements to effectively translating your customer experience vision into the appropriate Customer Experience Map Pool:

- Figuring out the right Experience Response Points and Customer Experience Maps...

- Covering all your identified customer audiences...

- Building Your Customer Experience Map Pool...

1. Figuring out the right Experience Response Points and Customer Experience Maps...

Think about all of the necessary Experience Response Points (the desired and expected customer responses and feelings you would like) needed to accomplish your Customer Experience Vision and delight your customers. The number of Experience Response Points you need for your vision dictates the minimum number of Customer Experience Maps needed in your Pool. You'll get a lot of help in making this determination from a tool we call the **Initial Transaction Assessment** (Chapter 6). The number of Customer Experience Maps in your Pool will greatly depend on the number of customer audiences to which you want your experience to apply. Remember, each map has only a single Experience Response Point.

Here's a chart of Customer Experience Maps with their respective Experience Response Points.

Customer Experience Map Chart – Lemonade Stand

Customer Experience Maps (CEM)	Desired Experience Response Point
CEM 1 – Lemonade signage	We need to attract the attention of drivers and pedestrians.
CEM 2 – Lemonade sample	We want to give each potential customer a sip of our delicious, cool lemonade in hopes they'll want to purchase a full glass.
CEM 3 – Lemonade offer	After their sample, we want to tell them how little it costs to purchase a full, tall glass of cool, refreshing lemonade.
CEM 4 – Lemonade fulfillment in cars the same side of the street	Handling our car customers will be different than our on pedestrian customers. Customers must perceive that buying from a car is just as easy as buying as a pedestrian, so it's worth stopping.
CEM 5 – Lemonade fulfillment cars on the opposite side of the street	Handling our car customers on the opposite side of the in street will first of all require they know it isn't a big deal. Customers must perceive that buying from a car is just as easy as buying as a pedestrian.
CEM 6 – Lemonade fulfillment at the stand	Our pedestrian customers will feel this is so simple to order and receive their cool, refreshing lemonade, they'll just stop.
CEM 7 – Lemonade payment	We want our customers to be able to give us coin or currency with no hassles about making change.
CEM 8 – Lemonade referral	We want all our customers to be delighted and want to tell their friends about our lemonade stand.

2. Covering all your identified customer audiences...

Know the profile of your customer audiences. Make sure your customer audiences are covered by the appropriate Customer Experience Maps. Not every Customer Experience Map will apply to every customer audience. For instance, if you were selling media advertising, printed material, or website construction, you might have a different Customer Experience Map for dealing with a VP of marketing than for dealing with a VP of purchasing. We discuss this topic extensively and provide some excellent tools in Chapter 5.

Here's an example of a Customer Audience Chart for the lemonade stand...

Remember, each map has only a single Experience Response Point.

Customer Audience Chart – Lemonade Stand	
Passing cars same side of street	Audience 1
Passing cars opposite side of street	Audience 2
Pedestrian adults	Audience 3
Pedestrian kids	Audience 4

3. Constructing your Customer Experience Map Pool

Combining your Customer Experience Map Chart with your Customer Audience chart builds your Customer Experience Map Pool. Building a Customer Experience Map Pool will save you tons of time in creating your **Experience Plan** (the assembly of the appropriate Customer Experience Maps for the delivery of specific customer experience). The Pool will help you document the Customer Experience Maps you need for your Experience Plan based on selected customer audiences. It will serve as your employee training guide on how to assemble an Experience Plan for each of your customer experiences you need to deliver. The Pool has great value in matching the Customer Experience Maps against the customer audiences for whom they're needed.

The magic of the Pool is that it shows you instantly *what is needed* and *who needs it*. The Pool is very powerful in helping you eliminate any unnecessary Customer Experience Maps and audiences. Here's an example using our lemonade stand...

Customer Experience Map Pool – Lemonade Stand

Customer Experience Map (CEM)	Customer Audiences			
	Passing Cars Same Side of the Street	Passing Cars Opposite Side of the Street	Pedestrian Adults	Pedestrian Kids
CEM 1 – Lemonade signage	X	X	X	X
CEM 2 – Lemonade sample	X	X	X	X
CEM 3 – Lemonade offer	X	X	X	X
CEM 4 – Lemonade fulfillment in cars on the same side of the street	X			
CEM 5 – Lemonade fulfillment in cars on the opposite side of the street		X		

Customer Experience Map (CEM)	Customer Audiences			
	Passing Cars Same Side of the Street	Passing Cars Opposite Side of the Street	Pedestrian Adults	Pedestrian Kids
CEM 6 – Lemonade fulfillment at the stand	X	X	X	X
CEM 7 – Lemonade payment	X	X	X	X
CEM 8 – Lemonade referral			X	X

This lemonade stand Customer Experience Map Pool indicates that you need to meet the experience needs of four distinct customer audiences and that it requires eight distinct Customer Experience Maps to meet those experience needs. You can see from the chart that you'll use Customer Experience Maps 1, 2, 3, 6, and 7 in the experiences for all the audiences in your vision, while Customer Experience Maps 4, 5, and 8 apply only to the specific experiences of four various audiences.

The Customer Experience Map Pool does a wonderful job in helping you determine...

- Your experience investment (cost of the lemonade, stand and signage, rent for the table and chairs, cooler, and umbrella).

- Your experience training (Bobby needs to know how much water goes into the lemonade pitcher per packet of lemonade, how to talk to the customers as they pass by, what the pricing is, how to do the thank-you and ask for referrals).

- Your experience expectations (counting the number of cars and wanting to have 5 percent of them stop for a refreshing sample and have 80 percent of those who stop purchase a large glass).

- Your required investment to implement your Customer Experience Vision (help at the stand, glasses, lemonade, ice, curly straws, provisions for additional lemonade in the event a school bus stops or your referral programs works and kids from two neighborhoods converge).

- Your customer delight measurement process (must ask each customer how they liked their experience).

A Customer Experience Map Pool also creates a solid foundation and helps document the process of creating an Experience Plan to deliver customer delight. Advanced lemonade stand owners would probably have done a competitive analysis to determine other stands in the neighborhood and how much they're charging. You would also want to consider making the stand convertible for those hot-chocolate days.

Here are four qualifications you'll find invaluable when deciding whether a Customer Experience Map should be placed in your Customer Experience Map Pool:

1. Does it contain an Experience Response Point needed in the overall experience?

2. Will it execute in a logical order with your other maps?

3. Does it create any conflicts with other maps?

4. If it were absent from the experience, would there be a significant impact on customer delight?

In many cases, less can be more. Irrelevant Customer Experience Maps only add confusion, inconsistency, and cost to your customer experience. They also create "experience noise," which is distracting and annoying. Experience noise will lessen your chances of achieving your Experience Response Points and make it hard for your customers to understand the experiences you're delivering, not to mention what it does to customer delight. On the flip side, missing maps – "map gaps" – can jeopardize the success of the overall experience.

Creating your Customer Experience Map Pool is a strategic process. The Customer Experience Maps in your Pool will largely determine your revenues, costs, and profits. Therefore, it's important to spend the time and effort you need to build an effective Pool.

Here's a checklist to help you build an effective Customer Experience Map Pool:

- Keep the required number of Customer Experience Maps to a minimum. Less is more. You'll find that having fewer Customer Experience Maps is far more effective and controllable and much less costly. Figuring this out can provide a good opportunity for some outside the box thinking.

- Review for **Map Gaps**. Walk through your entire Totally Awesome Customer Experience, from start to finish, as if you were the customer for each audience. Ask yourself, as a customer, what is missing.

Map Gaps:

The "void" between two Customer Experience Maps in a Totally Awesome Customer Experience where the customer experience is not contiguous.

- Get your customers involved whenever possible. Let your customers "test-drive" the maps and give you their input. It may be the most valuable input you receive. It's better to do this before you invest any more time and money in creating and delivering the experience. Have customers give you their input, using their own "customer experience language."

- Have uninvolved staff review the layout of the vision of your Totally Awesome Customer Experience from a customer's point of view. This process will give you excellent perspective.

- All members of the team need to provide their candid comments. Revise the Customer Experience Maps or even the vision and audiences as needed.

- Go through a series of reviews to make sure you have the right Customer Experience Maps for the right audience.

B. Building Your Customer Experience Maps

Once you decide which Customer Experience Maps you need in your Customer Experience Map Pool you're ready to move to building the individual Customer Experience Maps. Chapter 4 walks you through the step-by-step method of building your Customer Experience Maps using a tool called Customer Experience Mapping. Once you've built your Customer Experience Maps, you'll be ready to assemble them into the Experience Plans for delivery to any of your selected customer audiences.

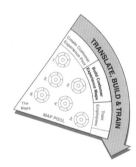

C. Training Your Employees to Use the Customer Experience Map Pool

Customer Experience Maps create the perfect medium for training employees. Each Experience Plan you intend to deliver to a specific audience requires certain employees to be involved. Revisit your Customer Experience Map Pool to match each Experience Plan required with the employees who will be involved in delivering it. This matching process will immediately establish your training requirements for each employee in your organization.

Here are six suggestions for making employee training effective and fun.

1. Create special training materials...

Organize your training materials in such a way that they present the Customer Experience Maps in the order in which they'll be delivered to a customer.

2. Invest the time...

After your employees read the Customer Experience Maps, take your time explaining your Customer Experience Vision (the maps should match the vision). Show them how to use the Customer Experience Map Pool to create different experiences for different audiences using the appropriate Customer Experience Maps.

3. Let employees be the customer and give you feedback...

Let the employees be customers. Have them tell you about their customer experiences and give you feedback. Consider omitting one of the critical Customer Experience Maps with some of the employees. See what happens. Take the opportunity to stress how dependent and integral all Customer Experience Maps are to the success of an experience.

4. Use a variety of tools to show everyone's role...

Communicates your employees' roles and responsibilities by means of some creative role-playing tools, graphics, and so on. Make sure they're well-documented.

5. Role-play, role-play, role-play...theory just isn't good enough...

Make people feel comfortable about approaching customers. If they feel comfortable in delivering experiences, they have less of a tendency to revert to the safe haven of operations.

6. Take an experience reality check...

From your role-playing experience, take a quick time-out to make sure your Customer Experience Maps reflect reality.

One key indicator of successful training is that your employees can easily select and execute the appropriate Customer Experience Maps for each experience and for the appropriate customer audience.

CREATING A TOTALLY AWESOME CUSTOMER EXPERIENCE STEP THREE – ASSEMBLE THE EXPERIENCE PLAN

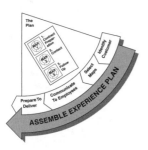

Your Customer Experience Map Pool, in effect, becomes your strategic tool for creating the Experience Plans for delivering the Totally Awesome Customer Experiences to any of your selected customer audiences.

Again, if you want to assemble an Experience Plan to deliver a Totally Awesome Customer Experience for pedestrian adults, buying lemonade at our stand, you'll need to select Customer Experience Maps 1, 2, 3, 6, 7, and 8 in your Experience Plan. To assemble an Experience Plan to deliver a Totally Awesome Customer Experience for passengers in cars, passing by on the same side of the street, you'll need to select Customer Experience Maps 1, 2, 3, 4, 6, and 7 in your Experience Plan. Once your employees know how this process works, it should be a snap for them to select the right maps for the customer audience they're serving and create a simple Experience Plan for delivery of the Totally Awesome Customer Experience.

Identifying the right customer audience, and appropriately selecting Customer Experience Maps for that audience, assembles your Experience Plan for the delivery of your Totally Awesome Customer Experience to that audience.

Customer Experience Map Pool – Lemonade Stand

Customer Experience Map (CEM)	Customer Audiences			
	Passing Cars Same Side of the Street	Passing Cars Opposite Side of the Street	Pedestrian Adults	Pedestrian Kids
CEM 1 – Lemonade signage	X	X	X	X
CEM 2 – Lemonade sample	X	X	X	X
CEM 3 – Lemonade offer	X	X	X	X
CEM 4 – Lemonade fulfillment in car on the same side of the street	X			
CEM 5 – Lemonade fulfillment in cars on the opposite side of the street		X		
CEM 6 – Lemonade fulfillment at the stand	X	X	X	X
CEM 7 – Lemonade payment	X	X	X	X
CEM 8 – Lemonade referral			X	X

The process of assembling an Experience Plan is to:

- Identify the customer

- Select the right Customer Experience Maps from the Customer Experience Map Pool

- Communicate relevant customer audience information to involved employees

- Prepare the appropriate resources for delivery

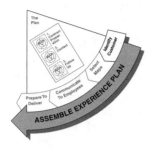

A. Identify the Customer

Although in creating your Customer Experience Vision you have identified all of the potential customer audiences in which you want to create Totally Awesome Customer Experiences, the exact customer experience you will deliver will be based on an Experience Plan for a specific customer or customer audience. The first step in building your Experience Plan is to identify the specific customer or customer audience your Totally Awesome Customer Experience is intended. This step sets the tone for the rest of the Experience Plan process.

There are a number of tools organizations can put in place to assist their employees in identification of the specific customer or customer audience. Smart Cards, for instance, have been developed that carry information about the customer's profile right in the card. Once an employee "swipes" the card it can provide knowledge about the customer that helps the employee quickly assemble the Experience Plan.

B. Select the Right Customer Experience Maps from the Customer Experience Map Pool

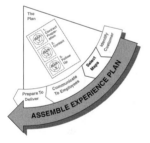

Everyone needs to learn how the Customer Experience Map Pool works and the contents of each Customer Experience Map. This knowledge provides any employee the ability to quickly tell which Customer Experience Maps will deliver the best experience for the customer or customer audience. This process can be manual or automated. This step in the Experience Plan process is the heart of the process, because the selection of the wrong Customer Experience Maps will jeopardize the quality of your Experience Plan and risk losing the Delight Vote from your customers.

C. Communicate Relevant Customer Audience Information to Involved Employees

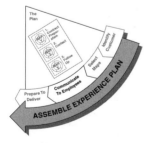

In addition to training your employees to quickly assemble an Experience Plan, you will need to develop methods of communicating customer knowledge to your employees during the delivery of a customer experience. These innovative communication methods must be set up to quickly and effectively communicate an Experience Plan, with all the related customer audience information, to your employees involved in the delivery of the Experience Plan. In our studies we have noted that the more customer information your employees have, the easier it will be for them to make the experience appear seamless to your customer. The communication of information also plays a big role in empowering employees to adopt a more flexible approach in interacting with your customers, helping them to negotiate some often tricky thought and feeling filters that could trigger negative Experience Voting Points.

D. Prepare the Appropriate Resources for Delivery

The best-laid plans can be easily foiled without the resources to execute them properly. Once you have your Experience Plan developed, you will know which Customer Experience Maps are involved. This knowledge will tell you, the people, technology and resources you are going to need to effectively execute all the Experience Touch Points called for by your Customer Experience Maps.

This step in the process is where the operational side of your organization must sync up with the experience side of your organization. The true mark of an experience-based organization is that its organization, acquisition, and deployment of resources are geared to executing Experience Plans, rather than fitting a customer experience into the defined operations of the organization.

The knowledge of how to assemble an Experience Plan gives staff and management the skills to quickly identify the audience, select the appropriate Customer Experience Maps, build an Experience Plan, and prepare the resources for its delivery. The mastering of this assembly skill set is a critical component to the effective management of an experience-based organization. We cannot overemphasize the importance of perfecting the process of assembling your Experience Plans.

DELIVERING A TOTALLY AWESOME CUSTOMER EXPERIENCE

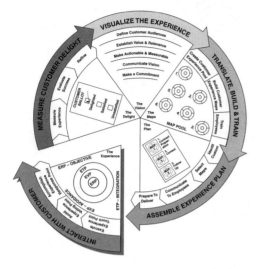

Step Four – Interact

- Execute Your Experience Touch Points with Your Customers
- Avoid Triggering Experience Voting Points
- Accomplish Your Experience Response Points

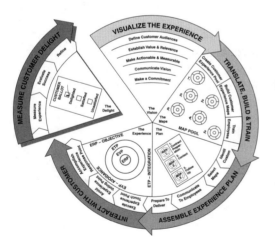

Step Five – Measure Customer Delight

- Measure the Customer Experience
- Evaluate the Success to Your Vision – The Delight Vote
- Refine

DELIVERING A TOTALLY AWESOME CUSTOMER EXPERIENCE
STEP FOUR – INTERACT WITH THE CUSTOMER

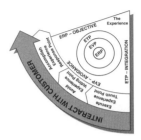

Now comes the fun! Turn on the experiences and execute your Experience Touch Points. You'll love to hear the comments and see the faces as you interact with your customers and continue to deepen your relationship with them through delivering the customer experience.

This step is your opportunity to delight your customers because you have all your employees focused, trained, and prepared with an arsenal of very powerful Customer Experience Maps. You'll find that enthusiasm, morale, and camaraderie will all improve because your organization is becoming experience-based.

Suffice it to say the key to interacting with your customer rests in your ability to coordinate all the different Experience Touch Points into a single, seamless and contiguous experience for your customer.

During this step you'll want to make it easy for employees to provide their feedback so you can constantly improve the experiences you deliver to your customers. This employee participation will make them part of the experience-based process and give them a feeling of empowerment in the process of delighting the customer.

Interacting with your customers as you deliver your Totally Awesome Customer Experience gives your organization the first opportunity to manage to the expectations of the customer's experience rather than to the expectations of your operational procedures. This interaction requires your management staff to be trained in managing each Customer Experience Map in your Experience Plan as well as the people and resources required to deliver those experiences.

Nothing is more fun than interacting with delighted customers, especially when they tell you how delighted they are with their experiences.

A. Execute Your Experience Touch Points with Your Customers

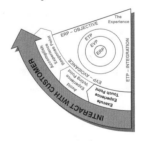

All of the Experience Touch Points from all of the Customer Experience Maps in your Experience Plan dictate the entire interaction you will have with your customer audience. Because of the critical nature of creating and delivering these all-important customer interactions, we have dedicated all of Chapter 5 to Experience Touch Points. Suffice it to say the key to interacting with your customer rests in your ability to coordinate all the different Experience Touch Points into a single, seamless and contiguous experience for your customer. This is what the customer cares about and is the key to receiving the customer's Delight Vote.

B. Avoid Triggering Experience Voting Points

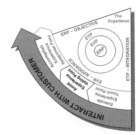

In Chapter 4 we will talk a lot about Experience Voting Points, the points where a customer decides if they want to continue with the experience. The one key thought to be stressed right here is that most critical Experience Voting Points aren't triggered because of the poor design and execution of a single Experience Touch Point. They are triggered because of the conflict among the Experience Touch Points being delivered throughout the customer's experience. In multi-departmental organizations, this is a huge issue because of the lack of interdepartmental coordination of Experience Touch Points.

Your customers, do not see departments, they see a single organization. Setting up effective communication and coordination systems among various departments that develop Experience Touch Points for a customer's experience is a very good investment. It will reward you many times over.

C. Accomplish Your Experience Response Points

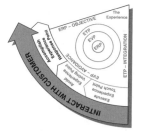

All the customer interaction in the world is not worth much if it doesn't accomplish the Experience Response Points identified in your Customer Experience Maps. It is the accomplishment of all the Experience Response Points that will determine your ability to delight your customers and receive their Delight Vote.

The management of Experience Touch Points must be done in light of what Experience Response Points you need to accomplish. Anything short of this focus will only cost you customers and money.

The interaction with your customer dictates the experience they will interpret. The empowerment of your employees to be flexible in keeping the interactions on track and positive is fundamental to your success. This is because at the end of the day, every customer experience is individual. The interpretation of the experience is individual, and the relationship currency you ultimately develop between your and your customers will be individual. This means you must empower your employees with the tools, training and trust to make their interactions with your customers as individual as possible without jeopardizing the organization's own healthy objectives. This is because customer loyalty is individual.

DELIVERING A TOTALLY AWESOME CUSTOMER EXPERIENCE STEP FIVE – MEASURE CUSTOMER DELIGHT

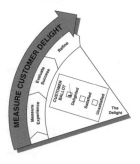

The last key element to delivering a customer experience is measuring customer delight. "If you don't keep score, you're only practicing." Our Awesome Customer Challenge is to create delighted customers and receive the Delight Vote. If you don't keep score, how will you know your customers are delighted?

You need to conduct two levels of measurement. The first level is measuring the planning and performance of your Totally Awesome Customer Experience. The second level is measuring the Delight Vote.

A. Measuring Your Totally Awesome Customer Experience

The purpose of measuring the delivery of your Totally Awesome Customer Experience is to determine if what you meant to do was done. You'll want to be able to consistently answer "Yes" to the following four questions in measuring the creation and delivery of your Totally Awesome Customer Experience:

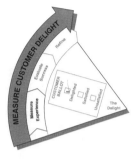

- Did the Customer Experience Map Pool contain the right Customer Experience Maps? This question measures whether or not audience definition and Customer Experience Vision translation were done properly.

- Did the Customer Experience Maps have the right Experience Response Points? This question measures whether or not the Experience Response Points in your Customer Experience Maps moved the customer towards delight in your overall customer experience.

- Did the Customer Experience Maps contain the right Experience Touch Points to generate the expected customer response and feeling? This question measures whether or not the right Experience Touch Points were designed to accomplish the Experience Response Point and to avoid potential Experience Voting Points.

- Were the Experience Touch Points delivered properly? Chapter 5 is dedicated to Experience Touch Points because of their importance in interacting with the customer. We give you more specific information about their measurement in that chapter.

B. Evaluate the Success of Your Vision – The Delight Vote

The success of any Customer Experience Vision is evaluated in terms of whether or not you received the customer's Delight Vote. You measure the Delight Vote quite differently than you measure traditional customer satisfaction. You measure customer delight using customer experience language, allowing the customer to have control over the measurement. The role of the measurer is to record the exact customer experience language and translate that information into operational language that the organization can then act upon. It's very important that your questions do not influence the customer's comments, as is so prevalent in customer satisfaction surveys today.

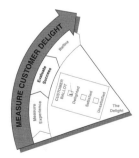

Here are some excellent questions you can ask when measuring the customer's experience in terms of the Delight Vote...

- Did we tell you that our mission is to make this a delightful experience and ask what we could do to make your experience delightful? (Set customer expectations.)

- Did we deliver the experience you told us you wanted? And if not, why not? (Were the expectations you set with the customer met by your delivery?)

- Were you delighted with the experience you had with our organization? (Let customers answer "Yes" or "No." This is really the Delight Vote and you must find out. Either they were delighted or they weren't. We're not interested in knowing if they were satisfied – only if they were delighted.)

- If your experience was delightful, please tell us why. If your experience wasn't delightful, please tell us why. (Let customers talk in their language; you can translate it later.)

- Tell us the two specific things in your experience that most delighted you. (It won't be ten things, so don't ask for ten things.)

- Tell us two things you would add to your experience that would increase your delight. (Push the customers to tell you in customer experience language what is important to them. You'll always be surprised by your customers' answers).

Customer Delight questions strictly focus on the Delight Vote and on evaluating how to improve the customer's experience.

Note how these questions differ from traditional, operational-oriented customer satisfaction questions such as: "Was the tone of our receptionist pleasant?" or "How many rings did you wait through before we answered the phone?" or "Was our salesperson's appearance professional?" Customer Delight questions strictly focus on the Delight Vote and on evaluating how to improve the customer's experience.

Measuring the Delight Vote is your opportunity to truly get your arms around a wonderful breakthrough in understanding your customer, especially in the area of measuring and collecting "customer feelings knowledge." This knowledge will help your organization transition from a Customer Knowledge Currency to a Customer Trust Currency.

CAUTION: If you're determined to ask the tough experience questions in order to measure customer delight, then you must be prepared to cheerfully implement the changes your results dictate.

There are two issues for your consideration in measuring the Delight Vote:

1. Being able to respond...

You're better off not asking customer delight questions if you don't plan to respond. This is Pandora's box. You must be able to respond to those results unless you're willing to risk eroding the trust in your relationship.

2. Tell everyone you're keeping score...

Let all your employees know you're keeping score. Don't surprise them by suddenly showing them a scorecard. Also, if you want accurate scores, set up an "it's safe to fail" environment. If your employees think they'll be penalized or punished because of the scores, they'll find ways to fix the scores. Find ways for penalties to be self-imposed or peer-imposed. Have clear, easy-to-understand paths for improvement. Improvement from the employee perspective needs to express itself through higher wages, better working environment, and so on. Let the employees help you decide the best ways to reward performance in these areas. Think rewards – not penalties. You'll get far better results, much faster.

Measure the right stuff using the right questions expressed in the right language, and you'll receive: valuable customer experience answers you can compare to your original vision.

C. Refine

Once you compile the customer experience results and evaluate the success of your vision in light of receiving the Delight Vote, you're prepared to refine the experiences for your customer. This is a ever-improving process. Armed with your Customer Experience Plan (Customer Experience Map Chart, Customer Experience Map Pool, and each Customer Experience Map) refining, updating, and communicating improvements based on the results of your Customer Delight Surveys will be an easy, natural process within your organization. Experience-based organizations base their future success on their ability to master the process.

ILLUSTRATION OF THE FIVE-STEP PROCESS

Chapters 7 and 8 contain complete case studies showing the detailed process of creating and delivering Totally Awesome Customer Experiences. This short illustration reviews the five-step process of creating and delivering a Totally Awesome Customer Experience. We deliberately simplified what would normally be a much more involved Customer Experience Mapping exercise, using an experience with "Sky Airlines." This Totally Awesome Customer Experience includes ordering tickets, dealing with airport arrival and baggage check-in, getting to the gate, boarding the plane, arriving at the destination, debarking the plane, and retrieving the bags to depart the airport.

We assume that Sky Airlines has done its Initial Transaction Assessment (Chapter 6). This Initial Transaction Assessment will have identified all the experience-based transactions they currently perform in getting their passengers from airport arrival to airport departure. This activity sets the stage for Sky Airlines to begin their five-step process of creating and delivering their Totally Awesome Customer Experience, starting with creating the Sky Airlines' Customer Experience Vision.

Step One – Visualize the Experience

Sky Airlines' Customer Experience Vision is to have their customers feel that they were treated as important, individual passengers. They need to believe that Sky Airlines is committed to on-time arrivals with no-hassle flying from the passengers' airport departure to the passengers' airport arrival.

Actual airlines traditionally segregate passengers into many different groups. In this illustrative review, Sky Airlines has only two groups: regular passengers and senior citizens. The two customer groups further divide into passengers having to check their luggage versus passengers who have carry-on luggage. This chart shows the passenger audiences:

Customer Audience Chart – Sky Airlines	
Seniors with luggage	Audience 1
Seniors with carry-on luggage	Audience 2
Non-seniors with luggage	Audience 3
Non-seniors with carry-on luggage	Audience 4

Sky Airlines communicated their vision to everyone who needed to know the vision. They can now define what Experience Response Points they need to translate their vision into the passenger experience.

Step Two – Translate, Build and Train

The next step in creating the passenger's experience is translating Sky Airlines' Customer Experience Vision into the Customer Experience Maps that correspond to the Experience Response Points originally identified in Sky Airlines' Initial Transaction Assessment. They're shown in the Customer Experience Map Chart on the following page.

Customer Experience Map Chart – Sky Airlines

Customer Experience Maps (CEM)	Desired Experience Response Point
CEM 1 – Obtaining a ticket	Customer orders and receives his or her tickets.
CEM 2 – Airport arrival with baggage check-in.	Passengers check their luggage, find the right gate, check in 60 minutes prior to the flight with the proper seat assignment, obtain the boarding pass, and wait to board. Sky Airlines wants the passengers to note how easy all these activities were. Someone was there helping them every step of the way. The key is a smooth transition.
CEM 3 – Senior customer airport arrival with baggage check-in.	Senior passenger needs assistance with luggage, with mobility, and with directions. Airline personnel quickly assume full responsibility for the arrival of a senior passenger, senior check-in, finding the right gate, and giving the proper seating and pre-boarding pass. Senior passenger issues are given VIP treatment showing care. Sky Airlines wants the passengers to thank them along the way.
CEM 4 – Airport arrival with carry-on baggage.	Passengers check in 60 minutes prior to flight, bags are appropriate for carry-on, each passenger has a proper seating assignment and a boarding pass. There are no passenger issues. All the self-instruction is fully noted each step of the way.
CEM 5 – Senior customer arrival with carry-on baggage	Senior passenger needs assistance with carry-on luggage, with mobility, and with directions. Airline personnel quickly assume full responsibility for the arrival of a senior passenger, senior check-in, finding the right gate, and receiving proper seating and pre-boarding pass. Senior passenger issues are given VIP treatment, showing care. Sky Airlines wants passengers to thank them along the way. Someone will assist the senior passengers with getting their bags into the overhead bins upon boarding.
CEM 6 – On-time flight.	Passenger boards safely, gets seated, plane takes off and lands on time. The airline wants to have the passenger comment on their efficiency and timeliness.
CEM 7 – Delayed flight/ prior notice.	Passenger is immediately notified of new departure time and assisted in rerouting. Passenger safely boards, takes off, and lands as soon as possible. The airline apologizes and looks for ways to help on the other end with phone calls, ground transportation, and so on. There were passenger issues, but they have been resolved. The airline wants the passenger to respond, "Sky Airlines'" people did everything in their power to minimize the delay."

Customer Experience Maps (CEM)	Desired Experience Response Point
CEM 8 – Delayed flight/ without prior notice.	Passenger is notified as soon as possible and cared for at the airport during the wait for the new departure time. Passenger safely boards, takes off, and lands as soon as possible. The airline apologizes and looks for ways to help on the other end with phone calls, ground transportation, and so forth. There were passenger issues, but they have been resolved. We want the passenger to respond, "They did everything in their power to minimize the delay."
CEM 9 – Departure from The baggage claim.	Passenger receives correct bags quickly and leaves airport. airline wants the customer to respond, "Wow, that was fast!"
CEM 10 – Senior customer departure from baggage claim.	Senior passenger needs assistance to the baggage claim area, help in retrieving the baggage, and help making it safely to a pick-up point. Senior passenger issues have been resolved. The airline wants the passenger to respond, "They helped me every step of the way until I got in the car to leave."
CEM 11 – Depart airport/ carry-on baggage.	The airport wants passengers to feel delighted and say, "I wish all my trips were this hassle-free."
CEM 12 – Senior customer airport departure with pick-carry-on baggage.	Senior passenger needs assistance retrieving carry-on baggage from storage compartment, and assistance to a passenger up point. Senior passenger issues have been resolved. The airline wants the passenger to respond, "They even helped me get my bags down out of the overhead bin and escorted me off the plane."

Sky Airlines will then combine their Customer Audience Chart and Customer Experience Map Chart into their Customer Experience Map Pool representing the passenger experience that Sky Airlines intends to deliver.

Customer Experience Map Pool – Sky Airlines

Customer Experience Map (CEM)	Customer Audiences			
	Audience 1 Senior With Luggage	Audience 2 Senior CO Luggage	Audience 3 Non-senior Luggage	Audience 4 Non-senior CO Luggage
CEM 1 – Obtaining a ticket.	X	X	X	X
CEM 2 – Airport arrival with baggage check-in.			X	
CEM 3 – Senior customer airport arrival with baggage check-in.	X			

Customer Experience Map (CEM)	Customer Audiences			
	Audience 1 Senior With Luggage	Audience 2 Senior CO Luggage	Audience 3 Non-senior Luggage	Audience 4 Non-senior CO Luggage
CEM 4 – Airport arrival with carry-on baggage.				X
CEM 5 – Senior customer arrival with carry-on baggage.		X		
CEM 6 – On-time flight.	X	X	X	X
CEM 7 – Delayed flight/ prior notice.	X	X	X	X
CEM 8 – Delayed flight/ without prior notice.	X	X	X	X
CEM 9 – Departure from baggage claim.			X	
CEM 10 – Senior customer departure from baggage claim.	X			
CEM 11 – Depart airport/ carry-on baggage.				X
CEM 12 – Senior customer airport departure with carry-on baggage.		X		

After carefully checking for unnecessary maps and "map gaps," Sky Airlines is ready to create their Customer Experience Maps, train their employees on both the maps and their Customer Experience Map Pool, and prepare to deliver their Totally Awesome Customer Experiences by assembling the appropriate passenger Experience Plan.

An Experience Response Point for each Customer Experience Map doesn't have to end in a letter to the president or public adulation. In this airline example, Sky Airlines might not want a passenger leaping from the seat and kissing the ground when the airplane reaches the gate. That might give the wrong impression to the rest of the passengers! All an effective Experience Response Point must do is advance the customer toward being delighted so your organization can receive the Delight Vote.

Step Three – Assemble the Experience Plan

Armed with fully developed and employee-trained Customer Experience Maps and Customer Experience Map Pool, Sky Airlines is now ready to assemble its Experience Plan for its passengers' Totally Awesome Customer Experiences. The first step is to identify the passenger from one of the passenger audience groups as they arrive at the airport. Next they must pass this information on to other staff members involved in delivering the experience to the passenger. Since all its employees have memorized and been trained on the Customer Experience Map Pool, building the Experience Plan by selecting the right Customer Experience Maps based on identified passenger audience should be a simple process. Now it's on to doing a great job in executing their Customer Experience Maps.

To further illustrate the point of assembling the right Customer Experience Maps for an effective Experience Plan, let's look at a McDonald's restaurant. A variety of different demographically profiled customers go to McDonald's every day. During each visit, there should be a Customer Experience Map for ordering, a Customer Experience Map for the delivery of the food, a Customer Experience Map for creating a positive eating environment, a Customer Experience Map for the Playland area, and so on. For example, the first person to interact with the customer should identify the audience and assemble the right Customer Experience Maps needed to build an Experience Plan to deliver a Totally Awesome Customer Experience. If the customer is a senior citizen, for example, the employee might not want to include the Customer Experience Map for the Playland area in the Experience Plan. If the customer is a senior citizen with grandchildren, then the Playland Customer Experience Map might be just the ticket.

You don't get points for perfectly selecting the wrong Customer Experience Maps for an Experience Plan.

Step Four – Interact with the Customer

Sky Airlines counts on every employee involved in delivering the passenger experience to do his or her part in executing all the right Customer Experience Touch Points at the right time. The employee must, of course, tap the appropriate Customer Experience Maps in the Experience Plan for each particular passenger group.

Step Five – Measure the Customer Delight

Sky Airlines needs to measure both the results from each Customer Experience Map and the Delight Vote coming from their passengers as they complete their Totally Awesome Customer Experience. After measuring the passenger experience, Sky Airlines needs to do something with the information to help them continue to improve passenger experiences in the future.

People don't like to answer surveys, but organizations need their feedback. Sky Airlines must innovate ways to collect their feedback in the least painful, most non-intrusive manner possible to measure the results of our Customer Experience Maps and the Delight Vote. Sky Airlines should limit its survey to four experience-based questions rather than making a passenger plod through the typical 23 operational questions survey ordeal. The questions Sky Airlines asks of its passengers should to be written in customer experience language. Passengers should be encouraged to respond to them in customer experience language.

The four customer delight questions are:

1. Were you delighted with your airline experience?

2. If your experience was delightful, please tell us why. If we only satisfied you, tell us why, and if we dissatisfied you, tell us why.

3. Tell us the two things about your airline experience that most delighted you.

4. Tell us the two things in your airline experience that didn't delight you and that we could improve to make your airline experience more delightful.

These results will help Sky Airlines pinpoint which Customer Experience Touch Points either delighted or failed to delight the passengers. Sky Airlines will learn which Experience Response Points they accomplished and which they didn't. Overall, they'll know if they received the Delight Vote from the passenger. One interesting thing about asking experience-based questions is that you can learn just as much from what customers don't tell you as from what they do tell you.

Once Sky Airlines collected the customer experience information from the four questions, they can tell...

- which Customer Experience Maps they need to examine for improvement.

- which Experience Response Points they consistently accomplish.

- the keys to differentiating themselves from competition.

- the most important aspects of the passenger's experience to invest in.

- the aspects of the passenger's experience they can downplay.

- how to migrate merely satisfactory aspects of a passenger's experience to delightful aspects in their experience.

Sky Airlines should thank each customer for helping them improve the experiences they deliver to their customers. The airline also needs to communicate to the customers the changes they make as a result of the customers' participation. This is a great opportunity for Sky Airlines to make the customer feel important, build a stronger emotional trust bond, and up-sell or cross-sell other services.

EXPERIENCE-BASED ECONOMICS

Let's face it. The fundamental purpose of a for-profit organization is to provide a return to its shareholders. This return is a result of the organization's making a profit. Profits are also the key to the growth of most organizations and the primary source of funding capital over the long term.

The oldest business formula is the profit formula...

$$\textbf{Revenues} - \textbf{Costs} = \textbf{Profits}$$

This formula also holds true for measuring the profitability of an experience. *Experience Revenues* are derived from the products and services your organization sells to its customers as a result of accomplishing any of the Experience Response Points in a Totally Awesome Customer Experience. *Experience Costs* are derived from all the Experience Touch Points used to deliver your Totally Awesome Customer Experience. The difference between your Experience Revenues and your Experience Costs equal your *Experience Profits*.

From there you can compute your Experience Return on Investment and look at opportunities to maximize your profitability.

Experience Revenues

Experience Revenues are generated when a customer votes to accept your offer through the experiences you're delivering. If the customer does not have a desirable experience, he or she never reaches the right Experience Response Point and no Experience Revenues are generated. Ideally, you want to deliver your most relevant and valuable offers through your most delightful Totally Awesome Customer Experience in order to have the best

Experience Revenue:

Experience Revenues are derived from the products and services your organization sells to its customers as a result of accomplishing any of the Experience Response Points in a Totally Awesome Customer Experience.

chance of receiving a positive customer response. The more perceived relevance and value your offers have to the customer audience, the greater acceptance they'll get from the customer. The result is higher revenues. In fact, the acceptance of the experience itself can play a dramatic role in increasing a customer's response to your offers.

In the economics of experiences, we concentrate heavily on something called **Customer Response Rate**. This is the percentage of time your offers are accepted by the audience to whom they were presented or intended. With all things being equal, the higher the customer response rate, the higher your revenues and the lower your costs per customer will be. The reverse also holds true: the lower your customer response rate, the lower your revenues and the higher your costs per customer.

Direct mail, for instance, generally has a customer response rate between 1.5 percent and 3 percent. That means that for every 100 offers you present to a customer for acceptance, only three people (3 percent) ever accept those offers. It also means you incurred the cost of the other 97 percent of those who did not accept your offer.

Here are five key variables that affect customer response rates:

1. Customer acceptability barriers to your offer .

2. Timing of the presentation of your offer.

3. Coordination of Experience Touch Points in both delivering your experiences and presenting your offers.

4. Relevancy of your offer.

5. Value of your offer.

The last two variables pertain directly to the offer itself. The first three variables relate to the experience in which you present the offer. The value of your offer often increases if the experience in which you deliver your offers is delightful. Therefore, coordinating all of your Experience Touch Points is essential in making the experience and your offers more acceptable.

"The bottom line is that customer response rates, which depend on acceptability, relevance, and perceived value, ultimately dictate the Experience Revenues you'll generate."

Experience Costs

On the cost side of the equation, the more effective and efficient your Experience Touch Points, the lower the costs of your overall experience. We

Customer Response Rate:

The percentage of your offers accepted by the audience to whom they were presented or intended.

Experience Cost:

Experience Costs are derived from all the costs of creating and delivering the Experience Touch Points that deliver your Totally Awesome Customer Experience.

explore Experience Touch Point costs in greater detail in Chapter 5. Your costs in your customers' Totally Awesome Customer Experience are incurred through the design and execution of your Experience Touch Points. The type, nature, frequency, medium used, and timing of Experience Touch Points are all variables that help determine their cost. The aggregate cost of all your Experience Touch Points determines the overall cost of your Totally Awesome Customer Experience. When you divide the total cost of all Experience Touch Points in your experience by the total number in the customer audience receiving your experience and offer, the result is your Cost of Experience Per Customer. This number is very helpful in establishing standards of performance and investment.

Experience Profit

Experience Profit:

The difference between your Experience Revenues and your Experience Costs.

The profit from a Totally Awesome Customer Experience is equal to the Experience Revenues from accepted offers minus all costs of generating the necessary Experience Touch Points to accomplish the Experience Response Points.

Experience Return on Investment

Experience Return on Investment:

The result of incremental Experience Profit divided by Incremental Experience Cost.

To determine whether you should invest more or less into your Totally Awesome Customer Experience, with the hope of increasing your Return on Investment (ROI) for that experience, use this formula:

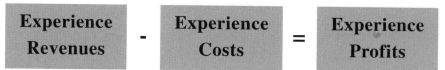

Experience Revenues − **Experience Costs** = **Experience Profits**

Here's how you get there...

1. First, determine present Experience Profit (Experience Response Point revenues minus present Experience Touch Points cost)...$1,000,000 − $700,000 = $300,000

2. Next, determine your new Experience Profit (New expected Experience Response Point revenues minus new Experience Touch Point costs)...$1,500,000 − $900,000 = $600,000

3. This makes it possible to determine your Incremental Experience Profit (New Experience Profit minus Present Experience Profit)...$600,000 − $300,000 = $300,000...and your Incremental Experience Touch Point Cost...$900,000 − $700,000 = $200,000

4. Then just divide

The result is your Return on Investment, expressed as a percentage. In the example above, the ROI is 150 percent.

Maximizing Your Profitability and Investment

Maximizing profitability requires that you employ the most effective and direct Experience Response Points while minimizing the number of Experience Touch Points necessary to successfully accomplish those Experience Response Points. This procedure will generate higher Experience Revenues, lower Experience Costs, and greater Experience Profits. However, we can't forget that the overall objective is to delight the customer.

Here are three critical tips to help you maximize your profits and investment in the experiences you deliver to your customers:

1. Invest in relevant Experience Touch Points

Never invest in Experience Touch Points that don't actively guide a customer toward a positive Experience Response Point. Hundreds of millions of dollars are wasted every year delivering irrelevant, uncoordinated, and ineffective Experience Touch Points. These Experience Touch Points confuse customers and increase your risk of triggering an Experience Voting Point. They also add cost without any offsetting revenues. As Maslow would say, "What is not worth doing, is not worth doing well."

For instance...ABC organization is now using 12 Experience Touch Points to arrive at the expected Experience Response Point. Each Experience Touch Point costs them $1,000. XYZ, using Customer Experience Mapping, needs only five Experience Touch Points to create and deliver their Totally Awesome Customer Experience. The Experience Touch Points for XYZ, however, cost $2,000 each.

The overall difference in profit is $2,000 ($12,000 − $10,000), even though the cost of the Experience Touch Point for XYZ was double in cost. The organization must view Experience Touch Points in aggregate through the Customer Experience Mapping process.

The other significant benefit is that the XYZ organization will have seven (12 minus 5) fewer Experience Touch Points to manage, significantly reducing the overhead/operational support costs for each Experience Touch Point also this smaller number of Experience Touch Points will reduce the risk of having the customer exit the experience before reaching the Customer Response

The process of creating and delivering Totally Awesome Customer Experiences and Customer Experience Mapping can help you derive the maximum value from your investment in your customers.

Point because of a poorly executed, irrelevant Experience Touch Point. Think about all the irrelevant Experience Touch Points you've encountered. You have to wonder why organizations are wasting their money.

2. Balance relevancy and value against "look and feel"

Weigh relevancy and value against experience "look and feel." Usually, a balanced combination of both is most successful. How many times have you received a really fancy mailer, only to find out that it wasn't relevant or valuable? It seems the more relevant and valuable the offer, the less packaging it needs to be accepted.

3. Less is more

Minimize the number of Experience Touch Points you need by trying to increase the effectiveness of each one. We look at this argument (Reach versus Richness) in more depth in Chapter 5. Minimizing the number of Experience Touch Points also decreases the risk of triggering Experience Voting Points.

The economics behind creating and delivering Totally Awesome Customer Experiences focuses on receiving the highest customer response rates for the least amount of Experience Touch Point cost. Customer Experience Mapping significantly lowers your Experience Costs because it improves customer response rates while lowering the number of Experience Touch Points needed to reach an Experience Response Point.

IMPROVING CONSISTENCY AND REPEATABILITY IN YOUR CUSTOMER EXPERIENCES

Many organizations are already trying to create and deliver Totally Awesome Customer Experiences. Yours might be one. Just because people haven't read this book doesn't mean that they're not creating and delivering Totally Awesome Customer Experiences. What we can add to the game is consistency and repeatability. If your organization is struggling to consistently and repeatedly create and deliver Totally Awesome Customer Experiences, you might want to take a look at our Top Ten list for some possible reasons for your difficulty.

1. You have no formal process for creating customer experiences. Customer experiences seem to be created randomly by people "doing their own thing."

2. Not everyone actually cares about creating or delivering customer experiences.

3. Your people don't realize that they're not delivering Totally Awesome Customer Experiences.

4. You haven't clearly defined your vision for customer experiences.

5. You haven't selected the right customer audiences for the customer experiences.

6. There is inconsistency or non-repeatability in the execution of customer experiences.

7. You haven't properly determined or set customer experience expectations for the customers or staff.

8. Experience Touch Points are poorly coordinated and/or incongruent.

9. Experience Touch Points are in conflict and triggering Experience Voting Points.

10. Your people display a lack of interest in being customer-focused.

We've divided our Top Ten list into further sub-categories that will make it easier for you to assess your own organization's trouble spots...

Belief and Motivation

You might consider that some organizations...

- are not customer-focused. Some may never be.

- don't realize that their most valuable assets are their customers.

- are ineffective in motivating their personnel.

- have employees who think that being customer-focused is just another new idea of the month that will go away like so many other initiatives.

- have employees who just don't care about a customer's experience.

Awareness

You might consider that some organizations...

- are unaware of the benefits derived from creating and delivering Totally Awesome Customer Experiences.

- think they're just doing fine.

- have very high product demand that is temporarily masking customer experience issues.

- have long volumes of meaningless bureaucratic reports or even the self-serving customer satisfaction surveys that cover up the truth about customer experiences.

- have customers who never complain, but just cease to be customers while the organization rationalizes customer turnover as part of their industry or market.

Lack of Tools or Structure

You might consider that some organizations...

- lack the tools necessary to do Customer Experience Mapping.

- don't have the know-how to define the standards for what a Totally Awesome Customer Experience should be.

- lack the infrastructure to support customer experiences even if they could create and deliver them.

- don't know how to do the actual creation, delivery, or measurement of customer experiences or customer delight.

- have a structure where inconsistent, tactically incorrect, and confusing Experience Touch Points happen as a normal course of trade and business.

- are forced to rely on the customer to fill in the missing parts of the experiences being delivered to them due to lack of people, technology, or process.

- are just operationally-oriented.

Commitment and Follow-Through

You might consider that some organizations...

- are customer-focused only through their vision or planning phases.

- have no one accountable or responsible for the creation and delivery of Totally Awesome Customer Experiences. They have no VP of Customers.

- think they have no time or resources to pay attention to customer experiences – operations done right will cover it.

Poor Execution of Experience Touch Points

You might consider that some organizations...

- plan poorly.

- train employees poorly.

- select the wrong people, processes, and/or technologies to use.

- have no established standards for employee performance.

- have inconsistent employee performance.

The trick is to work on correcting your biggest trouble spots. You'll want to assess how adopting the Five-Step Process of creating and delivering a Totally Awesome Customer Experiences might mitigate most of your trouble spots.

MANAGING YOUR EXPERIENCE VARIABLES

We often hear the excuse, "There are just too many variables out of our control to make a customer experience process work effectively." This is pure nonsense. Although customers are actually in control of the ultimate acceptance of their experiences, the fact is that you're in control of creating and delivering each experience for your customers. And while some variables in an experience are difficult to get your arms around, it only stands to reason that using a process will help.

Implementing the Five-Step Process will help your organization improve its control over these ten significant customer **Experience Variables**:

1. Customer audience selection. You can choose with whom you want to do business.

2. Experience selection. You can decide which experiences you want to deliver to which customers. For example, Nike can choose to deliver its basketball shoe experience to inner city youth by using Michael Jordan as a spokesperson.

3. Content and messaging method selection. You choose the best way to touch your customers (Experience Touch Points).

4. Employee selection. Which employees in your organization do you want to directly interface with customers? What attributes best suit that customer interaction? The hiring process also helps immensely.

5. Measuring customer delight.

6. Deciding on customer investment. You can better control the investment you make in creating and delivering a Totally Awesome Customer Experience.

Experience Variables:

The variables that impact the effectiveness of accomplishing Experience Response Points in a Totally Awesome Customer Experience

7. Offer creation. You know which offers you want to make to which customers. Your choice will determine your revenue from a Totally Awesome Customer Experience.

8. Waste. You can minimize your costs by carefully selecting only the Experience Touch Points that will evoke the appropriate response from your customers.

9. Selecting operations. You'll have a road map to tell you what people, technology, and processes you need to create, deliver, and support every Experience Touch Point. The remaining operations can be eliminated and costs reduced.

10. Vision and mission. You can keep your organization more focused on the goal of delighting customers!

Improved control over the creation and delivery variables of your customer experiences will only add to the accomplishment of more Experience Response Points. This kind of improvement will help created more delighted customers and inspire them to give your organization their Delight Vote.

MASTERING THE CUSTOMER EXPERIENCE LANGUAGE

We feel passionate about getting organizations to adopt a common customer experience language. Adopting a customer experience language fosters understanding and accelerates your efforts in implementation. Having a common language can be both powerful and directive. The adoption or integration of a new customer experience language can help immensely in developing an experience-based culture. The book deliberately overuses the customer experience language in an effort to help you become more familiar with the terms and their proper use.

In our case studies, we found that when everyone used the customer experience language, it significantly lessened misunderstandings, shortened conversations, and built team unity. We've prepared a Glossary of Terms for you in the back of this book with indexed references of key areas where the terms are used. The Glossary will also help you in your customer experience language adoption. The customer experience language sets up a contextual framework for defining a Totally Awesome Customer Experience.

THE MAGIC FORMULA

It's all about stopping the operationally misdirected efforts that merely satisfy your customers and starting to energize experience-based efforts that will delight them. This tenacious attitude and total resolve to be experience-based will help your organization leverage the new customer economy.

Millions of customers are buried in the quagmire of poor customer service, uncaring organizations, horrible offers, and inconsistent and uncoordinated experiences.

The magic formula lies in changing to an experience-based organization that combines customer-focused activities with the development of a Customer Trust Currency. This formula allows for the creation of delighted customers through creating and delivering Totally Awesome Customer Experiences. It's really just that simple. Do you remember *The Wizard of Oz*? It's one of the most watched films ever made. You know that yellow brick road thing? We think there's something there – definitely something there. We built a power tool called Customer Experience Mapping to help you travel the yellow brick road a bit more easily, and a whole lot faster.

Chapter 5

The Science of Customer Experience Mapping©...Using the Power Tool

"It's not about how cool your website is or how much content it has. It's about how you use the Internet to improve the entire customer experience."

David Pottruck,
CEO of Charles Schwab

Chapter 4 covers the nuts and bolts of Customer-Experience Mapping. The chapter starts with Customer Experience Maps as the fundamental component of a Totally Awesome Customer Experience. Next comes an explanation of how the Science of Customer Experience Mapping© helps you create your Customer Experience Maps and reduce your costs. We then look at each element of an effective Customer Experience Map and its role in making the map effective. The chapter finishes with noting how valuable Customer Experience Mapping is in your strategic planning process and its capabilities as both a key planning and documentation tool.

THE SCIENCE

The significance of Pottruck's remark is his astute recognition of the need to deliver the entire experience to a customer. Although each particular tool is important, it's the contribution that each tool makes to the overall success of the experience that really counts, not any one tool by itself. We can't overemphasize the importance of his remark.

It has been said, "If the only tool you have is a hammer, then every problem must look like a nail." The Internet is just one great tool to help us deliver experiences. Other tools include direct mail, television, radio, video, CD-ROM, personal sales calls, and magazine advertisements.

Customer Experience Mapping is a strategic power tool. It protects your organization from those random acts of excellence and chaos that cause customer confusion and hamper your efforts to create delighted customers. It does so by performing three critical functions to assist you in the creation and delivery of consistent and repeatable Totally Awesome Customer Experiences:

Customer Experience Mapping is a power tool that helps you place the necessary components into a customer interactive framework called a Customer Experience Map. A Totally Awesome Customer Experience is made from a series of contiguous and coordinated Customer Experience Maps.

1. It builds effective Customer Experience Maps that your employees can easily learn and follow, and that you can manage.

*The workflow of creating
a Customer Experience
Map is:*

*Build your Experience
Response Point*

↓

*Build your Experience
Touch Points*

↓

*Identify your potential
Experience Voting Points*

**The point that
defines how
you want your
customers to
respond and feel
(the Experience
Map's objective)**

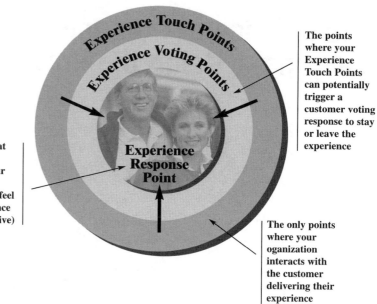

**The points
where your
Experience
Touch Points
can potentially
trigger a
customer voting
response to stay
or leave the
experience**

**The only points
where your
oganization
interacts with
the customer
delivering their
experience**

2. It links your Customer Experience Maps together into a contiguous
    string of Experience Touch Points, producing a seamless experience
    for your customer.

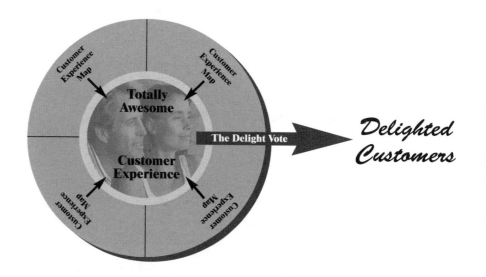

3. It documents both your Customer Experience Maps and their linkage so your experiences can be consistent, repeatable, and correctable.

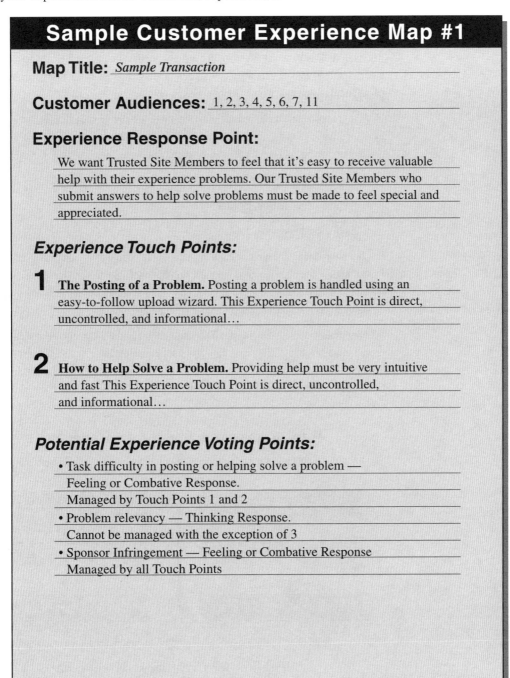

Sample Customer Experience Map #1

Map Title: *Sample Transaction*

Customer Audiences: 1, 2, 3, 4, 5, 6, 7, 11

Experience Response Point:

We want Trusted Site Members to feel that it's easy to receive valuable help with their experience problems. Our Trusted Site Members who submit answers to help solve problems must be made to feel special and appreciated.

Experience Touch Points:

1 **The Posting of a Problem.** Posting a problem is handled using an easy-to-follow upload wizard. This Experience Touch Point is direct, uncontrolled, and informational...

2 **How to Help Solve a Problem.** Providing help must be very intuitive and fast This Experience Touch Point is direct, uncontrolled, and informational...

Potential Experience Voting Points:

• Task difficulty in posting or helping solve a problem — Feeling or Combative Response.
  Managed by Touch Points 1 and 2
• Problem relevancy — Thinking Response.
  Cannot be managed with the exception of 3
• Sponsor Infringement — Feeling or Combative Response
  Managed by all Touch Points

BUILDING AN EFFECTIVE CUSTOMER EXPERIENCE MAP

A Customer Experience Map is the basic building block of a Totally Awesome Customer Experience. The purpose of a Customer Experience Map is to form a documented framework within which you can deliver the necessary Experience Touch Points to your customer. The Map lets you do so in such a way as to add relevancy and value in the creation and delivery of a Totally Awesome Customer Experience.

Every Customer Experience Map comprises three major interactive components in association with a Success Measurement Standard (we touched on these components earlier in the book). The three interactive components are:

1. Experience Response Points

2. Experience Touch Points

3. Experience Voting Points

The process by which you create a Customer Experience Map is not the way you deliver a Customer Experience Map!

Each Customer Experience Map can have only one Experience Response Point (its objective), but it can have multiple Experience Touch Points (points of customer interaction) and Experience Voting Points (points of customer conflict and decision).

We're going to examine each of the interactive components and success measurement standards in a Customer Experience Map, and then go through an example. As you saw in Chapter 3, the process by which you create a Customer Experience Map is not the way you deliver a Customer Experience Map!

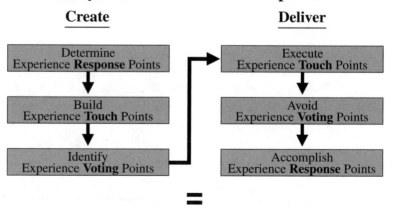

Totally Awesome Customer Experience

Create   **Deliver**

Determine Experience **Response** Points	Execute Experience **Touch** Points
Build Experience **Touch** Points	Avoid Experience **Voting** Points
Identify Experience **Voting** Points	Accomplish Experience **Response** Points

=

Workflow for **Creating** and **Delivering**
Totally Awesome Customer Experiences

On the path to a Totally Awesome Customer Experience, your customers eventually interact with all of your selected Customer Experience Maps. What they'll specifically interact with is a series of contiguous Experience Touch Points coming from the appropriate Customer Experience Maps. As this interaction takes place, you hope that these interactions will accomplish the Experience Response Point you planned, while steering clear of any Experience Voting Points. Remember our lemonade stand example?

Customer Experience Map Chart – Lemonade Stand

Customer Experience Maps	Desired Experience Response Point
CEM 1 – Lemonade signage	We need to attract the attention of drivers and pedestrians.
CEM 2 – Lemonade sample	We want to give each potential customer a sip of our delicious, cool lemonade in hopes they'll want to purchase a full glass.
CEM 3 – Lemonade offer	After their sample, we want to tell them how little it costs to purchase a full, glass of cool, refreshing lemonade.
CEM 4 – Lemonade fulfillment in cars on the same side of the street	Handling our car customers will be different than our pedestrian customers. Customers must perceive that buying from a car is just as easy as buying as a pedestrian, so it's worth stopping.
CEM 5 – Lemonade fulfillment in cars on the opposite side of the street	Handling our car customers on the opposite side of the street will first of all require they know it isn't a big deal. Customers must perceive that buying from a car is just as easy as buying as a pedestrian.
CEM 6 – Lemonade fulfillment at the stand	Our pedestrian customers will feel this is so simple to order and receive their cool, refreshing lemonade, they'll just stop.
CEM 7 – Lemonade payment	We want our customers to be able to give us coin or currency with no hassles about making change.
CEM 8 – Lemonade referral	We want all our customers to want to tell their friends about our lemonade stand.

Customers will see your signage, see your great smile, taste your sample, receive your offer to purchase a full glass, pay for the purchase, and receive your request to make referrals. They won't see what it took to assemble the sign, make the stand, rehearse the scripts, make the lemonade, haul everything to the corner, get the change, or other tasks you had to perform. They'll simply perceive their experience as a lemonade stand customer. The creation of a Customer Experience Map is in reverse order of its delivery.

In our lemonade stand example, you create your Customer Experience Maps by first identifying the Experience Response Points you need for the entire experience of all of your selected customer audiences. The lemonade stand Experience Response Points are "wanting your customers to stop," then "sample," then "purchase," then "pay," then "enjoy," and then "refer." Once you set your Experience Response Points, it's time to design your Experience Touch Points around those Experience Response Points identifying any potential Experience Voting Points, like "too much traffic to stop," "can't read the sign," "don't see the stand until it's too late," "kids having a bad attitude," "sample of lemonade is terrible," "nobody is interested – it's a game," and so on. This is the *creation* workflow.

The *delivery* workflow, on the other hand, is all about the execution of Experience Touch Points contained in your Customer Experience Map that let you accomplish the Experience Response Point while trying to avoid an Experience Voting Points.

It's a challenge to keep focused on *delivering* the customer experience when the process of *creating* the customer experience has the opposite work flow. This is because delivering a customer experience starts with Experience Touch Points, while creating a customer experience starts with identifying the necessary Experience Response Points.

CREATING CUSTOMER EXPERIENCE MAPS...

Recognizing the difference between how you *create* your Customer Experience Maps and how you *deliver* them is helpful in keeping you equally focused on the overall process of creating and delivering a Totally Awesome Customer Experience. This focus is an important key to managing an experience-based organization

You'll finally build a measurement system to track your experience success. Maybe it's having one kid count the cars and people that pass by, while the other kid counts how many stop, sample, and purchase. This provides you with the knowledge you need to improve your lemonade stand experience.

With that said, let's take a detailed look at the *three* major components required for creating a Customer Experience Map, outline the setting of your success measurement standards, and finish with a simple Customer Experience Map example...

The Experience Response Point Component...

We noted in Chapter 3 that the Experience Response Point is the objective of a Customer Experience Map. The Experience Response Point defines your expectations of how you want the customer to respond and feel. An Experience Response Point must contribute to the overall creation and delivery of your Totally Awesome Customer Experience. You achieve Experience Response Points as a result of careful and meticulous planning and execution of Experience Touch Points. The Customer Response Point is the primary measurement of the success of a Customer Experience Map within the overall experience.

The key attributes of an effective Experience Response Point are its relevance and value to the overall Totally Awesome Customer Experience. If an Experience Response Point lacks these attributes, the Customer Experience Map itself becomes ineffective and only adds cost to the overall customer experience, not to mention creating confusion for the customer.

Again, an effective Experience Response Point defines how you want the customer to respond and feel. Caring about how the customer responds and feels is an essential requirement in helping form an emotional trust bond between the customer and your organization. This bond is fundamental in building a Customer Trust Currency.

The response segment of an Experience Response Point defines how you want the customer to respond as a result of receiving your Experience Touch Points. The table below lists some typical responses:

The Experience Response Point is the objective of a Customer Experience Map

Typical Experience Response Point Action
Orders the product
Signs the sales contract
Fills out a delight survey
Tells a friend or associate
Makes another deposit to his or her mutual fund account
Walks off the plane smiling
Asks for the same service person
Orders the same meal
Asks for additional information
Asks for a proposal

The emotional segment of an Experience Response Point defines how you want the customer to feel as a result of having received your Experience Touch Points. The table below lists some typical responses:

Typical Experience Response Point Action
I'm excited about using the product
I made a great decision
I would love to tell someone how good I feel
I was just delighted
I feel they take care of me
That was quite pleasant
I had such a fun time
That was delicious
What a cool idea
I really trust them

In our research and case studies, we've found that the emotional segment of an Experience Response Point tends to drive the response segment of the Experience Response Point. This means that a customer's feelings are more powerful in driving his or her thoughts than the customer's thoughts driving his or her feelings. The result is a unique coupling of both feeling and action into building an effective Experience Response Point.

Here are some examples of Experience Response Points that properly couple the emotional segment and the action segment:

Effective Experience Response Points

Emotional Side (Feelings)	Coupler	Response Side (Action)
I am excited about using this product	...so he or she	Orders the product
I have made a great decision	...so he or she	Signs the sales contract
I would love to tell someone how I feel about my experiences	...so he or she	Fills out a delight survey
I was just delighted	...so he or she	Tells a friend or associate
I feel they really take care of me	...so he or she	Makes another deposit to his or her mutual fund account
That was quite pleasant	...so he or she	Walks off the plane smiling, having had no issues with a flight

Emotional Side (Feelings)	Coupler	Response Side (Action)
I had such a fun time	...so he or she	Asks for the same service person
That was so delicious	...so he or she	Orders the same meal
What a cool idea	...so he or she	Asks for additional information
I really trust them	...so he or she	Asks for a proposal

CAUTION: It's dangerous to use either the action response or feeling segment alone in selecting your Experience Response Point. If you choose only the action response segment, you're in danger of building experiences that are customer-manipulative. If you use only the emotional segment, you tend to lose focus and purpose. In either case, using only one in your Experience Response Point could detract from creating customer delight.

The Experience Touch Point Component

Experience Touch Points are the only points of interaction with a customer. They are the only means of conveying what you want your customer to do and how you want them to feel. Only a customer's interaction with your Experience Touch Points can accomplish an Experience Response Point. The Experience Touch Point is where the strategy within a Customer Experience Map is converted into customer interaction.

Experience Touch Points are the only points of interaction with a customer. They are the only means of conveying what you want your customer to do and how you want them to feel.

Relative to the science side of creating Experience Touch Points (the art side is described in Chapter 5) for an effective Customer Experience Map, here are some helpful guidelines. An Experience Touch Point should:

1. Guide the customer toward an Experience Response Point.

2. Avoid conflict with another Experience Touch Point in other Customer Experience Maps in the experience.

3. Require resources within your budget for people, technology, and process.

4. Be easily understood and perceived by the customer.

5. Be designed in conjunction with other Experience Touch Points.

6. Have standards for performance that are understood by all the employees involved in the Experience Touch Point delivery.

7. Be measurable in terms of its contribution to accomplishing the appropriate Experience Response Point.

All people have thought and feeling filters. We have different filters in terms of how we think and feel towards different aspects of life. That's why everyone is not named Bob. We have thought and feeling filters for issues such as religion, politics, family, friendship, car colors, and other matters. When an Experience Touch Point is delivered to a customer in perfect alignment with his or her thought and feeling filters, the customer moves closer to the Experience Response Point. On the other hand, an Experience Touch Point that's out of alignment with a customer's thought and feeling filters causes conflict. This conflict triggers what we call an Experience Voting Point. The type and degree of conflict between the Experience Touch Point and the customer's thought and feeling filters determines whether a customer votes to stay engaged or terminate the experience. The design or creation of an Experience Touch Point has a lot to do with making sure your Experience Touch Points are as well aligned as possible to your customer's thought and feeling filters. Experience Touch Points require imagination and creativity to achieve effective alignment.

In Chapter 5, we discuss creating and delivering effective Experience Touch Points and refer to it as the Art of Customer Experience Mapping.

The Experience Voting Point Component

Experience Voting Point Spectrum:

The first and only time you want your customers to vote is when they cast their Delight Vote at the end of their Totally Awesome Customer Experience.

The first and only time you want your customers to vote is when they cast their Delight Vote at the end of their Totally Awesome Customer Experience. If customers think or feel that they need to vote about their experience before completing it and casting their Delight Vote, your Experience Touch Points are not properly aligned with your customer's thought and feeling filters and have created conflict. Conflict is expressed as either customer confusion or anxiety. These points of conflict are called Experience Voting Points. An Experience Voting Point is really a decision point. It consciously or unconsciously gives the customer a place to pause and decide whether to proceed, suspend or disengage from their experience.

Below is the Experience Voting Point Spectrum. It describes potential responses when you deliver an Experience Touch Point to a customer. Under each point on the spectrum are four response aspects denoting "customer reaction," "what customers do," "what customers become," and "what customers need."

Experience Voting Point Spectrum

	No Response	Thinking Response	Feeling Response	Combative Response
Cust. Reaction	None	Confusion	Anxiety	Fight/flight
Cust. Does	Moves forward	Asks questions	Expresses doubts	No comment/criticizes
Cust. Becomes	A believer	A questioner	A doubter	A skeptic
Cust. Needs	Nothing	More facts/end the experience	Confirmation/end the experience	To end the experience

Here's a summary of the different Experience Voting Point responses in order of the most severe response to no response.

- **A No Response is the ideal situation.** This happens when all of your Experience Touch Points are accepted by your customer, or at least don't trigger severe enough responses to cause an Experience Voting Point.

- **A Thinking Response is triggered when your customers become confused.** Perhaps your message wasn't exactly on target, or you didn't answer all their questions, or they may not perceive your offer as relevant or valuable. It might be as simple as they can't see where the Experience Touch Point is leading them. Whatever the reason, the customer is confused, asks a lot of questions, and needs more facts. Depending on the severity of the Thinking Response, customers either stay in the experience and look for more facts, or simply judge it too much effort and leave. Many websites have this issue.

- **A Feeling Response creates anxiety.** This anxiety causes customers to express their doubts. Anxiety conjures up a perception of risk. Customers who are risk-averse, and there are many, become doubters. These customers require some kind of confirmation, preferably from a trusted third party, to get them back on track. If the anxiety is great enough, they'll simply end the experience. If the customers continue their experience, they'll be attentively looking for confirmation as they cautiously proceed forward.

- **A Combative Response causes customers to either fight or flee.** They'll either say nothing or criticize the organization openly. They've become your opponents and skeptical. They will leave the experience mentally, physically, or both. Triggering a Combative Response is the worst-case scenario. In terms of severity, it's followed by the triggering a "Feeling Response" and finally by a "Thinking Response."

As Robert Reid told us, "It doesn't take a PhD; it only takes a person with a pulse" to encounter an Experience Voting Point and respond to it. Our goal in delivering your Experience Touch Points is to avoid triggering any Experience Voting Points. The only vote you want to trigger is a Delight Vote at the end of the experience. In our imperfect world, this rarely happens. You can count on some of your Experience Touch Points triggering Experience Voting Points. The key is how you manage those Experience Voting Points once triggered. One of the values of Customer Experience Mapping is that it helps you identify the potential Experience Voting Points in a Customer Experience Map so you can develop a plan to manage them when they do occur.

Thinking Response

A state where the customer expresses the need for further information to assess the value of continuing with an experience.

Feeling Response

A feeling of anxiety where the customer expresses doubts regarding the value of continuing with an experience.

Combative Response

A spontaneous fight-or-flight reaction to an Experience Touch Point, causing the customer to either say nothing or criticize the organization openly, inevitably terminating the experience. That customer has become your opponent.

Managing a triggered Experience Voting Point is an exercise in reaction speed. You must quickly mitigate any issue causing anxiety or confusion while keeping the customer moving towards the Experience Response Point. Delays only heighten the severity of your customers' reactions. Having a plan in place, with all your employees trained in using it, will help you keep your customers on track while giving you an advantage over your competition.

An organization must know and actively manage its Experience Voting Points. Experience Voting Points represent all the exit doors from a customer experience. If you want your audience to see the final act of your play and cast their Delight Vote at final curtain, it's important to keep them in the theater.

A word about customer filters. A customer's acceptance of your Experience Touch Points greatly depends on the number of that customer's thought and feeling filters. The more he or she has, the more critical and less accepting your customer will be of your Experience Touch Points. This attitude can substantially impact your customer response rates. The various types of Experience Touch Points discussed in Chapter 5 are critical in dealing with different levels of customer filters. This is why Experience Touch Points represent the Art of Customer Experience Mapping. It's also important to remember when selecting your potential customer audiences.

Dr. Jakob Nielsen, a website usability expert, wrote, "The web changed the game. Things swung back toward the novice user – the user lacking knowledge of the system and the interface. With websites, there is no training. You hit the site and it's in your face. Thus, if you don't make a website effective in the first few seconds, you have lost the user." Dr. Nielsen is saying that certain Experience Touch Points trigger Experience Voting Points faster than others. He could not be more accurate.

Here's an example of multiple Experience Touch Points triggering two different Experience Voting Points.

> John, a Lexus customer, has just received a letter from the local Lexus dealership. The letter offers a special deal, to only Lexus customers, for a discount on an oil change. The offer stated the words "Expiration date" but there was no date! (Experience Touch Point 1). It triggers a very mild Thinking Response Experience Voting Point.
>
> John votes to stay with the experience and calls the dealership to inquire further about the offering. He speaks to a receptionist about the oil change special. (Experience Touch Point 2). He asks her if there is an expiration date and she says no. She then goes over the rest of the offering and quotes the same price as the one listed on the flyer.

John suddenly notices that she doesn't ask him if he is a Lexus customer. He tells her he has a Jeep Cherokee and asks if the special also applies to his vehicle. She tells him that it does. This triggers a not-so-good Feeling Response Voting Point that brings on anxiety because the two Experience Touch Points are in conflict. One Experience Touch Point makes a promise – the offer is special because he is a Lexus owner – while the other Experience Touch Point tells him he is not special and anyone can participate.

The anxiety expresses itself in John's feeling of being deceived. It's a severe enough feeling for John to end the experience and get his oil changed elsewhere. He perceives, or feels (not thinks), the offering is a gimmick and opts out. The conflict between the two Experience Touch Points has caused a loss of loyalty and trust. It most likely eroded brand as well. John later learns that the receptionist was not accurate in her statements and the discount did apply to Lexus owners only. But John has already voted.

John easily made it through the first Thinking Response Experience Voting Point with simple clarification. It was the Feeling Response Experience Voting Point that he didn't get past. We cannot stress enough the importance of having all Experience Touch Points coordinated and executed properly to avoid severe Experience Voting Points. We'll talk more in Chapter 5 about the importance of coordinating Experience Touch Points and their power to lessen the severity and type of Experience Voting Points.

Here's an example of a single Experience Touch Point creating a Combative Response Experience Voting Point:

Frank and Sally are going to dinner. They've already selected a restaurant. It's raining that night. When they arrive at the restaurant, they notice that the restaurant has no valet parking. The parking lot is full; no free parking spot is in sight. *No valet parking*, *no close parking*, and *rain* become Frank and Sally's first Experience Touch Point with the restaurant. This unpleasant situation immediately brings on a Combative Response Experience Voting Point for Frank. "They should have valet parking or umbrellas or something if they care about their guests on nights like these," grumbles Frank. "This is ridiculous." Frank's fight-or-flight response is now triggered. He now responds as an opponent to the restaurant. Without further comment, Frank and Sally vote to end their experience and drive to another restaurant with valet parking.

So what happened here? Simply put, the restaurant had not created a Customer Experience Map covering the Experience Response Point of "getting our customers into the restaurant, quickly and dry, when it's raining." The fact that you haven't thought of a Customer Experience Map that should be in an experience doesn't mean that no Experience Touch Points will be delivered to a customer. On the contrary, they will be delivered, but it won't be you delivering them. The Experience Touch Points and Experience Voting Points happen with or without you.

The really bad news is that you get blamed for them and didn't even know they occurred. Take Frank and Sally. They won't blame the weather for preventing them from dining at the restaurant; they'll blame the restaurant for not making it possible to get from their car to the restaurant.

How much business do organizations lose without even knowing that Experience Touch Points are taking place? If a website is hard to navigate, or a clerk is unfriendly, or the package is ugly, or the customer wasn't called back on time, or salespeople are late, or the food is cold, or employees of the organization are apathetic, or your customers are stuck in a parking lot in the rain, customers vote. They just rarely tell you about it. Frank and Sally didn't bother to phone the restaurant to complain while on their way to another restaurant – one that provides valet parking. They'll simply tell all their friends not to go to that restaurant when it's raining or snowing. That night the restaurant lost revenue they didn't even know they lost. More important, the loss could have been prevented.

Setting Your Success Measurement Standards

Although you would like to achieve every one of your Experience Response Points for every Totally Awesome Customer Experience delivered to every customer, it may not be realistic. Each Experience Response Point represents what you want to accomplish with your Customer Experience Map. You'll also want to measure how often you accomplish it. The "how often" becomes your standard for accomplishment. Maybe you'll be happy if you accomplish an Experience Response Point 50 percent of the time. Maybe the Experience Response Point is very difficult to achieve and five percent might be the right standard. You'll use the performance standards you set to evaluate the success or failure of your Customer Experience Map, and those standards will differ for every Customer Experience Map.

Here's a good example of setting performance standards for an outside sales experience. Let's say we've built five Customer Experience Maps covering the Totally Awesome Outside Sales Experience. They might look something like this...

Experience Response Point Performance Standards Chart

Customer Experience Map	Experience Response Point	Measurement Standard
Contacting a prospect	Getting the prospect to feel excited about having a face-to-face meeting with you	10% of the prospects want a meeting
Setting an introductory appointment	Having the prospect excited about seeing the solution you create	50% want to see the solution
Solution demonstration	Having the prospect want to save money immediately by asking you to prepare a proposal	60% want a proposal
Preparing a proposal	Everything looks great; and let's proceed to implement	70% have no objections want to sign the contract
Signing of a contract	Delighted about becoming one of your customers	80% sign the contract

If you create and deliver a Totally Awesome Customer Experience to 10,000 prospects, your goal is to sign 168 contracts (10,000 x 10% x 50% x 60% x 70% x 80%). Note: Each Customer Experience Map has a different Success Measurement Standard.

Once you set a Success Measurement Standard, you can now manage your Customer Experience Map to that standard and investigate discrepancies as they occur. You will continue to modify this standard as you learn more and improve your process.

A Simple Customer Experience Map Example

The experience is a visit to the dentist's office. Jane needs a procedure that makes her a bit nervous. She's only visited this particular dentist once, due to a recent change in insurance plans, and that was only for a cleaning. A number of Customer Experience Maps belong to this experience: for example, calling for an appointment, greeting upon arrival, filling out the paperwork, going from reception to preparing for dental work, dental work, checking out, leaving the office, and patient follow-up.

We're now going to extract the Customer Experience Map of *Going from Reception to Preparing for Dental Work* (see the following pages) to do a walk-through in detail.

We shouldn't expect an Experience Voting Point ever to be so severe that Jane would decide to get out of the dentist's chair and leave the office. The two Experience Voting Points, if triggered, have an impact on the overall Delight Vote of Jane's present visit, but most likely will exhibit themselves in Jane's future patronage, and the number of people with whom she shares the experience. (Please see the Customer Experience Map beginning on the following page).

Dentist's Customer Experience Map

Map Title: _Going From Reception to Preparing for Dental Work_

Customer Audiences: _A current patient facing a new dental procedure_

Experience Response Point:

Jane needs to feel familiar, welcome, important, relaxed, and confident prior to undergoing a new procedure. Achievement of this Response Point will be measured by positive patient comments and positive patient body language.

Experience Touch Points:

1 The hygienist calls Jane's name, escorts her to the procedure room, and makes her comfortable in the dentist's chair.

The Hygienist Role:
A. Prior to calling Jane's name, the hygienist knows her family members, regular checkups, age, how long it has been since they last saw Jane, which dentist and hygienist saw her, and some history about her dental care...something the hygienist can talk about to make Jane feel known and welcome.
B. The hygienist smiles and greets Jane by her first name, pronouncing the name correctly. She shakes Jane's hand (personal contact) and introduces herself. She confirms the purpose of Jane's visit today. This confirmation allows for the opportunity to get engaged in the experience and for the Jane experience to continue without interruption. The hygienist directs Jane into the procedure room. As they walk to the room, the hygienist talks about some familiar history, asking Jane some questions that allow Jane to feel important and talk.
C. The hygienist offers to take Jane's coat and personal items. She places personal items carefully on a table in the room. The hygienist then makes a comment about how awkward it is to get into the dentist's chair (because they are awkward and you feel like an idiot every time you try to get in one).

(continued)

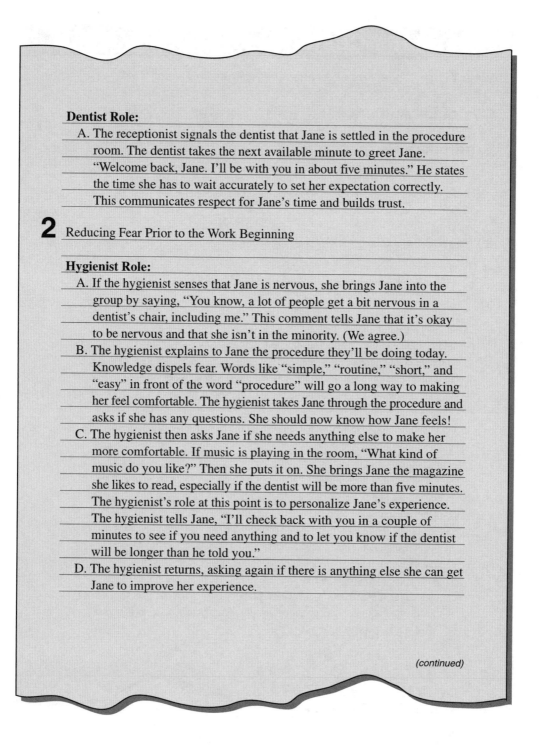

Dentist Role:

A. The receptionist signals the dentist that Jane is settled in the procedure room. The dentist takes the next available minute to greet Jane. "Welcome back, Jane. I'll be with you in about five minutes." He states the time she has to wait accurately to set her expectation correctly. This communicates respect for Jane's time and builds trust.

2 Reducing Fear Prior to the Work Beginning

Hygienist Role:

A. If the hygienist senses that Jane is nervous, she brings Jane into the group by saying, "You know, a lot of people get a bit nervous in a dentist's chair, including me." This comment tells Jane that it's okay to be nervous and that she isn't in the minority. (We agree.)

B. The hygienist explains to Jane the procedure they'll be doing today. Knowledge dispels fear. Words like "simple," "routine," "short," and "easy" in front of the word "procedure" will go a long way to making her feel comfortable. The hygienist takes Jane through the procedure and asks if she has any questions. She should now know how Jane feels!

C. The hygienist then asks Jane if she needs anything else to make her more comfortable. If music is playing in the room, "What kind of music do you like?" Then she puts it on. She brings Jane the magazine she likes to read, especially if the dentist will be more than five minutes. The hygienist's role at this point is to personalize Jane's experience. The hygienist tells Jane, "I'll check back with you in a couple of minutes to see if you need anything and to let you know if the dentist will be longer than he told you."

D. The hygienist returns, asking again if there is anything else she can get Jane to improve her experience.

(continued)

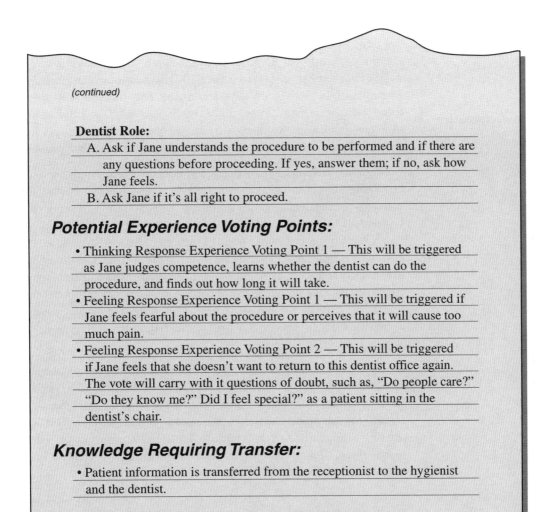

(continued)

Dentist Role:

    A. Ask if Jane understands the procedure to be performed and if there are any questions before proceeding. If yes, answer them; if no, ask how Jane feels.

    B. Ask Jane if it's all right to proceed.

Potential Experience Voting Points:

- Thinking Response Experience Voting Point 1 — This will be triggered as Jane judges competence, learns whether the dentist can do the procedure, and finds out how long it will take.
- Feeling Response Experience Voting Point 1 — This will be triggered if Jane feels fearful about the procedure or perceives that it will cause too much pain.
- Feeling Response Experience Voting Point 2 — This will be triggered if Jane feels that she doesn't want to return to this dentist office again. The vote will carry with it questions of doubt, such as, "Do people care?" "Do they know me?" Did I feel special?" as a patient sitting in the dentist's chair.

Knowledge Requiring Transfer:

- Patient information is transferred from the receptionist to the hygienist and the dentist.

It's critical that your Totally Awesome Customer Experience appears seamless to your customers, because your customers will cast their Delight Vote based on their experience as a whole.

LINKING YOUR CUSTOMER EXPERIENCE MAPS

The second primary function of Customer Experience Mapping is to link the appropriate Customer Experience Maps into a contiguous chain of maps that will deliver a consistent and seamless Totally Awesome Customer Experience. There can't be any gaps in your chain. The linkage between Customer Experience Maps coordinates all of the Experience Touch Points into a series of events, appearing seamless to your customer. A break in this linkage will have a negative effect on your chances of receiving the Delight Vote.

Contiguous linking of Customer Experience Maps requires a transfer of knowledge between one Customer Experience Map and another in order to make your experience appear seamless. The contiguous linking of Customer Experience Maps doesn't focus on the content of any one Customer Experience Map, but rather on the knowledge handoffs needed to continue a customer's seamless experience. One of the arts to Customer Experience Mapping is to create efficient handoff methods. The transference of knowledge usually takes place operationally and should go unnoticed by the customer. It's critical for the customer to see only one Totally Awesome Customer Experience; otherwise, you run the risk of triggering more Experience Voting Points.

If you find that your Totally Awesome Customer Experience doesn't flow, breaks down, or has noticeable gaps, you most likely have Experience Touch Points that are either missing, in conflict, or poorly performed. Customer Experience Mapping can help you detect which Experience Touch Points are missing or in conflict. You'll have to detect poor performance issues through management. This is one of the critical task CRM systems were designed to accomplish.

DOCUMENTING YOUR CUSTOMER EXPERIENCE MAPS

Think of how difficult it must be for organizations relying on random acts of employee excellence to delight their customers! Your Customer Experience Mapping documentation provides your company with a significant competitive advantage.

The third main function of Customer Experience Mapping is documentation. How many organizations today document their experience-based transactions and their customer interactions that go along with those transactions? If you don't document your experience path or experience results, how can they be repeated or improved?

Today, organizations do most of their documentation in the world of operations. They work under the illusion that performing good operations leads to delighted customers. Experience-based organizations use their documentation to consistently describe how to repeat the creation and delivery of their Totally Awesome Customer Experiences and use it to improve customer delight.

Customer Experience Mapping documentation also provides a solid framework and a common experience path that everyone can follow. It can be taught and understood by everyone in your organization. This commonality helps you maintain the common vision of your Totally Awesome Customer Experience and keeps you focused on creating customer delight.

CONVERTING CUSTOMER KNOWLEDGE CURRENCY INTO CUSTOMER TRUST CURRENCY

At the very beginning of this book, we spoke of the three types of Customer Relationship Currencies: informational, knowledge, and trust. Customer Experience Mapping helps transform Customer Knowledge Currency into Customer Trust Currency. It does so by helping you provide consistency, relevancy, value, and good feelings in repeated experiences delivered to your customers. The repeating of a delightful experience for your customers demonstrates that you can be trusted with their information and you'll use it only to provide them with even greater experiences. And the more your customers know that you're using their information on their behalf, the more information they're willing to share with you.

The continual use of Customer Experience Mapping in creating and delivering Totally Awesome Customer Experiences leads to the formation of an emotional trust bond that is fundamental to transforming Customer Knowledge Currency into Customer Trust Currency. Customer Trust Currency leads to customer loyalty and increased brand equity.Customer Trust Currency also paves the way for you to ask your customers even more about themselves without encroaching on their privacy. The level of customer knowledge you can obtain at the Customer Trust Currency level far exceeds the knowledge you can obtain at any other customer relationship currency level. The knowledge you obtain at the Customer Trust Currency level most often comes directly from the customer. It dramatically decreases your need for guessing and assuming. Remember, obtaining high-quality knowledge about your customers can significantly increase customer response rates.

INTEGRATING CUSTOMER EXPERIENCE MAPPING INTO YOUR STRATEGIC PLANNING PROCESS

Strategic planning is one of the key processes in most organizations. The end result of this process is a strategic plan, which outlines the financial and operational objectives for the year or next several years with a budgeted allocation of resources for people, processes, and technology.

Strategic plans tend to be operationally based. They begin with a mission or vision statement, and then break that statement down into specific objectives for accomplishing the mission. The objectives are further broken down into operating tactics that call out the resources required to meet the objectives. Even when you see "satisfying our customers" or "strengthening our brand" or "creating lasting differentiation" as part of the organization's mission objectives, you still know the approach to accomplishing those objectives will be operational in nature. In operational-based strategic plans, customers are viewed as "target markets," "target audiences," or "sources of revenue."

Take the time to really read your strategic plan. Take a yellow highlighter and mark how many times the plan actually says "delight" or "satisfy" the customer. You might be surprised what you discover. You can perform the same highlighter exercise on the annual reports of companies in which you have invested or are looking to invest because an annual report is the results of organization's strategic plan. As investors in both Mattel (the toy-making company) and Krispy Kreme Doughnuts, for example, we did the highlighter exercise on those two annual reports. Here's what we found:

The front cover of the Mattel annual report was completely white with a single word in black type: "Refocus." Krispy Kreme's front cover was very colorful, showing a large group of people smiling and laughing enjoying Krispy Kreme Doughnuts.

We opened the inside cover for each annual report and read the message from each organization's CEO. Here is our take on those messages.

Mattel's message, delivered by their CEO, did not once mention satisfying or delighting their customers. Part of the Mattel message read:

> Simply stated, our vision is to create and market the world's premier toy brands for today and tomorrow. We intend to reach our vision by building brands, cuttings costs, developing people, and keeping our promises. ...Looking ahead, we have four priorities for Mattel: strengthen core brand momentum in the US and abroad; to execute the financial realignment plan and deliver cost savings announced in September; to improve supply chain performance and customer service levels; and to develop our people and improve our employee development process.

Makes you wonder where "delighting kids" fits into all this planning for next year? Maybe they assume kids will be delighted with a great new brand, or the financial realignment, or improvements made to their supply chain. We should ask Katrina (age 8) or Alex (age 6) what they think about their Refocus. Most likely they'll just want to have a great experience buying and using their new toys. We wonder if Mattel management has seen the movie "Big" with Tom Hanks...could be good homework.

The Krispy Kreme annual report message, delivered by their CEO, Scott Livengood, starts out this way...

> For affirmation of Krispy Kreme's unlimited potential in the future and our connection with customers and communities today, you can go to one of our new store openings, especially the first store in a new market. There is no clearer expression of the depth and breadth of our special connection with the American public than the outpouring that occurs when a new Krispy Kreme opens its doors. It has the anticipation and emotion that you would expect if a long-lost family member returned home after years of separation. [Now for the winning line!] The key to our most recent success has been refining and upgrading our execution of the elements of the Krispy Kreme experience most valued by our customers through every channel of sales.

Wow! Did you feel the customer focus and Customer Trust Currency coming through? Do you have this kind of WOW factor working for you in your organization? Is there any doubt that Mr. Livengood believes customers are Krispy Kreme's most valuable assets? (We even like Scott's last name.) Have you ever tried a Krispy Kreme doughnut? If you haven't, you should. The entire Krispy Kreme experience is quite delightful. It's wonderful to see organizations letting customers participate in their own experiences and be the focal point of why they're in business.

The key to our most recent success has been refining and upgrading our execution of the elements of the Krispy Kreme experience most valued by our customers through every channel of sales.

Which organization would you say is more customer-focused? Which organization has an experience-based strategic plan? Which company has Customer Trust Currency working for them? Which company would you invest in? Which company's stock tripled last year?

The Art of Customer Experience Mapping...Creating and Delivering Experience Touch Points

"Imagination is more important than knowledge."

Albert Einstein,
genius, inventor, humanist...

Chapter 5 says, "Grab your palette and paintbrushes – it's art time." This chapter is all about the Art of Customer Experience Mapping, as well as creating Experience Touch Points (the points where you interact with your customers). You'll learn the Ten Rules of Creating Effective Experience Touch Points. We'll discuss how using different kinds, categories, and types of Experience Touch Points will increase the acceptability, relevance, and value of your product or service to your customers. On our soapbox, we preach about the importance of Experience Touch Point coordination and consistency in the creation and delivery of Totally Awesome Customer Experiences. We also explain how these two principles dramatically reduce costs. After touching on the aspects of Reach versus Richness in Experience Touch Points, the chapter ends with a discussion on how you measure an Experience Touch Point's success.

THE ART

If your strong suit is imagination, you finally hit the right chapter. Now don't go reading Professor Einstein's statement all wrong. Einstein never meant that knowledge wasn't important. He said imagination was more important. Imagination allows you to create new and wonderful ways to delight your customers.

Experience Touch Points are the only points where your organization interacts with your customers. They're the points where the customer learns who you are, what you do, what you stand for, the promises you make, and what you deliver. It's the point where the customer finds out if you're customer-focused or customer-manipulative. It's the point where you either build or erode trust, brand, and loyalty. It's the point where you can create customer delight.

Experience Touch Points occur everywhere. When a clerk offers help, a receptionist answers the phone, you receive a direct mail piece, an e-mail finds its way into your in-box, a phone solicitor calls during dinner, you're served a hot dog at a baseball game, a salesperson hands you a product

Every interaction your organization has with a customer or potential customer is an Experience Touch Point, whether you planned it or not.

brochure, you read a Seattle Mariners billboard as you drive, you see an advertisement on television, you're still up at 2:00 am mindlessly staring at an infomercial, your best friend tells you about her new skis, you overhear a conversation about a new hotel in San Francisco, you receive your new computer – and so forth and so forth. They're all Experience Touch Points.

Have you ever complained about poor customer service, had an really awful sales representative, suffered disrespect at the hands of a disinterested or belligerent store clerk, found out your name had been sold to about two thousand companies from which you have absolutely no interest in getting offers, had a lousy restaurant meal, a bad taxi ride, soggy French fries, pizza delivered cold, waited an hour in the doctor's office, can't understand your attorney or accountant, or learned they just ran out of the thirty-first flavor at Baskin-Robbins? These are also Experience Touch Points.

This chapter is devoted to one objective: helping you create and deliver the most effective and delightful Experience Touch Points possible.

- First, we'll look at the discipline you need to create effective Experience Touch Points. This step includes looking at the various flavors of Experience Touch Points from which you have to choose.

- Second, we'll discuss the power in the combination of characteristics of different Experience Touch Points and when best to use them.

- Third, we'll discuss how to select and sequence your Experience Touch Points in such a way as to progressively guide your customer smoothly towards an Experience Response Point.

- Fourth, we'll discuss the importance of Experience Touch Point coordination, consistency, and excellent execution to achieving your desired impact.

- Fifth, we'll examine the roles Reach (how many you can touch) and Richness (how deeply you can touch them) play in your overall Experience Touch Point strategies to create your desired customer response results.

- Finally, you'll want to know if your Experience Touch Points were effective in reaching your Experience Response Points, so let's finish off the chapter by discussing how to measure the effectiveness of Experience Touch Points.

The creation and delivery of Experience Touch Points is an art. It takes both creativity and discipline to execute effectively. The creativity requires imagination and customer knowledge to make your Experience Touch Points acceptable and valuable to your customers. The discipline requires you to focus on relevancy and direction toward the accomplishment of your Experience Response Point. Organizations spend billions of dollars every year in creating and delivering Experience Touch Points to customers. Some are effective and some are not. John Wanamaker said, "I know half the money I spend on advertising is wasted, but I can never find out which half." That comment says it all. Customer Experience Mapping could have helped John to determine which half.

Experience Touch Points are where all of your excellent strategic work in building your Customer Experience Maps converts into tactics and practice. In other words, they're where "the rubber meets the road." Clausewitz once said on military strategy, "Everything in strategy is very simple, but that does not mean everything is very easy." Having a simple Experience Response Point doesn't mean that you'll have an easy job in crafting your Experience Touch Points to accomplish it. It's challenging, but it's also very rewarding.

THE DISCIPLINE BEHIND EXPERIENCE TOUCH POINTS

How many commercials, ads, flyers, conversations, sales calls, point-of-purchase displays, and billboards do you experience every day? How many times have you thought or commented, "That's clever, but I really wonder how it will help them acquire more customers? I'm not sure I understand the message and what they're asking the customer to do." The discipline side of creating and delivering effective Experience Touch Points has the objective of keeping your Experience Touch Points focused and relevant. The creativity side has the objective of creating perceived value and acceptability.

Here are three great Experience Touch Point tools to help you with the discipline side.

1. The "Touch Point Ten." This tool is a checklist of ten solid rules for creating effective and valuable Experience Touch Points.

2. The "Audience Audit." This tool helps you identify and refine relevant audiences, transforming demographic, psychographic, and feeling information into customer knowledge.

3. The "So What? Test." This test is the ultimate focus test.

The "Touch Point Ten"

- **Rule One** – Keep your Experience Touch Points simple, understandable, and relevant. Confusion triggers Experience Voting Points.

- **Rule Two** – Never deliver an Experience Touch Point when the experience requires a capability your customers don't have. It will only frustrate and confuse them.

- **Rule Three** – Minimize any elements requiring the customer to make assumptions. Otherwise the outcome will be unpredictable.

- **Rule Four** – Discontinue any Experience Touch Point that does not appear to be working. Continued use of ineffective Experience Touch Points only antagonizes and irritates customers, triggering Experience Voting Points.

- **Rule Five** – Create an Experience Touch Point for as specific a customer audience as the delivery medium will allow.

- **Rule Six** – Always build an Experience Touch Point that adds trust and improves your emotional trust bond with the customer. This goes a long way in building your brand and loyalty, also insulating you more from the competition.

- **Rule Seven** – Always collect feedback quickly. It will immediately help you decide what to do next as well as improve your Customer Experience Map.

- **Rule Eight** – Create an Experience Touch Point under the assumption that customers still know more than your organization about what they like. Humility creates opportunities.

- **Rule Nine** – Be careful about creating an Experience Touch Point that follows your competition. First, they're already ahead of you, and second, they may be headed in the wrong direction.

- **Rule Ten** – Appeal to as many of the customer's senses as practically possible. Think outside of the box and have fun. Not everything has to cost a lot of money to be effective.

The "Audience Audit"

Audience Audit:

A tool to help refine the profiles of selected audiences by demographics, psychographics, and feelings in creating effective and delightful Experience Touch Points.

The second Experience Touch Point tool on the discipline side is the **Audience Audit**. The purpose of the Audience Audit is to first help you further identify and refine the attributes of your selected audience (discussed in Chapter 3) and second, to increase your customer knowledge about that customer audience.

1. Audience Identification and Refinement...

Delivering the right experience to the right customer audience demonstrates your focus on relevancy. Relevancy in your experiences and offers will dramatically increase your customer response rates. If you create and deliver a fabulous Experience Touch Point to the wrong audience, you're wasting your efforts. What makes it worse is that you aren't any closer to accomplishing your Experience Response Point than you were before. We cannot overstress the importance of relevancy to your Experience Touch Points.

Identifying and refining your audience may sound easy – but hundreds of millions of dollars are spent each year on identifying the right customer audience. Marketing directors are ecstatic when a customer response rate from a direct mail campaign creeps over five percent. The ideal audience is an audience of one, where you understand everything about the customer. In the real world we often settle for more aggregated forms of identification, such as customer groups or even customer populations.

Customer audience identification comes from asking the right questions and recording the relevant answers about your customers. Earlier in the book we cited how often customer satisfaction surveys fall short of asking the right questions and therefore record the wrong answers. Irrelevant customer information never becomes customer knowledge. Often, you start out having no customer knowledge. But if, little by little, you obtain more knowledge while building customer trust, you'll eventually be able to leverage that customer trust and knowledge into Customer Trust Currency. We find that increased customer trust allows you to ask "high criteria" questions (questions that are more direct and specific to that customer) and get honest direct answers without being considered intrusive. It's important, then, for organizations to progress from a simple Customer Information Currency to a Customer Trust Currency.

The more customer knowledge you have, the more you can segment or personalize your audience. As customer audience segments become smaller, you'll need more information to discern critical differences in audience needs. The most difficult audience to identify is the "audience of one" – the individual customer. Once you have knowledge about the individual customer, you hold the best opportunity to obtain very high response rates from that customer.

2. Customer Knowledge...

Obtaining customer knowledge requires the diligent collection of demographic, psychographic, and feelings information. Customer knowledge will help you build more relevant and valuable offers to better meet your customers' needs and delight them. It also will help you create and deliver better Experience Touch Points.

Irrelevant customer information never becomes customer knowledge.

Information isn't knowledge – it's just information. Information requires a reference point to become knowledge. It's the aggregation of information around a key reference point that generates knowledge. For instance, if you're an airline, the information on someone's height, weight, diet, daily routine, social activities, affiliations, economic status, education, and similar demographics will generate a completely different customer knowledge base than if you're a weight-loss clinic. Why? Airlines have different reference points than weight-loss clinics. Your reference point will help you filter the information that's important in helping you delight your customers.

Customer knowledge is extremely valuable when you're creating offers. Customer knowledge dramatically increases your ability to better fulfill your customers' needs and delight them. A customer-focused organization uses customer knowledge to add value and increase the participation and control customers have in their experiences. A customer-manipulative organization uses customer knowledge to find out the best way to control customers and sell them what they have to offer.

The three types of customer information include demographics, psychographics, and feelings. Changing your Customer Relationship Currency from either Customer Information Currency or Customer Knowledge Currency to Customer Trust Currency requires the inclusion of customer "feelings" information. You need it to help form the emotional trust bond between you and your customer. This emotional trust bond requires a customer knowledge base built from all three types of customer information.

Demographics

Demographic information includes the basic facts about customers: for example, their age, height, weight, race, hair color, gender, family status (dad, mom, kids), income, education level, occupation, locality, and so on. Although it might seem amazing, demographics is still the most prevalent type of information used in performing segmentation. Mainly because demographic information is the easiest and quickest to obtain. Demographic information becomes customer knowledge when you discover a link between that information and your customers' needs.

Psychographics

Psychographics deal in the pattern of behavior or lifestyle. Creating knowledge about customers' activities can be powerful in helping understand how to delight them. Psychographics focuses on understanding activities such as

---

Changing your Customer Relationship Currency from either Customer Information Currency or Customer Knowledge Currency to Customer Trust Currency requires the inclusion of customer "feelings" information.

Demographics:

Information about your customers such as their age, height, weight, race, hair color, gender, family status (dad, mom, child), income, education level, occupation, locality, and so forth.

Psychographics:

Information pertaining to the pattern of behavior or lifestyle of a customer such as "how you recreate," "how you shop," "how you dress," "how you take care of yourself," "how you handle your spiritual needs," and so forth.

"how you relax," "how you shop," "how you dress," "how you take care of yourself," or "how you drive." Psychographics information becomes customer knowledge when you discover a link between that information and your customers' needs.

Feelings

This is by far the hardest of all information to gather and understand. It's one thing to determine someone's income bracket, his age, the kind of car she drives, or her food preferences. It's another to understand someone's feelings. Words such as reward, punishment, love, hate, unpleasantness, disappointment, pain, delight, or pleasure can all describe how a person feels about either products, services, experiences, or organizations. Feelings push a customer either towards or away from a product or service. Rarely do customers fail to have feelings about their experiences.

Organizations that focus on gathering "feeling" information create the ability to draw the customer closer to the organization with an emotional trust bond. Customer delight is a result of fulfilling both the physical and emotional needs of a customer. If you omit the feeling side, the best you can achieve is traditional customer satisfaction – and you miss the opportunity to create customer loyalty, a stronger brand, and a significant differentiation. We cannot emphasize too strongly the value of collecting "feeling" information.

The "So What? Test"

The third discipline-side Experience Touch Point tool is the "So What? Test". The "So What? Test" asks whether your Experience Touch Point does anything to help you accomplish your Experience Response Point. If not, it doesn't pass the "So What? Test". So what if it's clever? So what if it's creative? So what if it's artistic? So what if it makes people laugh or cry? So what if it's good enough to win a Cleo Award? So what if your boss created it? So what if your advertising consultants like it? If your Experience Touch Point doesn't get you any closer to your Experience Response Point, you don't pass the "So What? Test". The test is just a simple and powerful way to stay focused.

The best time to apply the "So What? Test" is after you design an Experience Touch Point and before you deliver it. It's the nature of all artists to fall in love with their art. The "So What? Test" helps keep us focused on the real purpose behind our Experience Touch Points: the accomplishment of our Experience Response Points. That's why the test is so valuable.

Feelings:

Information pertaining to the emotive side of fulfilling a customer's needs.

Feelings push a customer either towards or away from a product or service. Rarely do customers fail to have feelings about their experiences

"So What? Test":

A powerful tool to help Experience Touch Point artists stay focused on the real purpose behind their Experience Touch Points.

The "So What? Test" also grants the immediate moral authority for anyone in the organization to ask whether an Experience Touch Point is helping to accomplish an Experience Response Point. Use the test often. Use the test with humility. Just use the test. We guarantee it.

THE CREATIVE SIDE...YOUR EXPERIENCE TOUCH POINT PALETTE

Any artist would be limited with only one color in his or her color palette. An artist's palette needs many colors to express creativity, whether the artist is painting on canvas or rendering on a computer screen. It leverages imagination and creativity.

The Kind, Category, and Type of Experience Touch Point

There are two kinds of color: additive and subtractive. *Additive* color deals with colors created by light sources, such as computer screens and televisions, where lights are combined to produce other colors. Our eyes have red, green, and blue cones that enable us to enjoy the beauty of the color spectrum. *Subtractive* color deals with color pigments and starts with a reflective surface, such as paper, fabric, walls, or tables. where pigments subtract portions of white light to enable us to enjoy other colors from those surfaces.

Along with kinds of color, there are two categories by which we can perceive color. Either an object's surface absorbs light or it reflects light. An apple looks red because it *absorbs* green and blue and *reflects* red back to our eyes.

There are also types (attributes) of color; *hue, saturation* and *lightness,* sometimes called brightness or intensity. These attributes, along with the way we see and view color, make up the infinite spectral range of color we can see and communicate in our visual palette.

Just as there is a visual color palette, there is also an Experience Touch Point Palette. There are kinds of Experience Touch Points: *direct* and *indirect.* There are categories of Experience Touch Points: *controlled* and *uncontrolled.* And there are types of Experience Touch Points: *informational, influential,* and *impacting.* The combined array of kind, category, and type of Experience Touch Point creates your Experience Touch Point Palette.

"Kind" refers to *how you deliver* your Experience Touch Points. Of the two kinds, *direct* means that you directed the efforts of delivering the Experience Touch Point to your audience, and *indirect* means that you didn't.

"Category" refers to the *content and value* of your Experience Touch Point. Controlled and uncontrolled Experience Touch Points have to do with "who controlled the creation of the content" for an Experience Touch Point. Of the two categories, *controlled* means that you directed the activities that created the content for the Experience Touch Point, and *uncontrolled* means that you didn't.

The "type" of Experience Touch Point *controls the level of impact* your Experience Touch Point has in eliciting a customer response. We call it "intensity." *Informational*, *influential*, and *impacting* are the three different degrees of intensity.

An *Experience Artist* has the freedom to choose how to deliver an Experience Touch Point, what it will contain, and with what intensity to deliver it. The combination of kind, category, and type of Experience Touch Points form a very broad and powerful Experience Touch Point Palette to help you express your imagination and creativity. Your artistry in its use will help guide your customers to an Experience Response Point while avoiding Experience Voting Points.

You exhibit all your artistry through creating and delivering a Totally Awesome Customer Experience. If customers love your art, they'll give you the Delight Vote. Your Experience Touch Point Palette is shown in the right column.

Let's look at some examples of Experience Touch Points we're all familiar with...

- **The wonderful phone solicitation you get just as you sit down to dinner with your family.** You know the ones. What fine array of kind, category, and type did the solicitation artist bless us with? It's direct, controlled, and impacting. Why? This Experience Touch Point was *direct* because the delivery was under the solicitor's complete direction, *controlled* because all of the content in the script and offering were created by the solicitor organization, and *impacting* because they're going to force you to either commit or hang up. Let's do another...

- **Getting information from an Internet site.** What array of kind, category, and type did the website artist use? It's direct, controlled, and informational. Why? This Experience Touch Point was *direct* because it was presented by the organization, *controlled* because they created and own the site content, and *informational* because it requires no commitment or decision to gain access to the information. Some websites try to be influential and impacting. It all depends on their design and deployment.

Experience Touch Point Palette

Kind
Direct & Indirect

Category
Controlled & Uncontrolled

Type
Informational, Influential & Impacting

"Kind" is how your Experience Touch Point will be delivered (direct or indirect.) "Category" is the control you have over content and value. "Type" is the intensity of your Experience Touch Point in evoking a customer response.

EXPERIENCE TOUCH POINT PALETTE

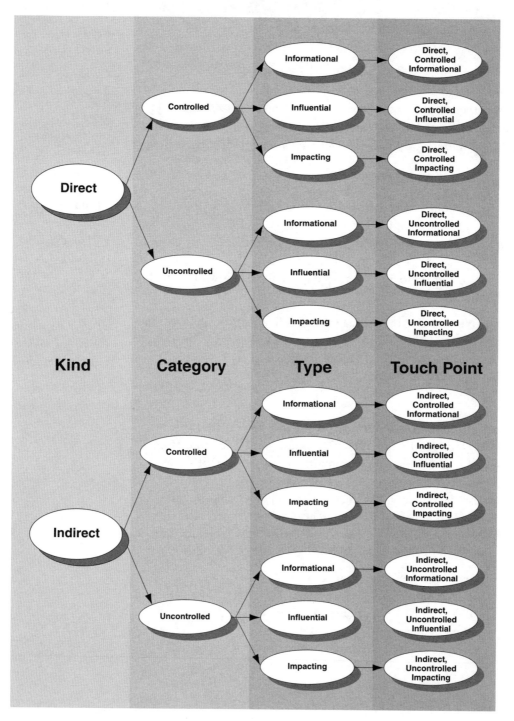

Let's look now at an indirect kind...

- **Your customer reads a magazine article about your organization (in a magazine that all your customers read).** This example is indirect, uncontrolled, and influential. Why? This Experience Touch Point was *indirect* because the delivery was not under your direction, *uncontrolled* because the content was created by someone else, and *influential* because the author stated certain opinions in the article that could influence his readers and your customers.

It's easy to use your Experience Touch Point Palette. The combination of kind, category, and type provides a very rich and powerful palette for your artistic touch.

Here's a little more insight into kind, category, and type. We hope this discussion will help you make decisions about the "colors" you use for your Experience Touch Points.

Understanding the Kinds of Experience Touch Points – Direct and Indirect

Direct and indirect Experience Touch Points have everything to do with your direct control over how your Experience Touch Points are delivered to your customers.

Direct Experience Touch Points are directive. The customer perceives that you have control over their delivery.

Indirect Experience Touch Points are non-directive. The customer perceives that you have no control over their delivery.

Three main attributes govern both direct and indirect Experience Touch Points. They are *engagement*, *impression*, and *retention*.

- *Engagement* is simply the degree of choice a customer has in receiving an Experience Touch Point. Direct and Indirect Experience Touch Points can be either engaging or non-engaging. For instance, a direct mail package is engaging because someone else placed it in your mailbox. A website is non-engaging because it requires you to locate and navigate. Some other examples of engaging are solicitors' phone calls, a sales appointment, or an e-mail. Some non-engaging examples would be television, a magazine article, or a radio commercial.

- *Impression* refers to your immediate thoughts and feelings when an Experience Touch Point is delivered. This is the Wow! effect, or that "first impression thing." Some examples are walking into the foyer of a new home you're looking to purchase, the cover of a magazine, or the opening line in a radio commercial. Impression is very important to quickly establishing acceptability with the customer.

- *Retention* is how long your Experience Touch Point lives. A car brochure may be around your house for months, while a radio spot has disappeared in thirty seconds. Retention measures how many repeat opportunities your Experience Touch Point has for delivery.

Here are the artistic benefits of using direct or indirect Experience Touch Points...

Artistic Benefits of Direct and Indirect Touch Points	
Direct Touch Points	**Indirect Touch Points**
Controllable efforts	Higher acceptability
Lower risk of delivery failure	Greater credibility
Controllable timing	Lower costs

Understanding the Categories of an Experience Touch Point – Controlled and Uncontrolled

Controlled Experience Touch Points are often seen as more subjective than objective, because you created the content and have a natural bias.

The advantage of an uncontrolled Experience Touch Point is that your customers perceive it as objective and authoritative.

Controlled Experience Touch Points are all the messaging mediums, (brochures, flyers, advertisements, seminars, tradeshow booths, e-mails, press tours, products, services, sales scripts, brand logos, tag lines, etc.) a company produces to interact with the customer via an Experience Touch Point. Here your organization has complete control over what you produce and pass on to the customer. Controlled Experience Touch Points are often seen as more subjective than objective, because you created the content and have a natural bias.

Uncontrolled Experience Touch Points literally define the world of publicity (word-of-mouth and public relations), such as analyst reviews, write-ups, articles, TV interviews, radio discussions, or product comparisons. Uncontrolled Experience Touch Points use content created by others outside your organization. The advantage of an uncontrolled Experience Touch Point is that your customers perceive it as objective and authoritative.

The power of category attributes in an Experience Touch Point rests in the actual value of the content delivered to the customer, regardless of whether it's controlled or uncontrolled.

Value plays a strong role in moving your customer closer to the Experience Response Point. Most organizations feel more comfortable in using controlled Experience Touch Points, but there are some outstanding uses for uncontrolled Experience Touch Points. Here are the artistic benefits of using either controlled or uncontrolled Experience Touch Points...

Artistic Benefits of Controlled and Uncontrolled Touch Points	
Controlled Touch Points	**Uncontrolled Touch Points**
Flexibility, easy to produce	Higher perceived objectivity and authority
Control of content	Lower costs
Lower risk of errors	Unlimited reach potential

Understanding the Types of an Experience Touch Point – Informational, Influential, and Impacting...

Each Experience Touch Point calls for a response from your customer. Responses might even be as passive as "they downloaded the file" or "they received the brochure" or "they got your materials" or "they saw the advertisement." Knowing the different types in your Experience Touch Point Palette helps you proactively manage Experience Voting Points through understanding your customer's thought and feeling filters. This understanding determines Experience Touch Point acceptability.

For instance, what would happen if a phone solicitor said, "I apologize for bothering you so late, but I would appreciate it if you could keep an eye out for some important information you'll receive from Bob's Insurance because you're a special XYZ bank member. Again, sorry for the inconvenience this evening." Would this informational approach elicit a different customer response than the cram-down method the phone solicitor used earlier? Would customer response rates differ between the two methods?

Normally, direct sales activities such as cold phone solicitation have low customer response rates, between 1 percent and 3 percent. Is it worth potentially upsetting 97 percent to 99 percent of your customers just to get a few to buy?

The "type" of Experience Touch Point determines acceptability and refers to how effectively your message gets through your customer's thought and feeling filters. Of the three basic types (informational, influential, and impacting), informational types have the highest acceptability, while impacting types have the lowest.

We show all three types below on an acceptability continuum, along with their attributes. On one end of the Acceptability Continuum, informational attributes are neutral filters, perceived as being objective/subjective, low risk in triggering an Experience Voting Point, and likely to be acceptable. Their drawback that is they don't evoke strong decision responses from the customer. On the other end of the acceptability spectrum are impacting attributes which have filters on alert, are perceived as aggressive, and carry a high risk of triggering an Experience Voting Point (EVP) where the customer is naturally skeptical. It does, however, evoke a very strong customer decision response that quickly leads to the accomplishment of your Experience Response Point.

Experience Touch Point Acceptability Continuum

	Informational	**Influential**	**Impacting**
Filters	Filters neutral	Filters active	Filters on alert
Perceived As	Objective/subjective	Suggestive	Aggressive
Risk in trigger EVP	Low	Average	High
Acceptability	Likely	Cautious	Skeptical
Response Motivation	Lowest	Average	Highest

Here are some additional insights into informational, influential, and impacting Experience Touch Points.

- *Informational* Experience Touch Points are perceived by the customer as simply supplying information or knowledge. You can best use this type of Experience Touch Point to support influential and impacting Experience Touch Points, which are more action and response oriented. Informational Experience Touch Points carry the lowest risk of triggering an Experience Voting Point.

- *Influential* Experience Touch Points are perceived by customers to be guiding them towards some type of decision. This type of touch point works in conjunction with other influential, informational, or impacting Experience Touch Points to actively guide the customer to the Experience Response Point. Influential Experience Touch Points carry an average risk of triggering an Experience Voting Point.

- *Impacting* Experience Touch Points are perceived by the customer to be directing or forcing a decision. Organizations typically use this type of Experience Touch Point to evoke decisions from the customer about the Experience Response Point. Impacting Experience Touch Points carry a high risk for triggering an Experience Voting Point.

Keep in mind that your customers might not always perceive your Experience Touch Points in the way you planned. For example, if American Century Investments (ACI) does a direct mailing of a mutual funds prospectus to their customers, ACI is hoping the prospectus will be influential. Yet if the customer thinks the prospectus is merely informational, then it is informational. Remember, the customer is the only one who votes on your Experience Touch Points, so you need to make allowances for their wrong perceptions.

When Patricia Seybold said, "Customers will be in control of your business," she was dead on! Controlling the acceptability of your Experience Touch Points is very powerful and not subject to much negotiation.

THE POWER WITHIN YOUR EXPERIENCE TOUCH POINT PALETTE

The power comes from the combination of kind, category, and type Experience Touch Points. Articulate use of this power creates greater acceptability, relevancy, and value in your Experience Touch Points.

There are twelve combinations of kind, category, and type as depicted in The Experience Touch Point Palette. Each Experience Touch Point has a "when best to use" advantage. Knowing when best to use each of these Experience Touch Points can leverage your creative skills as an Experience Artist. It will also help you to achieve your Experience Response Points much more quickly and for less cost.

The left column of the When Best to Use the Experience Touch Point Chart (pages XXXX) shows the Experience Touch Points. The right column shows when it's best to use each one, along with a brief example of an Experience Touch Point that fits the kind, category, and type combination. This chart is a helpful guide to use when getting started.

Direct Experience Touch Points Chart

Touch Point   "When Best To Use"

Direct, Controlled Informational

Use when beginning a new relationship. Trust is low and your customer will more readily accept objectivity in content.

The customer calls your company looking for additional information and a product brochure. You send the information with a welcome note that encourages reading and asking for additional information or a conversation. Most websites are in this group or the influential group, in addition to prospectuses, technical white papers, FAQs, and so on.

Direct, Controlled Influential

Use when you have built some trust and sense that one or two key determining factors are needed for the customer to make a decision to help complete the Experience Response Point. Be cautious of triggering an Experience Voting Point here.

You create an insert that goes into your annual report for all your big investors, encouraging them to participate in the next round of funding. It points out some significant reasons they should invest and indicates the percentage of other investors who have already invested or have expressed an interest in investing. Direct mail typically falls into this group.

Direct, Controlled Impacting

Use when trust is high, your relationship is strong, and time is of the essence. Recommendations in making key decisions are welcomed.

You send an e-mail to all of your customers telling them about new specials for the month with an accompanying link for their orders. Most ongoing selling is in this group, as are advertisements wanting to rekindle "top of mind" positioning.

Direct, Uncontrolled Informational

Use when trust is low to average and credibility is an issue. You want to provide directed outside verification to help build trust. Good to use prior to progressing to a direct controlled Experience Touch Point.

The Wall Street Journal did an article on your product, comparing it to other products in the market and giving it a ranking. You send it along with a handwritten note to your customer, saying you thought they might be interested in this article. Most active sending of outside party materials falls into this group, as does taking plant tours.

Direct, Uncontrolled Influential

Use when you need perceived objectivity in presenting one or two key determining factors to help the customer make a decision or influence them to take the next step in accomplishing your Experience Response Point.

You invite your client to lunch with one of your other clients who had the same issues before becoming your customer. Infomercials fall into this group, as do home parties in multilevel marketing companies.

Direct, Uncontrolled Impacting

Use when trust is average, relationship does not yet have an emotional trust bond formed with the customer, and you locate and use a strong third-party endorsement whose opinion is well respected and accepted.

You present the clinical study information from five independent studies along with a cured patient at a dinner meeting of doctors, clearly demonstrating superior results from your new drug. You follow it up by handing out a copy of the study and asking for an appointment next week.

Indirect Experience Touch Points Chart

Touch Point   **"When Best To Use"**

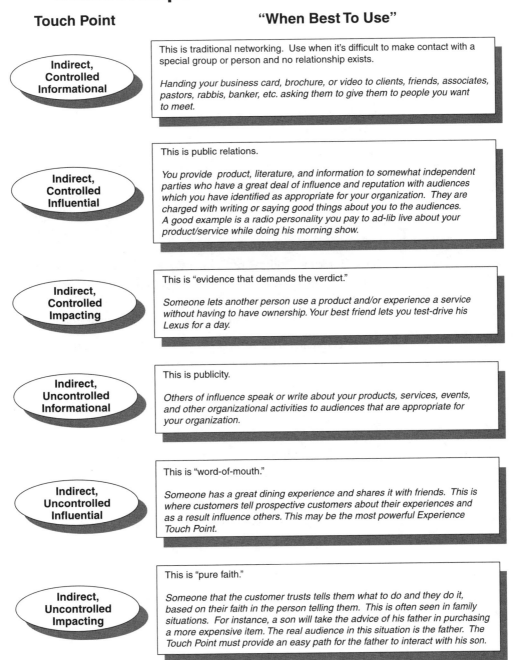

Indirect, Controlled Informational

This is traditional networking. Use when it's difficult to make contact with a special group or person and no relationship exists.

Handing your business card, brochure, or video to clients, friends, associates, pastors, rabbis, banker, etc. asking them to give them to people you want to meet.

Indirect, Controlled Influential

This is public relations.

You provide product, literature, and information to somewhat independent parties who have a great deal of influence and reputation with audiences which you have identified as appropriate for your organization. They are charged with writing or saying good things about you to the audiences. A good example is a radio personality you pay to ad-lib live about your product/service while doing his morning show.

Indirect, Controlled Impacting

This is "evidence that demands the verdict."

Someone lets another person use a product and/or experience a service without having to have ownership. Your best friend lets you test-drive his Lexus for a day.

Indirect, Uncontrolled Informational

This is publicity.

Others of influence speak or write about your products, services, events, and other organizational activities to audiences that are appropriate for your organization.

Indirect, Uncontrolled Influential

This is "word-of-mouth."

Someone has a great dining experience and shares it with friends. This is where customers tell prospective customers about their experiences and as a result influence others. This may be the most powerful Experience Touch Point.

Indirect, Uncontrolled Impacting

This is "pure faith."

Someone that the customer trusts tells them what to do and they do it, based on their faith in the person telling them. This is often seen in family situations. For instance, a son will take the advice of his father in purchasing a more expensive item. The real audience in this situation is the father. The Touch Point must provide an easy path for the father to interact with his son.

APPLYING YOUR EXPERIENCE TOUCH POINT PALETTE

Time to don the artist's smock, cap, and grab your color palette. We're going to create some art! Now comes the real fun.

It takes great understanding and a feeling for your customer audience to predict customer responses. This is where having developed a Customer Trust Currency is really important because it gives you a greater direct knowledge of what's effective and ineffective with your customer audience. You also have their trust.

Take, for instance, a direct, controlled, impacting Experience Touch Point. It carries the highest risk of triggering an Experience Voting Point. Why? Because you're in the customer's face, presenting an offer or information that calls for a decision. If you use this Experience Touch Point and the customer's trust level in your organization is low, you'll trigger an Experience Voting Point. Depending on how invasive your Experience Touch Point, you'll trigger a Thinking, Feeling, or Combative Response Experience Voting Point. In contrast, if the customer's trust level is high, a direct, impacting Experience Touch Point may not trigger an Experience Voting Point and the customer will simply move towards the Experience Response Point.

The effectiveness and acceptability of your Experience Touch Points are significantly impacted by your organization's level of Customer Relationship Currency.

Remember the phone solicitation example (page XXXX)? Let's give it a real artist's critique.

Ring, ring…"Hello."

"Is this Jerry Mallet?"

"No, not unless he's just won the lottery. But it could be Gary Millet." The subject hung up, of course. The caller didn't even get his name right!

Let's try it again…ring, ring…"Hello."

 "Is this Mr. Gary Millet?"

"Why, yes, it is. I want to thank you for interrupting my dinner." Obviously, the caller didn't know who Gary was.

Let's try one more time. "Hello."

"Gary?"

"Yes."

"This is Jenny, over at Bob's Insurance. This is a courtesy call on behalf of XYZ Bank. They want to offer their loyal XYZ Bank cardholders a very special mortgage insurance policy as part of their ongoing commitment to their loyal bank customers."

The script is all right up to this point. However, then Jenny launches into her canned script without pause until she asks, "Can we go ahead and sign you up for a free $2,500 life insurance policy, Gary?"

"No. Not interested." The subject hangs up. Many people hang up during Jenny's script because Jenny shows a lack of respect for the listener by not allowing the listener to respond or interact with the experience.

Let's break down this Experience Touch Point. Here's what happens:

- The company calling isn't even owned by XYZ Bank. It's Bob's Insurance.

- XYZ Bank has apparently sold your name to Bob's Insurance

- The words "courtesy call" mean that Bob's Insurance has purchased permission to use XYZ Bank's name as a "front."

- XYZ might be getting a kickback from sales made by Bob's Insurance.

- The solicitor is calling at a time you'll most likely be home. They never leave messages.

- The solicitor tries to maintain the script at all costs because she doesn't really understand the offer being made in the first place and doesn't want to get lost.

- The solicitor is paid based on manipulating the customer to accept the offer, not on delighting the customer.

- The solicitor disengages by simply hanging up when any phone call gets too far from the established norms.

- Bob's Insurance is counting on the percentages game to achieve the number of needed responses to cost-justify this Experience Touch Point.

How did we do? Here's what the solicitor is trying to do with the customer while delivering the Experience Touch Point...

- Uses the word "courtesy call" to lessen the intensity (disguise impacting as informational).

- Uses the name XYZ Bank as much as possible to try to artificially elevate the customer's trust, hoping the customer will have an emotional

Your artistic challenge as an Experience Artist: to use your imagination and customer knowledge to guide the greatest number of customers to an Experience Response Point...doing it with the least number of Experience Touch Points for the lowest cost...while triggering the fewest Experience Voting Points.

trust bond with XYZ Bank that will lead to higher acceptability (because no one knows Bob).

- Uses the phrase "loyal cardholders" to give the appearance of exclusivity and relevancy.

- Uses the phrase "special offer" to indicate value.

The phone solicitor hit all the right elements. The call touched relevance, value and acceptability. So why wasn't Gary happy?

The insurance company attempted to elevate Gary's trust in an artificial and phony manner. The approach was customer-manipulative. Most customers can detect the lack of sincerity and just hang up because the solicitor instantly triggers a Combative Response Experience Voting Point. A small percentage – perhaps three percent – will accept the free offer, with two percent later rejecting the real offer.

Interestingly enough, an indirect, uncontrolled, impacting Experience Touch Point was being delivered to the customer from XYZ Bank – and the bank didn't even know it. The message delivered to the customer was, "Your information is not safe with us; we sold it to Bob. So don't trust us with anything else, unless you want the same thing to happen."

XYZ Bank potentially lost credibility with the 97 percent of their customers that Bob's Insurance called who did not respond positively. The XYZ Bank Experience Touch Point most likely triggered a Feelings Response Experience Voting Point in a good number of XYZ Bank's customers.

There was also no progression or sequencing of Experience Touch Points that would lead the customer to build a higher level of trust. This is another reason why the acceptability level is so low in phone solicitation and direct mail. Experience Artists need to be sensitive to the steps required to elevate customer trust. Done correctly, elevating trust can significantly increase customer response rates.

Managing Experience Voting Points and moving a customer quickly to the desired Experience Response Point takes artful selection of Experience Touch Points. Relevance, value, and acceptability of your Experience Touch Points determine your customer's response. If you misjudge what is relevant or valuable, your audience will trigger a Thinking Response Experience Voting Point. If you misjudge the acceptability of your Experience Touch Point, your audience will trigger a Feeling or Combative Response Experience Voting Point.

Customer Trust Currency helps suppress customer acceptability filters and lessen the risk of triggering Experience Voting Points. The suppression in customer acceptability filters allows you to use more influential and impacting Experience Touch Points.

Many great marketing gurus and salespeople are Experience Artists. They've mastered the art of delivering Experience Touch Points. They manage the Experience Touch Points like a symphony conductor manages his or her orchestra. We cannot overemphasize the importance of strategically selecting the appropriate combination and sequence of Experience Touch Points.

Selecting the combination and sequence of Experience Touch Points in a Customer Experience Map is the Art of Customer Experience Mapping.

Making Your Experience Touch Point Selection

Even artists have rules on color selection. Here are our Touch Point selections:

Ideally, we want to accomplish all of the Experience Response Points without triggering a single Experience Voting Point until we ask for the Delight Vote.

- First, deal with acceptability. If the Experience Touch Point strikes hard against a customer's thought or feeling (acceptability) filters, it will most likely trigger a Feeling or Combative Response Experience Voting Point, spelling almost immediate disaster – the customer wants to end the experience.

- Second, pay attention to relevance. If your customer can't identify with your Experience Touch Point, it will trigger an immediate Thinking Experience Voting Point.

- Third, present your value honestly. Once past acceptability and relevance, the customer will examine the value. Be careful to present value in the customer's language and terms, not yours. Make it easy for the customer to understand and decide. This is the perfect spot to strengthen your brand, build trust, and establish differentiation.

You might find this checklist of questions helpful as you begin to select the right Experience Touch Point from your palette...

- What is your customer trust level?

- How much customer knowledge do you have?

- How much do you trust your insight?

- What are the past successes and failures of others?

Here's how this works. How you answer each of these questions will govern the degree of intensity and subjectivity your Experience Touch Point should contain. For instance, the more trust a customer has in you, the more impacting and controlled your Experience Touch Points can be. The more customer knowledge you have, the more likely you can craft an Experience Touch Point that is influential because of its high relevancy and value.

When you hit the insight question, you're most likely beginning to guess about the customer, so try to couple your insight with knowledge to use it more effectively. If you don't have much trust, customer knowledge, or insight, you might want to consider using less intense and controlled Experience Touch Points for gradually building the trust and knowledge. The fourth question simply provides a starting point by asking what has worked and not worked in the past – there might be some good lessons to be learned.

Experience Touch Point Sequencing

The sequencing of Experience Touch Points helps to build trust with your customer, making the next Experience Touch Point you deliver more acceptable.

Sequencing the delivery of your Experience Touch Points is just as important as selecting them. The sequencing of Experience Touch Points helps to build trust with your customer, making the next Experience Touch Point you deliver more acceptable. Sequencing helps you reach your Experience Response Point while avoiding time-consuming Experience Voting Points. Your sequencing skills as an organization can greatly help you accelerate trust-building.

Sequencing is an important tool because customers have a lot of thought and feeling filters against gimmicks and so-called "good deals." Customers want to avoid being manipulated, but appreciate guidance. Sequencing helps you guide your customers. For instance, if you're just beginning your relationship with a customer, you should start with a sequencing of a direct, uncontrolled, informational Experience Touch Point, then a direct, controlled informational Experience Touch Point, followed by a direct controlled, Influential Experience Touch Points, ending up with a direct, controlled, impacting Experience Touch Point. If you started with a direct, controlled, impacting Experience Touch Point, you run a very high risk of triggering an Experience Voting Point and having your customer terminate the experience.

THE VALUE OF COORDINATED, CONSISTENT, AND WELL-EXECUTED EXPERIENCE TOUCH POINTS

Conductors know their orchestras. They're masters at getting each musician playing his or her part at the right time, turning a bunch of notes on a sheet of paper into beautiful music. Everything must be coordinated, consistent, and well-executed in order to make the music beautiful. Anything less produces noise – and noise is annoying, confusing, and frustrating. As an Experience Artist, you are the conductor of your Totally Awesome Customer Experiences – and the audience is listening.

When creating Experience Touch Points, put yourself in the customers' shoes. See what they see, feel what they feel, and try to perceive what they perceive. Think about how you would like an organization to build trust with you. Remember, sequencing is a trust-building exercise, and trust is generally built one step at a time.

The Value of Coordinated Experience Touch Points

All of your Experience Touch Points need to be linked to a Customer Experience Map through an Experience Response Point. Just as an orchestra conductor doesn't want to hear errant notes now and then throughout the performance, you should have no rogue Experience Touch Points wandering around. Customer Experience Mapping makes sure there is linkage of all Experience Touch Points to both their Experience Response Point and between the Customer Experience Maps themselves. Having rogue Experience Touch Points can undermine the effectiveness of other great Experience Touch Points. This situation leads to what we have called **Experience Noise.**

So what happens when Experience Noise takes place?

Experience Noise causes trust and brand erosion for your organization, while causing annoyance, confusion, and conflict for your customers. Experience Noise often triggers an Experience Voting Point. Experience Touch Points need synergy, not conflict.

We recently asked the senior vice president of marketing for an IT organization how often her organization coordinates Experience Touch Points on a new product launch. She smiled and told us, "Sometimes we don't even get the product literature to the field before the product is on the shelves. When we do manage to get the literature to the field ahead of the product, we seldom have time to instruct the field on the best way to use the literature in their sales process. Most of the time we're doing well to just get it over the fence to them and let them run with it."

We then asked her if she thought new product adoption might increase if every Experience Touch Point on a new product launch were mapped and coordinated. She told us, "Tibet is a bit east of here and I have no idea where Nirvana might be – but any time you can have a coordinated sequence of customer touches, your message is understood much faster and held as top of mind much longer than when touches appear random to the customer." She added, "We have a lot of departmentalization in this organization, so it makes it extra tough to get all of our customer touches coordinated. It's often a political thing, you know."

Experience Noise:

An instance when two or more Experience Touch Points contradict each other. The conflict may or may not trigger an Experience Voting Point. For example, your frequent flyer program treats a new passenger who flies 100,000 miles in the first year better than the frequent flyer who only flew 50,000 miles last year, but has flown over 3 million miles on your airline.

Experience Noise occurs frequently and costs organizations billions of dollars a year. It would be far better to deliver fewer Experience Touch Points that are well-coordinated than more Touch Points that cause Experience Noise. It would also be a lot less expensive and increase customer response rates to Experience Response Points.

Consistent performance builds brand equity. It's essential that you deliver all Experience Touch Points consistently across all interactions with the customer.

The Value of Consistent Experience Touch Points

We asked the CEO of a mid-size bank, "Do you think your customers receive the exact same experience from all of your tellers?" After the laughter died down, we all just looked at each other, all thinking the same thing. When Experience Touch Points are inconsistently delivered, they can represent a different experience altogether. Once again, when this happens, Experience Noise occurs.

Brand equity and customer loyalty are built through consistently delighting customers. If Experience Touch Points don't have consistency, they undermine the entire process of creating and delivering Totally Awesome Customer Experiences. It's consistent delivery of brand experiences that fulfills a brand promise and builds brand equity.

The biggest value that John Stockton and Karl Malone bring to the Utah Jazz NBA basketball team is their consistency. Stockton delivers about 10 assists per game and Malone delivers about 24 points and 13 rebounds. They've done this game in and game out for over 12 straight years. How many players have won the hearts of their fans by being inconsistent? Not many come to mind. In baseball, Reggie Jackson was known as Mr. October. You could depend on Reggie to be at his very best during the playoffs and the World Series. In the Olympics, not many athletes are awarded gold medals for inconsistent performance!

We asked the senior vice president of a financial investment firm's fund management group, "Do you think one of your customers would have the same experience when visiting your Internet site, your call center, and their personal representative?"

He said, "As much as I'd like to think so, it's not likely."

We followed that question up with this one: "How important is it for you to maintain consistent brand experiences that match your brand image in the marketplace?"

He responded, "Brand in the financial services industry is crucial to business. We all deal with commodities, so our brand is extremely important in differentiating ourselves from our competition. This is an area we need to pay more attention to in the future."

We followed that question with, "Do you feel that not having all Experience Touch Points consistent and coordinated has had any impact on your customers and their interpretation of your brand and overall revenues?"

He answered, "It obviously has an impact. We just don't know what that impact is...one thing is for sure; it can't be positive, and it's probably costing us much more than we'd like to admit."

It's better to have average Experience Touch Points delivered consistently than have a few spectacular Experience Touch Points and many poor Experience Touch Points delivered inconsistently.

The Value of Properly Executing Experience Touch Points

The best plans on the drawing board are only as good as their execution in the field. Good execution of Experience Touch Points relies on the following factors:

- Delivering consistent, well-planned, coordinated Experience Touch Points that guide customers towards a common Experience Response Point.

- Having the right people, technology, and processes in place to execute the Experience Touch Points.

- Making the commitment to train everyone involved in all of the Experience Touch Points being delivered.

- Seeking feedback to know if your Experience Touch Points have been planned and executed properly.

When an Experience Touch Point is executed poorly, the organization may experience what we call an **Experience Lapse**. An Experience Lapse often leads to an immediate Experience Voting Point. Whether the customer leaves that experience depends highly on his or her past experience with the organization and trust in the organization. If the customer's trust level is high enough, that customer will stay in the experience. When a customer stays in an experience after an Experience Lapse, we call that an **Experience Token**. The Experience Token keeps the customer in the game.

Here's an example of an Experience Lapse that Blaine had at Nordstrom (of all places):

> I've shopped for years at Nordstrom with nothing but positive experiences, thus driving positive brand and trust. However, on this last experience, the entire transaction took me about an hour to complete. It had nothing to do with me – only the internal systems of Nordstrom (Experience Lapse). Through the

Experience Lapse:

A condition when an Experience Touch Point is executed so poorly that it triggers an Experience Voting Point.

Experience Token:

A condition when the customer forgives the organization for an Experience Lapse.

entire process the customer service person was friendly and pleasant, but wasn't doing what I really wanted: solving my problem. At the end of the hour-long process, all they said was that they were sorry it took so long. That did nothing to help my experience. They didn't offer to solve the problem off-line (it was a computer glitch) and take care of it after I left, or offer me anything in return to make me feel better about the wasted hour...just "I'm sorry."

This experience soured me on their store and showed me that as long as everything goes well, they're very pleasant and the experience is great. The store is always neat, professional, well-laid-out, and the people are very friendly and helpful in finding what I need. But when things go wrong, that's the true test of the customer experience. That's what brand and trust are built upon. Will I go back to Nordstrom? Most likely (Experience Token) they'll get another shot at me since they've built up so much loyalty. However, if something occurs again, I'm gone. There are too many good competitors today to subject myself to this kind of customer experience.

Here's the scoop on Experience Lapses and Experience Tokens: If a customer believes the cause of an Experience Lapse is an individual employee, it lessens the severity of the Experience Lapse. If the customer perceives the Experience Lapse as management- or ownership-related, an experience exit vote is more likely. You need to strategically deliver your Experience Touch Points in such a way as to always demonstrate management's commitment to the customer and avoid placing the fate of the organization's brand equity and customer loyalty into the hands of individual employees. This strategy gives the organization every chance to have an Experience Token when an isolated employee incident causes an Experience Lapse. Keep in mind that too many "isolated" Experience Lapses will simply be perceived as management's lack of good business practices and customers will leave the relationship anyway.

REACH VERSUS RICHNESS

The goal of any Customer Experience Map is to get as many customers as possible to the Experience Response Point. Experience Touch Points are the way you get them there.

Here are the two schools of thought as to potential strategies to use...Reach versus Richness.

Reach Strategy

A reach strategy counts on the sheer mass of delivering enough Experience Touch Points to achieve your Experience Response Point goals. For example, if you send a direct mail campaign consisting of 1,000,000 pieces of mail, you can traditionally expect 30,000 customers to respond – a three percent response rate. The idea behind Reach is to deliver enough Experience Touch Points to provide an acceptable number of respondents (regardless of the response rate percentage). Reach depends on a very low cost per Experience Touch Point to be successful.

Reach focuses on achieving the number of respondents needed (assuming a fixed response rate) to be successful. A Reach strategy increases the size of the customer audience in order to achieve the desired number of respondents targeted. This strategy works as long as increasing the audience size is not cost-prohibitive or you don't run out of available audience. Reach strategy contends that all Experience Touch Points delivered to non-respondents still deliver a brand impression that may be valuable in the future.

Richness Strategy

In contrast to the Reach strategy is the Richness strategy. Pepper's and Rogers's studies suggest that an organization can achieve dramatically higher customer response rates through delivering Experience Touch Points with greater relevancy and higher value to segmented audiences or even individual customers. For instance, rather than mass-mailing to 1,000,000 customers, you would send 500,000 pieces to 100 different customer audiences of 5,000 customers and try to obtain an increased response rate of, say, 10 percent, which would yield 50,000 customer responses.

Richness requires greater customer knowledge and generally has higher costs per delivered Experience Touch Point. The idea is that the increased customer response rates more than offset the additional cost per Experience Touch Point. The Richness strategy is sensitive to the idea that Experience Touch Points received by customers not interested in your offer may not cause a favorable brand impression; rather, they may cause "noise" and erode brand.

Choosing a Strategy

As an Experience Artist, you'll need to determine the best strategy for you to accomplish your Experience Response Points. Ideally, a strategy will combine both Reach and Richness. Many new technologies are making a combined strategy more and more possible as well as cost-effective.

Here are a few questions you might find helpful in determining which strategy to use in creating and delivering your Experience Touch Points:

- Do we project that the additional revenue created from higher customer response rates will clearly cover the increase in cost of delivering segmented or personalized Experience Touch Points?

- How difficult and expensive is it to obtain the necessary demographics, psychographics, or feeling information and convert it into customer knowledge?

- Is our customer knowledge sufficient to logically segment and differentiate customer audience by relevancy and value?

- Does our organization have the physical capability to create and deliver segmented or personalized Experience Touch Points?

- Do we think non-respondents perceive our Experience Touch Points to be "noise?"

- What Experience Touch Point delivery options do we have that help blend Reach and Richness?

MEASURING YOUR ART

Artists measure their work by noting the audience response. If your paintings sell or you receive standing ovations or people buy your CDs, you know they like what you're doing.

Experience Touch Points are much the same. They are experience art. You create and deliver them for your customers to enjoy and respond. Their responses should help you guide them toward accomplishing an Experience Response Point, which will ultimately lead them to having a Totally Awesome Customer Experience. This will result in customer delight and the accomplishment of our Awesome Customer Challenge.

To effectively measure an Experience Touch Point, you only need to answer four basic questions:

1. Did the Experience Touch Point move the customer closer to the achievement of the appropriate Experience Response Point?

2. Did the Experience Touch Point conflict with any other Experience Touch Points?

3. Did the Experience Touch Point result in the expected response from the customer?

4. Did you avoid Experience Voting Points?

Use your artistic skills to craft the questions to your customer that will answer these four basic questions. Remember to let your customers answer in customer experience language.

Enjoy the Art...You'll Be Great!

Through the first five chapters, we've shown you the benefits of meeting the Awesome Customer Challenge of transforming merely satisfied customers into delighted customers. We've outlined the changes your organization must make to become experience-based. We've talked about the process of creating and delivering a Totally Awesome Customer Experience, and we've explored both the art and science behind Customer Experience Mapping. We're now ready to discuss how your organization can start to realize these benefits. You're now at the point of "Just Doing It!"

The next chapter has but one main purpose: to provide you some insight into how you might want go about implementing the process of creating and delivering Totally Awesome Customer Experiences within your own organization.

Chapter 7

Do It...Making the Dream Come True in Your Organization

> *"If you can dream it, you can do it.*
> *Always remember that this whole thing was started by a mouse."*
>
> Walt Disney

Chapter 6 is Ready, Set, Go. It's time to talk about implementing Totally Awesome Customer Experiences within your organization. The implementation process starts with helping you perform your Initial Transaction Assessment. This process documents where you are and ends with your rollout – in other words, where you want to be.

MAKING THE DREAM COME TRUE

Walt Disney created Disneyland, one of the greatest customer delight stories of all time. Disney had the ability to combine his knowledge with the feelings of children (by the way, that's all of us) with the goal of delighting them to "make his dream come true." Disney's organization continues to create and deliver Totally Awesome Customer Experiences that people will never forget. Disneyland is a remarkable example of being extremely experience-based. Disney's dream was not to satisfy kids; his dream was to delight them...and to see the delight on each child's face. It was a brilliant dream.

Phil Knight, the founder and CEO of the athletic gear organization Nike, had a dream. His dream started a sports business revolution in the 1970s: changing old-fashioned tennis shoes into highly specialized sports equipment. At the same time, he promoted the Nike brand as a symbol of athletic prowess and achievement. Nike's success made Knight one of America's wealthiest men. His dream was to offer his customers high-quality running shoes that could be designed in the United States, manufactured in Asia, and sold in America at lower prices than the then-popular West German-made running shoes.

His dream has evolved into creating and delivering memorable experiences for customers through their association with the best athletes in the world. Nike personifies a brand experience. Nike has transformed a basic product beyond its product value into an experience value, which is why people are willing to pay $150 for a pair of athletic shoes and feel absolutely delighted.

Did you know that Nike was started with only $500 and a dream?

Southwest Airlines is an anomaly in the airline industry. They have too much fun. Their dream is to delight customers by opening up the world of travel with inexpensive, hassle-free transportation. We think Herb chose airplanes instead of Harley-Davidsons to get them there.

Southwest Airlines is another incredible success story. Herb Kelleher's organization has converted their Customer Knowledge Currency into Customer Trust Currency, bringing them one of the highest customer loyalty ratings in the industry. This is what Herb had to say about their dream...

> We started back in 1971 with three planes serving three Texas cities. In the short-haul markets, most people will drive those distances instead of fly. A lot of people figured us for road kill at the time. But today we've got over 300 airplanes in 55 cities. We like mavericks and people who have a sense of humor. We've always done it differently. You know, we don't assign seats. Used to be we only had about four people on the whole plane, so the idea of assigned seats just made people laugh. Now the reason is, you can turn the airplanes quicker at the gate. And if you can turn an airplane quicker, you can have it fly more routes each day. That generates more revenue, so you can offer lower fares.
>
> –Herb Kelleher, CEO, Southwest Airlines

The comment we always hear from people, whether or not they fly Southwest, is, "We love how Herb keeps the big guys honest." People trust Southwest to keep their fares affordable and consistent.

Phil Knight, Walt Disney, Dave Thomas, Herb Kelleher, David Pottruck, Fred Smith, and many other CEOs of organizations we've spoken about in the book are all customer-focused executives. They're constantly challenging their organizations to adopt the dream of becoming experience-based through creating and delivering Totally Awesome Customer Experiences to delight their customers. They're building a Customer Trust Currency in their organizations that will provide them a strong brand, significant differentiation from their competition, and loyal customers.

This chapter is all about making your dream come true. We want to discuss building the commitment to become an experienced-based organization. We want to show you how to implement the process of creating and delivering Totally Awesome Customer Experiences inside your organization.

We realize that many organizations are fraught with political and structural issues that create barriers to moving forward rapidly. We also realize that people have a zillion other things on their plates already. We know that undertaking the implementation of anything on an enterprise level takes incredible courage, passion, patience, and planning. But we also know that any barrier can be overcome if there is a strong commitment to fulfilling your dream.

FIRST THINGS FIRST...COMMITMENT

We recommend that you answer the following questions very honestly before you decide if your organization is ready to move forward with becoming experienced-based and implementing the process of creating and delivering Totally Awesome Customer Experiences.

- How committed are the CEO and executive team to being customer-focused and adopting a Customer Trust Currency?

- How committed is middle management to being customer-focused and adopting a Customer Trust Currency?

- How committed are the rank and file to being customer-focused and adopting a Customer Trust Currency?

We hope that all your answers are "fully committed."

If you're a real diehard Utah Jazz basketball fan, then you'll remember when the franchise moved from New Orleans to Salt Lake City. In those early days, you may have attended games with 5,000 fans in the stands and thought, "Wow, a big crowd tonight!" If you were there, you were definitely committed (or maybe you should have been committed).

When the Jazz first arrived, you could count on their commitment to be consistent – consistently poor. They were one of those teams that never made the playoffs year after year after year. We had Pistol Pete Maravich, though, and despite our inability to assemble a winning team, Pistol Pete was a Totally Awesome Customer Experience in and of himself. Back then, the radio stations would give away Jazz tickets in contests where the winner would get a couple of tickets to the Jazz game and the runner-up would get a season pass. (You know the kind of tickets we mean.)

It took the Jazz nine seasons to post an above .500 season and another five seasons to get over .600. The first season the Jazz moved to Utah, the Jazz had 23 wins and 59 losses for a .280 average. They didn't even have enough money to change the uniforms or name. Utah Jazz? Yeah, right.

In the spring of 1986 Larry Miller, a local car dealer, purchased the Jazz in an attempt to stop the team from moving from Salt Lake City. He also made a commitment to his customers to do whatever it took to bring a winning franchise to Utah. With the incredible selection of John Stockton in 1984 and Karl Malone in 1985, and the hiring of Jerry Sloan in the 1988–1989 season, the Jazz had a consistent, solid anchor on which they've built an incredible franchise for more than a decade.

During these seasons, the Jazz have been delivering many Totally Awesome Customer Experiences for their fans and the entire Utah community. It turns out the Stockton-Malone duo will go down in the history books as the most dynamic one-two combination of players in the history of basketball. In the 1996–1997 season, the Jazz finally made it to the NBA Finals against Michael Jordan and the Chicago Bulls.

Making it to the finals was a Totally Awesome Customer Experience for all Utah Jazz fans. Losing in the sixth game wasn't as awesome, but it set the rematch that took place the following year. Unfortunately, once again the magic of Michael Jordan defeated the Utah Jazz, despite the Jazz having the home court advantage and the best record in the NBA prior to playoffs. That year Karl Malone was named MVP (Most Valuable Player).

Short of winning the NBA championship, the Jazz organization has done everything a professional sports franchise could do to create and deliver Totally Awesome Customer Experiences. To Utah Jazz fans, the Utah Jazz is a championship franchise made up of champions, both on and off the court.

It was the commitment of the ownership, coaches, and players that made the Utah Jazz franchise what it is today: very successful. They've accomplished their goal of being consistent winners, consistently good community citizens, and consistent providers of exciting basketball. The kind of support they show the community is reflected in the type of players and staff the Jazz has assembled – and the community returns that loyalty and support.

As to Michael Jordan's commitment, what can anyone say that hasn't already been said?

If your leadership is not committed…wait. Be patient. Work to get their commitment before you proceed. You only have one chance to make a first impression. It's essential to do it right. If you don't have their commitment, fall back to building "customer focus awareness" as your strategy. One of the best ways to work toward receiving management's commitment is to prove that becoming experienced-based indeed improves profitability. Pass out some books, invite people in for a seminar, put together a portfolio of great ROI (Return on Investment) examples, have management talk to customer-focused companies that are using Customer Trust Currency and have the documented successes. Don't proceed with your implementation before you have commitment.

So what's first? Commitment is first – always has been and always will be. The question is, who is committed and how committed are they to becoming experience-based? You'll have to decide the answer to this one for yourselves and then proceed.

BECOMING AN EXPERIENCE-BASED ORGANIZATION

During our research, case studies, and work with various organizations, we discovered a very dominant, constant, and recurring issue: most organizations are operational-based, not experience-based. Most organizations base their programs, strategies, structures, hiring practices, and investments on operational and financial objectives rather than on customer experience objectives.

We didn't find one single organization (among dozens we researched) that had a high-ranking officer with the title of Chief Customer Experience Officer. We found many organizations that had a Chief Operating Officer. The closest we came was Colleen Barrett, Executive Vice President Customers, Southwest Airlines. We believe that two of the biggest benefits of this book are helping your organization realize the competitive advantage in becoming experience-based and then helping your organization to become experience-based. We know that when your organization finally sees itself from the viewpoint of its customers rather than from the viewpoint of its operations, it will be a truly eye-opening revelation. You'll discover new wonderful and profitable opportunities to leverage your most valuable assets – your customers.

We found that most organizations are operational-based, not experience-based. Most organizations base their programs, strategies, structures, hiring practices, and investments on operational and financial objectives rather than on customer experience objectives.

When you do your first Initial Transaction Assessment, you'll learn firsthand exactly what we mean by being experience-based. We guarantee it will positively impact both your customers and your entire organization.

EFFECTIVELY IMPLEMENTING THE FIVE-STEP PROCESS

Assuming that you've hurdled most of the critical game-stopping political, structural, and commitment barriers to implementation, let's move on to the four phases of implementation:

Phase One – Perform an Initial Transaction Assessment (Where are you?)

Phase Two – Decide which Totally Awesome Customer Experiences to which you want to apply the Five-Step Process (Where do you want to go?)

Phase Three – The power of the pilot program…Getting off the ground (how you get there) and presenting the case study for deciding rollout (Is it worth the trip?)

Phase Four – The rollout (the big kahuna)

Phase One – Perform an Initial Transaction Assessment (Where Are You?)

Every transaction in an organization is a customer-related transaction, because if there were no customers there would be no need for transactions.

Before we jump into the "how-to" of completing an Initial Transaction Assessment, let's define what we mean by the word "transaction." A transaction is any major process carried out by an organization in order to conduct its business. Although not every transaction needs to be revenue–based, it's important to note that all transactions have cost.

Experience-Based Transaction:

A transaction that contains some level of customer interactivity. These transactions govern customer product and service offerings and revenue production.

Transactions might be ordering goods and services, delivering goods, waiting on a customer, sending out literature, making a sales call, processing a loan application, creating an advertisement, helping a customer on the phone, having a customer visit your website and leave his or her e-mail address, processing an order, processing a claim, manufacturing products, or any other such activity. These are all transactions.

We've identified two basic customer-related transaction types: experience-based transactions and operational-based transactions.

Experience-based transactions contain some level of customer inter-activity. These transactions govern customer product and service offerings and revenue production. Understanding your current experience-based transactions tells you what you're doing today with your customers. It's also the foundation for what you want to do with them tomorrow.

Performing an assessment of experience-based transactions is fundamental in choosing the Totally Awesome Customer Experiences you will want to create and deliver. The assessment will also help you determine the Customer Experience Maps necessary to support your selected Totally Awesome Customer Experiences.

Operational-Based Transaction:

A transaction that supports experience-based transactions. It does not contain any direct customer interactivity. Its purpose is to internally perform work to provide support for delivering goods and services to the your customers, both internal and external. Operational transactions represent cost to your organization.

Operational-based transactions support experience-based transactions and don't contain any direct customer interactivity. They provide support for delivering goods and services to your customers. Operational transactions represent cost to your organization. Business engineering concepts help you increase the efficiency and effectiveness of operational transactions in order to reduce costs and facilitate faster, easier business with your customers.

A recent Jupiter Research Report called *Creating Loyalty and Building Profitable Relationships* states, "Transactions are the first step to loyal relationships. This means organizations must assess the transactions they have with their customers."

You can increase your profits by focusing on increasing experience-based transactions and reducing operational-based transactions. Experience-based transactions give you increased opportunities to delight your customers while building revenue opportunities. Operational-based transactions only increase costs. Improving the value of your experience-based transactions increases customer response rates and revenues. Using Customer Experience Mapping to identify the operational transactions necessary to support your experience-based transactions helps you eliminate any unnecessary operational transactions and reduce the overall cost base of your entire organization.

The results of the Initial Transaction Assessment form the baseline for your present interactions with your customers. You should begin your Initial Transaction Assessment in areas in which you believe creating and delivering Totally Awesome Customer Experiences will be most beneficial.

Here are the eight basic segments of performing your Initial Transaction Assessment:

1. Define your vision and mission statements for your organization. This information will provide perspective in determining if your transactions are aligned to the accomplishment of your vision and mission objectives.

2. Use any available documents, interviews, policy/procedure manuals, flow charts, and so on to determine the transactions in a particular area.

3. Categorize the transactions into "experienced-based" and "operational-based" transactions.

4. Identify as closely as possible each experience-based transaction as to its detail, such as audience segment, purpose, associated Experience Touch Points, customer offerings, monthly transaction volume, revenues, costs, and other relevant information.

5. Identify each operational-based transaction as to its purpose, which experience-based transaction it supports, the transaction volume and the cost of each transaction (which is the sum of all activity costs required to perform that transaction).

6. Evaluate your inventory of operational-based transactions to determine if any of the operational-based transactions can be converted into experienced-based transactions. The advantage of converting an operational-based transaction to an experience-based transaction is

The value of an Initial Transaction Assessment is in identifying all of the organization's transactions in relationship to their value to the customer and the organization.

that experience-based transactions can potentially generate revenues that can help you offset costs, promote brand, and increase Experience Touch Point opportunities. An example of converting operational-based transaction into an experience-based transaction might be to integrate a very high-touch, personalized marketing offering into monthly customer statements.

7. Confirm the results and accuracy of your Initial Transaction Assessment.

8. Generate a summary report with a detailed transaction inventory to use in selecting the Totally Awesome Customer Experiences you want to create and deliver.

Phase Two – Decide Which Totally Awesome Customer Experiences You Want to Create and Deliver (Where Do You Want to Go?)

Smaller businesses or a website may need to deliver only a single Totally Awesome Customer Experience. Larger organizations most likely have many.

The Initial Transaction Assessment is the best way to decide which Totally Awesome Customer Experiences you want to create and deliver first. We also guarantee, since this decision is highly strategic and important, that everyone will have his or her own opinion on the choice. Your decision on which Totally Awesome Customer Experiences to select for a pilot program will be significantly different from the ones you select and prioritize for your rollout. In Phase Three, you'll find some good suggestions on selecting the contents of a successful pilot.

You might find the questions in the Implementation Prioritization Chart helpful in determining priorities in implementing your Totally Awesome Customer Experiences in your rollout.

Implementation Prioritization Chart

Importance Ranking (1–18)	Prioritization Questions
	Who are our most valuable customers?
	What is the highest area of customer attrition today?
	In which areas of the business do we get the most complaints?
	Which customers trust us the most and the least?
	Which customers are most vulnerable to competitive raiding?
	How easy is it to achieve Customer Trust Currency for each customer audience?
	In which area of our business can we most quickly assemble the people, processes, and technology to implement?
	In which areas of the business do we have the most customer-focused people?
	Which management teams will be most receptive to new ideas and making new commitments?
	In which areas of the business do we have the infrastructure to support the implementation and measurement of customer delight?
	Which customers provide us the highest profile and "getting to market first" advantage?
	Which areas of our business are trend-oriented (cutting-edge) rather than fad oriented (temporary)?
	Which markets or market segments will be first in offering Totally Awesome Customer Experiences, winning the "first in mind" race with our competitors?
	In which areas of our business do we have the most difficulty in differentiating ourselves?
	Which of our customer groups are more emotional and strongly driven by their perceptions?
	With which customers can we most easily own the word "trust" in their minds?
	How many of our competitors are customer-focused rather than customer-manipulative?
	In which areas of our organization would an initial failure not permanently damage any chance for future attempts?

We suggest you prioritize the criteria you want to use for making your selections, publish it, and stick with it.

Phase Three – The Power of a Pilot: Getting You Off the Ground and Presenting the Evidence for a Rollout Decision

*Our advice is to always do a **Pilot Program** first.*

Smaller companies can begin their rollouts straightaway. Here is our advice if you're a larger company.

1. If the CEO and executive team is totally committed to being customer experience-focused, do a pilot implementation.

2. If middle management is totally committed to being customer experience-focused, do a pilot implementation.

3. If you're totally committed to being customer experience-focused and have the authority, do a pilot implementation.

4. If you can feel the energy from the rank and file as being customer experience-focused, do a pilot implementation.

If you've had the luxury of experiencing such activities as change management, process reengineering, continuous improvement, process improvement, SAP, CRM, or any other such initiatives, you know exactly why we suggest doing a pilot implementation. If you haven't experienced this level of organizational torture, all we can say is *trust us on this one*.

A pilot is a great approach to proving the concept and accumulating real test case data you can use as evidence to decide on a complete enterprise rollout. Success leads to success. Quick wins are good. As successes mount, the course of action becomes clearer for all to see. People love to win and they rally around success. Success is the easiest way to evoke permanent change. Enthusiasm is contagious! A pilot can blaze a path for quicker and deeper overall adoption by the organization.

Selecting and Perfecting the Pilot

Select a pilot that gives you total control of an area. The pilot implementation is a journey of all or none. This means that you can't embark on a pilot with the idea you'll accumulate some interesting ideas to incorporate into what you're presently doing in the organization. You can't use a pilot just to see how it works so maybe the next pilot will be successful. Nor can you set up a pilot so you can implement what you like and leave the rest out. A pilot *must* be designed to hit the ball out of the park and provide every opportunity to do so. A pilot will work *only* if you have total control over it. You must either have complete control over the pilot or don't start one at all.

If you're ready, here are a few prerequisites to making your pilot a big success.

1. Insist on complete control over the customers, team members, and resources required to create and deliver a Totally Awesome Customer Experience.

2. Select the right team members. They must also be wildly enthusiastic about the pilot.

3. Select a highly visible and valuable experience to build your pilot around.

4. Get permission to do the case study write-up and presentation to those above you in the organization.

5. Select a pilot sponsor with outside Board of Directors or executive management influence.

Some of these prerequisites may not be necessary if you're the CEO or president of the organization. These guideposts are just a solid process to bring your organization and management staff through the pilot as believers in your dream of being experience-based and delighting customers through creating and delivering Totally Awesome Customer Experiences.

*Your **Pilot Program's** results will provide the evidence that "demands the verdict."*

A bit of caution here. Implementing Customer Experience Mapping on an enterprise level is not equivalent to a mass rollout of pilots. An enterprise implementation takes a much more strategic effort. Catching fifty 40-lbs. salmon is not quite the same as catching a 2,000-pound shark...it takes a bit more to reel it in.

Presenting the Case Study for a Rollout Decision

The benefits of the pilot are to successfully prove the concept and make it easy to make a go/no-go decision for the rollout. It also gives you the opportunity to reward the trust people extended in supporting your dream. We recommend that you pause for a moment to recognize their trust and efforts.

Your pilot results represent the evidence that "demands the verdict." The pilot results will also provide insight into key strategic directions where Totally Awesome Customer Experiences should be created and delivered.

Prepare a pilot case study document. It provides excellent influence and evidence in helping you make your decision to do a rollout. The pilot case study document should contain the five following sections:

The Executive Summary

In this section, describe the Totally Awesome Customer Experience you created and delivered to the target customer audience. Also include what your vision was, what results you expected, and the actual results. Highlight the key measurable result elements of delighted customers (to include key emotional or trust testimonials) and any quantitative information such as improved customer response rates, increased market share, customer loyalty, and ROI (Return on Investment).

The Initial Transaction Assessment Results – "Where Are You?"

This section outlines the current experience-based transactions in your pilot area. It should also include an honest inventory of what the customers' experiences are today and the customers' perception of those experiences. Don't rely on customer satisfaction information to describe the customers' experience. You might have to ask either the customers or those working directly with the customers.

The Totally Awesome Customer Experience – "Where Do You Want To Go?"

This section defines the vision behind the Totally Awesome Customer Experience you want to create and deliver for the pilot. This section should describe the expectations for both the customer and your organization. Refer to Chapters 3–5 when doing your pilot.

The Results of the Pilot – "Was It Worth the Trip?"

This section needs to answer such questions as, "Did the results meet expectations?" or "Do the results of the pilot provide the evidence that demands moving forward with the rollout?"

Recommendations – "Where Do We Go From Here?"

This section makes specific recommendations about the rollout in terms of time lines, responsibilities, prioritization of next steps, and so on.

The physical presentation of your pilot case study is an experience itself with your management team. Don't waste it. Do your own Customer Experience Map for the case study presentation experience. It will be powerful and impressive.

A successful pilot is wonderful. An unsuccessful pilot is a close second. An unsuccessful pilot is just a good try, not a giant mistake. It isn't the New Coke experience. Unsuccessful pilots can be revised and executed again. Enterprise rollouts don't have that luxury. If you have the cooperation and commitment of the management and your team, you'll be given a few chances to execute a successful pilot. You'll usually get only one chance to make a successful rollout in the enterprise.

Phase Four – The Rollout

After a successful pilot program, there will be an irresistible urge to extend this process rapidly to every area of the company, especially in a large corporation. It's full steam ahead, everyone! Wrong strategy!

The time period after a decision has been made to do a rollout is the most vulnerable time for an organization. This period is when everyone in the organization is excited about the pilot results and wants to implement the concepts, processes, and tools as quickly as possible, everywhere in the organization. But rollouts take focus – lots of focus. Organizations are famous for starting programs they never quite complete. Just ask the pioneers of rollouts in SAP, ECRM, and CRM. (By the way, do you know how to identify the pioneers? They're the people with the arrows in their backs.)

"Victorious warriors win first and then go to war, while defeated warriors go to war first and then seek to win." – Sun Tzu

A rollout can't be all things to all people, in all areas, at the same time. One senior VP in the company must take control and lead the rollout team. Stay narrow, stay focused, and for the first few attempts, still call them pilots just in case the first few attempts bomb. This way you won't get the nay-sayers out in force trying to label this as just another "flavor of the month" program. *Stay apolitical!* We recommend phasing in your rollout plan and playing devil's advocate when identifying each new phase in the rollout. Go into the rollout process understanding that no solution will be perfect and that there will always be a new set of challenges that you may not have anticipated. The key is to identify as many issues up front with everyone involved.

Rollouts have very little to do with the processes themselves. It's all about the perceptions of both customers and employees that make it happen or not happen. You might find it wise at first to include several key Experience Touch Points for employees in each Customer Experience Map you create. You might just want those employees to be part of your customer audience selection.

The key to a successful rollout is creating trust from both external customers and from employees. Continue to use and appreciate their help and commitment to succeed with your dream.

Reis and Trout, in their book *The Twenty-Two Immutable Laws of Marketing*, discuss the law of line extension. They say:

By far the most violated law in our book is the law of line extension. What's more diabolical is that line extension is a process that takes place continuously, with almost no conscious effort on the part of the corporation. It's like a closet or a desk drawer that fills up with almost no effort on your part. One day a company is tightly focused on a single product that is highly profitable. The next day the same company is spread thin over many products and is losing money.

This is very similar to the pilot/rollout scenario. One day you're all working together to make a few pilots work. The next day you're doing a rollout that's out of control, consuming large amounts of resources and returning very little value. The main message here is that tightly focused organizations plan and target better while concentrating on what is important. They have the courage to dominate what they start!

Creating a Totally Awesome Website Plan...
A Customer Experience Mapping Case Study

"The most important thing is to discover the three main reasons users
come to your site and make these things extremely fast and obvious to do.
Less common actions should certainly not be any more complicated
than necessary, but priority should be given to the key user goals."

Dr. Jakob Nielsen, Web Usability Czar and
Author of Designing Web Usability: The Practice of Simplicity

Chapter 8 is incredibly unique. We demonstrate the power of creating and delivering Totally Awesome Customer Experiences and Customer Experience Mapping in planning a website: not just any website, but our own new website. You'll enjoy reading the comments from the planners and designers.

USABILITY, A PART OF CUSTOMER ACCEPTABILITY

We just love people who think customers are the key to success. Dr. Nielsen is obviously one of those enlightened souls who believe that delighted customers are the most valuable assets of an organization. Dr. Nielsen estimates that more than a trillion dollars have been wasted on not understanding the creation and delivery of Totally Awesome Customer Experiences over websites. Dr Nielsen wrote...

> Wasn't a study done recently that estimated the size of the Internet economy at around a trillion dollars? Whatever the number is, that's also my estimate of the loss due to poor usability, since all the studies show that users cannot find what they're looking for half of the time. In other words, whatever business a site does now is only half of the business it would do if users could always find what they were looking for.

> If we only look at individual sites, I actually believe the loss is much greater than 100 percent of their current business. Sites also lose money because they don't follow the writing style guide for online content, so users don't feel comfortable buying. And because they design poor shopping carts and checkout procedures. They further antagonize users by not disclosing shipping and handling fees. I think that a site that followed all of my guidelines would increase sales by 500–1,000 percent.

Welcome to the Wonderful World of Using Customer Experience Mapping for Planning Totally Awesome Websites

Walk with us through the play-by-play as we show you how we used Customer Experience Mapping to produce the Customer Experience Maps to plan our own website: Customer Experiences Inc. (CEI) at...

http://www.customerexperiencesinc.com

CEI as an organization had already gone through the four phases of the implementation process of creating and delivering Totally Awesome Customer Experiences (Chapter 7). One customer experience we selected as an organization was that of creating and delivering a Totally Awesome Customer Experience from our website.

OUR WEBSITE EXPERIENCE OVERVIEW

Let us start by introducing Tim Harris, COO of Tela Interactive, a website design firm located in Pittsburgh. Tim and his crew were instrumental in helping us do this case study on Customer Experience Mapping of our website. You'll have a chance to enjoy Tim's and his team's comments later on in this chapter.

Prior to beginning our first planning session, we asked Tim and his crew to carefully read Chapters 1 through 6.

Our first session began with a discussion on how to use Customer Experience Mapping to create and deliver a Totally Awesome Customer Experience for a website.

We talked about the challenges the Internet posed over using a brick-and-mortar medium to create and deliver a Totally Awesome Customer Experience. We discussed the sensory limitations of having only sight, sound, and size. We also dealt with all the navigational issues.

We also acknowledged the advantages of using the Internet as our medium for delivering an experience. We knew that once we created the right Customer Experience Maps, the experience would be delivered the same way every time. This will make for very consistent Totally Awesome Customer Experiences. We also know this is hard to accomplish in the brick-and-mortar world. We finished the session with an excellent perspective of how we want to visualize our guest's experience through our website. We were ready to proceed with the process of creating and delivering a Totally Awesome Customer Experience for the CEI website.

We started session two by following the five-step process of creating and delivering a Totally Awesome Customer Experience (Chapter 4), beginning with visualizing the experience for the website. This session helped us crystallize all the elements of our Totally Awesome Customer Experience. Using conference calls and e-mail, we brainstormed, created examples, scanned in diagrams, and looked at dozens of websites. We didn't end the session until everyone had completely agreed on our overall vision for the website experience. Here is the vision we all agreed upon:

Specifically, our mission to complete this vision is to accomplish four objectives:

1. Learn how to improve the customer experiences you create and deliver to your online customers.

2. Provide tools to facilitate the process of creating and delivering Totally Awesome Customer Experiences.

3. Create a quick-and-easy avenue to ask for help from other Trusted Site Members or CEI directly.

4. Facilitate the opportunity to contribute to a community interested in creating and delivering Totally Awesome Customer Experiences.

Our vision is to build a website where our Guests and Trusted Site Members will feel and be safe, be enriched by our content and offers, participate as part of a specialized community – where information is turned into knowledge and knowledge into trust, and everyone will always be delighted they stopped by to see us.

In the third session, we started with the Customer Audience Chart and combined it with the Customer Experience Map Chart to create our Customer Experience Map Pool. The Pool would serve as our guide throughout the rest of the Customer Experience Mapping process. Once everyone approved the Pool, we were ready to do our Customer Experience Mapping and create the actual Customer Experience Maps.

Over the next five sessions, we performed Customer Experience Mapping to create the ten Customer Experience Maps in our Pool. Our goal was to create two Customer Experience Maps per session. Each session's progress was documented in writing and e-mailed to everyone for review before the next session. This process kept our team on the same page with the same reference materials. During these sessions, Gary used a big whiteboard to capture brainstorming ideas during our conference calls. Once the Experience Response Point for a Customer Experience Map had come together, it was e-mailed to everyone. It would have been easier had everyone been in the same room, but it's nice to know the process can be done remotely.

During this Customer Experience Mapping phase of building our website, Tim pointed out how easy it was to detect potential conflicts and how fast programming can be once all the Customer Experience Maps are completed. We thought Tim's best statement was, "I've never been involved in the conceptual design of a website that has gone so smoothly and stayed so focused with less disagreement than this site. Even when we encounter problems, they're easy to work through because of the Customer Experience Mapping process. It has truly been enlightening."

The tenth session concluded our website design planning case study. With Joel Daynes and Graham Northrup, senior web developers from Mercury Media Works, we discussed the physical design and programming of our website and the strategy behind each of the Customer Experience Maps we need first, second, third, and so forth in developing our site.

Once the physical design and programming for the site is complete, we'll be ready to finish the assembly, delivery, and measurement of our Totally Awesome Customer Experience for our Guests and Trusted Site Members of the CEI website.

All in all, the building of the website plan was a totally awesome experience for us.

OBSERVATIONS AND INSIGHTS FROM THE TEAM

- "It was initially challenging to think differently. I had to give up some old ways of thinking about website planning and design in order to embrace this new thought process. Once I did it, the process went two or three times faster than traditional site planning efforts."

- "Following the new process allowed more time for creativity. We weren't constantly worrying about where we were in a session."

- "It got rid of a lot of nonsense and things we didn't need. Everything had to pass the "So What? Test." I love that test."

- "This was the first real website I had planned while feeling that I understood the customers and what we needed to do to delight them. It makes me wonder for whom we planned all those other websites."

- "I was amazed, because at the end of every session everyone was still on the same page. That was remarkable. All of us have done website planning and design, so when this occurred it was one of those self-awareness deals where suddenly you say, '*Wow!*'"

- "Using customer experience language greatly helped our communications and lessened our misunderstandings. We all knew what a Direct, Controlled, Impacting Experience Touch Point meant. This was a really big deal in moving quickly forward."

- "It was a lot more fun when we knew that our vision and mission objectives were to focused on delighting the visitor. It's amazing how easy it is to get caught up in the operational side of designing a site for easy programming rather than for delighting the visitor. Easy to lose focus. Customer Experience Mapping helped us retain that focus."

- "Programming will now became secondary. We felt that when we were done with Customer Experience Maps, the physical designers and pro-grammers would have a much easier time building the site."

- "The first two or three Customer Experience Maps took us a long time and it was awkward at first. Once we got the process down, though, we made up for lost time. It's just a different way of thinking that we weren't used to."

- "What the hell were we doing before?"

- "You know, we had talked about a lot of stuff similar to Customer Experience Mapping before, but this tool really put all those thoughts together for me."

- "Those Guests better be delighted or we'll...just kidding."

THE NUTS AND BOLTS OF OUR SESSIONS

This section contains a detailed description of all the sessions we described in the Overview. This level of detail will help you to see all the specifics we went through in our process of creating and delivering a Totally Awesome Customer Experience for Guests and Trusted Site Members of our website. Enjoy...

Session 1 – We Discussed the Process of Creating and Delivering a Totally Awesome Customer Experience Using a Website Medium.

Tim's team all reviewed Chapters 1 through 6. We reviewed the customer experience language. Our discussions were specific to how best deliver an experience over the Internet. We reviewed many different websites, making specific comments on the delight achieved and the degree of difficulty the operating side of the website posed versus the delight derived from the experience site. We spent a lot of time asking questions like:

- What makes you want to return to this site?

- Did we lose the original purpose of the site as we became immersed in the site?

- Did the site ask and answer the questions the true audience for the site would have?

- What are the three major reasons why anyone would want to visit the site in the first place?

- Does the technology get in the way of the site's purpose and interfere with the customer's delight?

- What brand impressions of the organization do we walk away with after we sign off the site?

- Is this a site you would recommend to your colleagues or friends?

Session 2 – Visualize the Experience (Step One of Creating and Delivering a Totally Awesome Customer Experience)

We made absolutely sure all team members felt comfortable with the customer experience language before proceeding. It significantly increased our speed.

Remember the checklist of musts for the vision (Chapter 4).

- Must have defined customer audiences.

- Must be simple, with both perceived and real value for your customer and your organization. The customer must be delighted.

- Must be actionable and measurable. This means the vision can be translated into easy-to-implement Customer Experience Maps and be measurable in terms of customer delight and receiving the Delight Vote.

- Must be written in simple, straightforward language so it can be communicated effectively to team members and customers.

- Must have the commitment to make it happen.

Defined Audiences for the Vision

Our selected audiences are executives, managers, and entrepreneurs of organizations who are initially looking for better methods of interacting with their customers to improve customer service, to provide satisfaction, and to deepen relationships. We want to quickly help our Guests realize what we do and how we can help organizations make a giant leap beyond customer satisfaction into customer delight. Once we determine that they're within our defined site audience, we need to quickly identify our audience and help them along their path to customer delight.

If we don't know the Guests, let's introduce ourselves. Let's show them around our house and give them the option to continue with our help or explore the site on their own. For those who need help or don't want the hassle of finding things on their own, we will eventually want to have personal assistants that remember sessions, have personalities, and have only one duty: to delight the customer. We want to encourage them to use a personal assistant for their first visit.

If we do know them, let's welcome them back and see where we can re-engage them into their last experience with us. They may want to use a personal assistant they previously liked or get acquainted with a new one. Maybe they just want to proceed on their own to finish something from an earlier visit.

Simple, Valuable and Relevant Vision

We constructed this website to help executives, managers, and entrepreneurs of organizations who want to improve their customer experiences. It's important that we respect their time; therefore, we must help them access relevant locations on our site quickly and with minimal effort.

Actionable and Measurable Vision

The rest of our vision was describing what we felt was possible with our Guests and Trusted Site Members.

Communication of the Vision

We decided that our minimum site communication level, for both language and grammar, should be set at about the tenth-grade level. This makes the language simple and quickly readable, allowing people to move around faster on our site.

All members of the team will have a full written copy of all Customer Experience Maps, along with the vision and any other documentation that makes their job easier.

Commitment to the Vision

We asked all members of the team if they were prepared to move forward with their parts in making the CEI site possible. Each team member answered, "Yes." We were all very excited.

The detailed segments of the CEI vision are:

- We must first help our new Guests understand our philosophy about trust, privacy, and community. They need to know that the information of our Trusted Site Members is always safe and will not be shared. We also want them to know the truth about how we will use their information to help create and deliver Totally Awesome Customer Experiences.

- We will also tell our Guests how they can choose from ten experience transactions on our site:

The CEI vision is to build a website where our Guests and Trusted Site Members will feel and be safe, be enriched by our content and offers, participate as part of a specialized community – where information is turned into knowledge and knowledge into trust, and everyone will always be delighted they stopped by to see us.

1. Welcome

2. Problem-solving

3. Giving knowledge to the customer

4. Assembling and saving knowledge for the customer

5. Receiving knowledge from the customer

6. Affirming knowledge with the customer

7. Commerce

8. Offerings and proposals

9. Contacting people

10. Customer delight feedback

This also happens to be our entire site map.

• We want everyone to understand what's available and how to get there fast. Since we want their experience with us to be continuous and seamless, we must be able to remember what they did last time and help them store what they need to resume their experience next time.

• We also want to make it easy to ask for services and to get proposals and offerings. We want to build trust through the use of a single form and consistent format for any outbound communication to our Guests and Trusted Site Members. It will reinforce our brand image by providing brand experiences that meet our brand promises.

• We will only send relevant information with value. If we have nothing relevant to send, then we'll send nothing and let them know this as well. This sets the expectation that whenever we do send something, it will be important, valuable, and relevant.

• We will not be overly clever with oh-wow! graphics that wear out after the first visit and only waste time in the future. Instead, let's be trustworthy and trustable. We will always respond to our Guests and Trusted Site Members within a reasonable period of time. Our answers will be honest, relevant, and helpful.

• We will not over-stimulate our Guests or Trusted Site Members. We will be a site that is relaxing and a safe haven from all the clutter and noise of other sites. We'll keep our content fresh and easy to obtain. Our content will always be oriented toward the needs of the customer, showing that we support our concepts and our beliefs with our actions. Good thoughts and ideas, regardless of their origin, will be featured.

- Our choice of colors will characterize trust, openness, and ease of viewing for many different sessions. Our brand needs to be prominent and clear.

- Most of all, our website will assemble the right Customer Experience Maps for creating and delivering a Totally Awesome Customer Experience to each Guest or Trusted Site Member who comes to our site.

- The key to the CEI website is trust. No secrets, no guessing, no feeling stupid, no cluttered pages of warehouse-type selections that end in confusion and frustration. The CEI site must be a customer's site, plain and simple.

Tim and his team are the first group to use the Customer Experience Mapping process to plan a website. Tim participated in the creation of our vision and was instrumental in guiding us away from Experience Touch Points we could not practically deliver via the Internet.

We'll measure customer delight everywhere possible through the use of online feedback, outbound experience surveys, and usage analysis.

Upon review, our vision met all the musts of a Totally Awesome Customer Experience Vision, and we obtained consensus from the entire team to move forward into translating our vision and building our Customer Experience Maps.

Session 3 – Translated the Website Vision into Our Customer Experience Map Pool (Part of Step Two of Creating and Delivering a Totally Awesome Customer Experience)

We started this session by listing all of our defined audiences and assigning each of them an importance rating.

As noted in our vision, we're interested in executives, managers, and entrepreneurs looking to improve their interactions with their customers through creating and delivering Totally Awesome Customer Experiences. We broke them down by customer audience number, description, and importance rating on a scale of 1 to 5, with "5" being the highest level of importance and "1" being the lowest.

Please note that any Guest not in our defined customer audience is designated a "1" in importance, not a "0." This is because he or she could influence other people in our desired audience, so we must pay attention to anyone visiting. It's our responsibility to determine whether that person is a viable Guest or Trusted Site Member. Everyone is important to us, but some are more important than others.

Customer Audience Chart – CEI Website

Audience #	Description of the Audience	Audience Priority
1	Executives, managers, and entrepreneurs just browsing the website.	2
2	Executives, managers, and entrepreneurs looking for help in solving a problem in the area of customer experiences.	3
3	Executives, managers, and entrepreneurs looking to provide suggestions or recommendations to help solve a problem in the area of customer experiences.	4
4	Executives, managers, and entrepreneurs searching for information in the area of customer experiences.	3
5	Executives, managers, and entrepreneurs looking to provide information in the area of customer experiences.	3
6	Executives, managers, and entrepreneurs assembling/saving information in the area of customer experiences.	3
7	Executives, managers, and entrepreneurs looking for affirmation of information in the area of customer experiences.	4
8	Executives, managers, and entrepreneurs looking to purchase products or services.	5
9	Executives, managers, and entrepreneurs looking for offerings and proposals in the area of customer experiences.	5
10	Executives, managers, and entrepreneurs looking to contact us, contract our customers, or be contacted for various reasons.	3–5
11	Executives, managers, and entrepreneurs looking to share their experiences.	5
12	All non-customer audience Guests	1

Customer Experience Maps Chart – CEI Website

Customer Experience Map Name	Number
Welcome	CEM 1
Problem-solving	CEM 2
Giving knowledge to the customer	CEM 3
Assembling and saving knowledge for the customer	CEM 4
Receiving knowledge from the customer	CEM 5
Affirming knowledge with the customer	CEM 6
Commerce	CEM 7
Offerings and proposals	CEM 8
Contacting people	CEM 9
Customer delight feedback	CEM 10

Next we simply created our Customer Experience Map Pool.

Customer Experience Map Pool – CEI Website

CEM	Audience Number/Priority (PI)											
	1	2	3	4	5	6	7	8	9	10	11	12
	PI 2	PI 3	PI 4	PI 2	PI 3	PI 3	PI 4	PI 5	PI 5	PI 4	PI 4	PI 1
CEM 1 Welcome	X	X	X	X	X	X	X	X	X	X	X	X
CEM 2 Prob Solv	X	X	X	X	X	X	X				X	
CEM 3 Give Kn	X	X		X		X	X					
CEM 4 Assble	X	X		X		X	X					
CEM 5 Rec Kn	X		X		X						X	
CEM 6 Aff Kn	X			X		X	X		X			
CEM 7 Comm	X	X		X		X	X	X	X			

CEM	Audience Number/Priority (PI)											
	1	2	3	4	5	6	7	8	9	10	11	12
	PI 2	PI 3	PI 4	PI 2	PI 3	PI 3	PI 4	PI 5	PI 5	PI 4	PI 4	PI 1
CEM 8 Off/Prop	X	X		X		X	X	X	X			
CEM 9 Contact	X	X	X	X	X	X	X	X	X	X	X	
CEM 10 Feedback	X	X	X	X	X	X	X	X	X	X	X	

Upon completion of our Customer Experience Mapping Pool, we carefully examined the Pool to see if we could eliminate redundancy through consolidating audiences who use the same Customer Experience Maps and have the same relative importance. We found that Audiences 3, 5, and 11 and Audiences 6 and 7 fit the redundancy criteria for consolidation. Note that Audiences 3, 5 and 11 all have high importance (4, 5, 5 respectively), and Audiences 6 and 7 have average importance.

After consolidation, we had nine audiences instead of twelve. The value of consolidating audiences is that it saves time, effort, and cost in the Customer Experience Mapping process, employee training, and execution.

The Customer Experience Map Pool now looks like this:

Customer Experience Map Pool – CEI Website (Revised)

CEM	Audience Number/Priority (PI)								
	1	2	3, 5, 11	4	6, 7	8	9	10	12
	PI 2	PI 3	PI 5	PI 3	PI 4	PI 5	PI 5	PI 4	PI 1
CEM 1 Welcome	X	X	X	X	X	X	X	X	X
CEM 2 Prob Solv	X	X	X	X	X				
CEM 3 Give Kn	X	X		X	X				
CEM 4 Assble	X	X		X	X				
CEM 5 Rec Kn	X		X						

CEM	Audience Number/Priority (PI)								
	1	2	3, 5, 11	4	6, 7	8	9	10	12
	PI 2	PI 3	PI 5	PI 3	PI 4	PI 5	PI 5	PI 4	PI 1
CEM 6 Aff Kn	X			X	X		X		
CEM 7 Comm	X	X		X	X	X	X		
CEM 8 Off/Prop	X	X		X	X	X	X		
CEM 9 Contact	X	X	X	X	X	X	X	X	
CEM 10 Feedback	X	X	X	X	X	X	X	X	

We then reviewed the Customer Experience Map Pool for "map gaps." Once the review was complete, we proceeded to do our Customer Experience Mapping for each of our identified 10 Customer Experience Maps. Within each of our Customer Experience Maps, we wanted to note the audience it applied to, the Experience Response Point we wanted to achieve, the Experience Touch Points we used to achieve our Experience Response Point, and the Potential Experience Voting Points we needed to manage.

Sessions 5 through 9 – Build Our Customer Experience Maps (Part of Step Two of Creating and Delivering a Totally Awesome Customer Experience Continued)

We've included a few sample maps from the ten Customer Experience Maps for your review. This will allow you to hit our website pages as we build them to see how the Customer Experience Maps translate to reality.

CEI Website Customer Experience Map #1

Map Title: *Welcome*

Customer Audiences: All

Experience Response Point:

We want our qualified audience Guests to register as Trusted Site Members while helping unqualified Guests quickly exit our site, sending a message to those they believe are qualified about our site.

Experience Touch Points:

1 **The Look and Feel of Website Impression**. The CEI site will be warm, friendly, inviting, uncluttered, and lend a sense you can do things quickly and effectively. We will immediately project the word and image of trust to our Guests. This Experience Touch Point will be Direct, Controlled, and Influential or Informational.

2 **Our First Message**. We want first-time Guests to immediately discover if they are on the right website. We want to discourage non-audience browsers from further interaction, treating them with respect but suggesting that they might use their time better elsewhere. We would appreciate their telling someone who needs our help where they can find us. This Experience Touch Point will be Direct and Impacting.

3 **Who are you?** Assuming they stay, we need to know our Guests in order to best help them. We first need to know whether they're Guests or Trusted Site Members. If cookies (with their permission) have already been placed for identification purposes, we can identify them quickly and use this Experience Touch Point to personally engage them immediately. If they don't have cookies, we need to ask them to log in or select themselves as Guests. We also need to distinguish whether a Guest is there for the first time. This Experience Touch Point will be Direct and Impacting.

(continued)

(continued)

4 **The Invitation for a Tour**. Guests are invited to take a tour, or skip the tour and navigate on their own. We also need to tell our Guests they can do everything on our site other than problem-solving, knowledge-giving, assembly, saving and affirmation, or special offerings, and they can contact CEI. We want to encourage our Guests to become Trusted Site Members. This Experience Touch Point will be Direct, Controlled, and Impacting.

5 **Registering as a Trusted Site Member**. We will engage our personal assistant to help ask the appropriate registration questions. Answers will be self-directing to the next question as appropriate. Personal assistants will eventually speak different languages. We want to display information about the benefits of being a Trusted Site Member as we ask our registering questions. We will provide Guests a mini-tour during the registration process. We need to interlace questions of familiarity into the conversation to make this Experience Touch Point personal. This Experience Touch Point needs to be Direct, Controlled, and Impacting.

6 **Taking the Tour**. Our personal assistant introduces himself or herself to our Guests. He or she talks about CEI and the vision behind the site. The personal assistant tells our Guests they can stop the tour at any time, resume the tour, leave the tour, or repeat part of the tour. The tour explains how each segment of the site helps deliver our vision. The tour highlights the benefits to our Guests and Trusted Site Members. It is also our opportunity to know each Guest better. We will collect customer knowledge throughout the tour, using high criteria questions. The tour ends with our asking them to be Trusted Site Members and posting the information gathered against the minimum standard to be a Trusted Site Member. We will ask them to supply any additional information necessary before they leave the site. The tour will be pre-guided and animated. This Experience Touch Point is Direct, Controlled, and Informational.

7 **Navigation of Selection of Site Segments**. Navigation must always be easy and intuitive. We want our Guests or Trusted Site Members to quickly and effortlessly get where they need to go or retrieve what they need. This Touch Point will be Direct, Controlled, and Informational.

8 **Trusted Site Member Interaction**. We will give our Trusted Site Members a choice between using a personal assistant or going directly to different site segments. Regardless of their choice, we want to help them recall their last session. We will ask them if they want a summary recap. If they don't elect to use the personal assistant, we'll give them their last session information from "Alice" who says, "You might find this useful," and then let them proceed. If they're using a personal assistant, we'll ask them which assistant they would like to use and then bring forward the last session information along with a personal greeting. This Experience Touch Point will be Direct, Controlled, and Impacting.

9 **Using the Personal Assistant for the Web Session**. Using analysis tools, we will provide Trusted Site Members with suggestions from correlated database information and provide recommendations on content. We'll ask them if they want to look at the Trusted Site Member offerings. This Experience Touch Point will be Direct, Controlled, and Impacting.

Potential Experience Voting Points:

- Site Appeal — Feeling Response.
  Managed by Experience Touch Point 1
- Site Relevancy — Thinking Response.
  Managed by Experience Touch Points 2, 3, 4, 5, 6
- Site Navigation — Feeling Response or Combative Response
  depending on severity. Managed by all Experience Touch Points

Knowledge Requiring Transfer:

- None required, as it is all controlled within the same program.

CEI Website Customer Experience Map #7

Map Title: *Commerce*

Customer Audiences: 1, 2, 4, 6, 7, 8, 9

Experience Response Point:

We want our Guests and Trusted Site Members to tell us and their friends that purchasing from the CEI site was easy and hassle-free. We want them to tell us it was easy to find what they wanted, to order, to pay, and to track their purchases.

Experience Touch Points:

1 **The Shopping Cart.** The Guests or Trusted Site Members can easily select what they want to order from logical categorization. Each item will provide a crisp, easy-to-understand description with additional information if requested. Placement into the shopping cart or removal in a single click. We will walk them through the friendly payment process using a personal assistant. An e-message confirmation goes out thanking them, acknowledging their order, and giving them a projected delivery date along with a tracking URL (thumbnailed as "Track Your Purchase"). Everything they needed for this order will appear as smart attachments in the e-message. If the product is one of our partner products, we will use a co-branded wrapper for the e-message. This Experience Touch Point is Direct, Controlled, and Impacting.

2 **The Order Tracking.** The URL in the e-message gives them an instant link to our order-tracking screen where they can track their own order rather than calling or e-mailing our center. This Experience Touch Point is Direct, Controlled, and Informational.

3 **Shipping Confirmation and Thank You.** Upon shipping, an e-message will go to our Guest or Trusted Site Member, telling them it has shipped and once again thanking them for their order. We put in direct contact URL

(continued)

(continued)

if they have any questions, comments, or concerns that will recognize them personally upon use. This Experience Touch Point is Direct, Controlled, and Informational.

4 **Customer Delight Questionnaire**. Ten days after the delivery of their purchase, we will send an e-message with a brief customer delight questionnaire (only five customer delight questions), asking for their help. The questions will be in the form of a questionnaire smart attachment, but linked to a web page gathering the information directly into our database. Any issues detected will be immediately addressed. This Experience Touch Point is Direct, Controlled, and Impacting.

Potential Experience Voting Points:

- Task Difficulty in Finding, Ordering, or Paying —
  Feeling or Combative Response
  Managed by Experience Touch Point 1
- Task Difficulty in Tracking Their Order —
  Feeling or Combative Response
  Managed by Experience Touch Point 2
- Order Receipt – Thinking Response Point
  Managed by Experience Touch Point 3
  Managed by shipping company we select
- Product Delight – Thinking or Feeling or Combative Response
  Managed by the product promises and delivery itself
  Managed by Experience Touch Point 4

Knowledge Requiring Transfer:

- None required, as it is all controlled within the same program.

CEI Website Customer Experience Map #8

Map Title: *Offers and Proposals*

Customer Audiences: 1, 2, 4, 6, 7, 8, 9

Experience Response Point:

We want to help our Guests and Trusted Site Members to have quick access whether they can help or need help. We want them to see our services as valuable in leveraging to their skills and efforts to accelerate their vision. We want to make it easy and positive for them to ask for help.

Experience Touch Points:

1 **Find Their Interests and Help Points**. We need to find out specifically what help they need. We can do this by asking some probing, high-criteria questions. This Experience Touch Point is Direct, Controlled, and Impacting.

2 **Presentation of Services**. We perform a preliminary match of their needs to our capabilities and display what we think can help. They can also browse for solutions. We eliminate all "consulting speak." We will always speak to our audiences in their customer experience language. We will tell them directly what we can do for them, how long it normally takes, how much it most likely will cost, and what their participation needs to be in getting it done correctly. This is a good place for testimonials from people having had this service performed and their impressions as to the results they achieved. This Experience Touch Point is Direct, Controlled, and Impacting.

3 **Proposal Request**. We ask our Guests and Trusted Site Members if they would like us to prepare a proposal for them. If yes, we give them a specific time when they can expect it to be completed and what to expect when they receive it. This Experience Touch Point is Direct, Controlled, and Impacting.

(continued)

(continued)

4 **Proposal Sending and Presentation**. We will send a proposal either via an e-message or fax, and it will be presented through a WebEX type presentation or over the phone. The proposal will never be delivered "cold." This isn't personal enough and we can't answer their immediate questions. This will be a little difficult with a fax, but it can be managed. We will ask if we can proceed after presentation. This Experience Touch Point is Direct, Controlled, and Impacting.

Potential Experience Voting Points:

- Presentation of Services — Thinking, Feeling, and Combative Response Managed by Experience Touch Point 1
- Proposal Request — Thinking, Feeling, and Combative Response Managed by Experience Touch Points 2 and 3
- Proposal Receipt and Presentment — Thinking, Feeling, and Combative Response Managed by Experience Touch Point 4

Knowledge Requiring Transfer:

- None required, as it is all controlled within the same program.

Session 10 – Concluding the Design and Beginning the Programming

Our tenth session was all about the physical layout, design, and programming of our website. We were curious to see how easy it would be for designers/programmers to understand our Customer Experience Maps and translate them to a physical existence. During this session, we presented Joel and Graham with all 10 Customer Experience Maps, asking them to read them over, ask questions, and then comment on whether or not the Customer Experience Mapping process would help them in their physical design and programming of the CEI site.

Graham's comment:

> Customer Experience Mapping enhances and refines the thought process behind planning for the customer's experience. We have discovered through this process that there is more to building a customer-delighting website than simply providing the customer with various forms of information.

Joel's comment:

> Customer Experience Mapping has helped us focus on the integration of technology with the visitor's experience in browsing or engaging the website. Gone are the days of high-tech websites that fail to reach their potential for serving customers and accomplishing desired responses. The speed in which we were able to grasp the vision and feel for what CEI wanted in their website was incredible. It was a matter of hours, not a matter of days. Not only will it enhance the value of their site, but cost them a lot less money to build it.

Joel and Graham recommended that we do our website in three phases. Phase One is getting the site operational, defining the website's look and feel, and laying out the basics for all 10 Maps. It will provide our guests and Members the ability to seek help, communicate, become familiar with the principles presented in our book, and give feedback. Phase Two will implement our vision of integrated navigation based on the Five-Step Process. This navigation will seamlessly run through all sections of the website. Phase Three will be the automation phase, where technology will be used to improve the "human" characteristics displayed by our website in interacting with our customers.

As the team walked through each Customer Experience Map, you could visualize how it would flow for the Guests and Trusted Site Members. This process made it much easier to talk about the technology because it wasn't the dominant subject. Technology was finally playing the supporting role that technology should always play. The session was dominated by the thought and feelings of the Guests and Trusted Site Members.

This last session marked the beginning of Phase Two in the creation of the CEI website and the successful use of Customer Experience Mapping in its design planning.

A NEW UNDERSTANDING ABOUT WEBSITE PLANNING

"Great solutions have nothing to do with technology itself. They have to do with knowing what you want to accomplish, then using technology to help you get there."

Bill Rozier, VP of Marketing for NetTest, has a saying: "Great solutions have nothing to do with technology itself. They have to do with knowing what you want to accomplish, then using technology to help you get there." Until we went through this particular case study, perhaps we didn't understand the real truth behind Bill's statement.

Likewise, experiences have little to do with the technology itself. The role of technology is to help deliver an experience to the customer in which the customer does not notice the technology. The value of technology is that it provides a greater reach and the opportunity to enrich an experience. You achieve success when you deliver the customer experience without the customers' being concerned about the technology itself. Technology without an experience purpose behind it dies a quick death.

Marketers, managers, owners, and executives have allowed operationally oriented people to create the majority of the websites in the world. This predominance of operational thinking has created operationally functional sites (mainly informational), but not "human sites." That's why Dr. Nielsen believes that so much time and money has been wasted. The Internet is just a different medium. It's not a new business philosophy. If your website can't deliver delightful experiences to your customers, you eliminate one of the rich experience mediums your competition can use as differentiation.

The other issue we discovered on the Internet was fear on the part of potential customers: fear they'll feel stupid, fear they'll waste their time, fear people are tricking them or planting bizarre stuff on their desktops (or worse), fear their privacy has been or will be invaded. The Internet has the ability to amplify all the good and bad relationship items of which people are afraid. Personal privacy tops that list.

Over the next few years, significant ethical issues will surround the Internet, not the least of which is "the right to know."

The Right to Know – Customer Knowledge Versus Customer Privacy

"People aren't skeptical about what you know about them, as long as they know you care about them and will use that knowledge with respect."

The late David Evans, CEO, Evans and Sutherland

Chapter 9 covers an issue that's growing geometrically in importance: a customer's privacy. We discuss the ethical issues of gathering customer knowledge for use in creating and delivering Totally Awesome Customer Experiences while exploring how the concepts like CRM (Customer Relationship Management), data mining (customer knowledge), and customer privacy all interact in this highly explosive arena. You'll learn about a new path we think leads all of us out of the customer privacy woods. This new path offers a new perspective for the use and implementation of customer knowledge to help you increase customer trust, delight, and privacy.

CUSTOMER PRIVACY: A PROACTIVE CORPORATE RESPONSIBILITY

The following excerpt is from an article entitled "Trust is key in growing the digital economy." We found this article in the June edition of *Computerworld*. These are edited remarks from a speech that Dick Brown, chairman and CEO of Electronic Data Systems Corporation, delivered before The Economic Club of Detroit on May 7, 2001.

> A fundamental human value underlies all of today's emerging technological capability. That value is trust, and it's being threatened. As business leaders, we can't ignore those who are concerned about the degradation of privacy and security on the Internet. They won't accept it, and neither should we.
>
> The digital economy can't prosper in a world separate from our civilized society and the fundamental values upon which it's based. So when it comes to business over the Internet, your word has to be your bond.
>
> There's no one authority that polices Internet communities, no extensive system of laws to protect you. The responsibility to police the Internet falls squarely on business leaders, government leaders, and consumers. It will be the creation of an environment of trust that either ensures the validity of the digital

*Businesses that create
and maintain trust by
protecting privacy will be
the market leaders in the
digital economy.*

economy or stifles it growth. So, will we adhere to a fundamental principle of mutual trust, or will a breach of trust be the
digital sin that undoes our brave new e-world, dooming its
hopes for exponential progress?

A recent story in *The Wall Street Journal* told of a man who had
looked up personal details of hundreds of his old high school
classmates. He was easily able to find information on their
homes, mortgages, property values, and even credit history. It
was an intrusion into their private lives through the misuse of
personal data and an abuse of trust. Even though it wasn't
against the law to access the information, it was a breach of the
individuals' expectations of privacy.

Last year, one in three Internet users was the victim of a privacy
or security breach. No surprise! In a survey published in *The
Wall Street Journal*, 94 percent of the respondents are still concerned about threats to their privacy on the Internet. How many
privacy violations will it take for trust to completely disappear?
The digital economy has significantly widened the scope for
privacy abuse. And we won't have to wait long before all our
customers demand absolute, no-fail privacy protection. Privacy
will become a fundamental driver in determining the success of
the digital economy.

Businesses that create and maintain trust by protecting privacy
will be the market leaders in the digital economy. By not taking
action, we are permitting unacceptable behavior. If we continue
to look the other way, the problem will only intensify.
Successfully incorporating privacy practices requires strong
CEO leadership and commitment throughout the enterprise. All
of us in industry must commit to these issues. If we don't, government will. Already, there are more than 20 bills on privacy
before Congress, even more in the state legislatures. The privacy
issue demands not a government answer or a business answer
but a personal answer.

If you want to establish a relationship with an individual consumer
or business, it must be based on mutual trust or it will always
be suspect. That mutual trust requires you to honor, respect and
protect one another. We can't look at people's personal information as something that can be bartered in the marketplace.

No action is no option.

There has been explosive growth in integrated databases, the Internet, and business technologies over the past ten years. Advances in data collection and storage, widespread use of bar codes for most commercial products, and the complete computerization of many business and government transactions have provided organizations with an unbelievable amount of information. Organizations can now use this information to further their knowledge about customers, markets, competition, and even the economy itself. The ability to create these reservoirs of information has generated an urgent need to create new techniques that can assist organizations in transforming this data into useful knowledge. Two such techniques that transform Customer Information Currency into Customer Knowledge Currency are CRM (Customer Relationship Management) and data mining.

As a result of this rapid advance in transforming Customer Information Currency into Customer Knowledge Currency, customer privacy issues have also arisen. Customer privacy will be one of the biggest issues facing organizations over the next few years. There are urgent needs for some tough ethical decisions to be made surrounding the issues of customer privacy, such as the use of customer knowledge to manipulate customer-buying habits, the lack of trust in fostering customer/vendor relationships, and the sharing of customer data. Now more than ever, customer-focused solutions are needed to temper what could be an overwhelming public outcry in favor of legislative answers to these issues.

In this chapter, we want to explore customer knowledge-gathering techniques such as CRM, data mining, and customer profiling used in deepening customer relationships. We also want to discuss how customer knowledge aids Customer Experience Mapping in improving your return on customer investment, and increasing customer response rates. We'll examine the economics surrounding customer knowledge acquisition. Finally, we'll discuss how all of these aspects of customer knowledge affect customer privacy and the creating and delivering of customer experiences. One thing is for sure: these topics will remain interesting for many years to come.

CUSTOMER RELATIONSHIP MANAGEMENT (CRM)

CRM is an elusive concept and a poorly branded word. Every organization defines it differently, based on its own needs.

Many people believe CRM is just a tool, but in reality CRM is a philosophy. CRM is rooted in the belief that improving the personal relationships the organization has with its customers will strengthen its position, brand, and differentiation. We have seen hundreds of organizations get caught up in the technology of CRM, completely forgetting about the basic structural and customer-related processes necessary to make the technology effective. CRM technology should support the CRM process, not the other way around. CRM should not be an initiative run by the Information Services department.

There are many different degrees of CRM implementation success. The degree of success greatly depends on the organization's customer focus and level of Customer Relationship Currency. An organization that is customer-focused with a Customer Knowledge Currency might judge successful CRM implementation to be one that improves the way it determines customer needs, tailors its offering and increases its response rates. To design and implement the most highly effective and successful CRM system requires the organization to be experience-based supporting a robust Customer Trust Currency.

We define CRM as an organization's ability to leverage its knowledge of its customers in an attempt to continually and progressively deepen that relationship. An organization's customer focus and level of customer relationship currency will ultimately determine the implementation's success.

Here are some examples of organizations using the CRM process to deepen relationships:

- When you log onto Amazon.com, the first thing they do is give you a list of suggested books, based on your purchase history. Amazon wants their customers to know they're trying their best to be helpful in showing them books that will delight them.

- When you phone Fidelity Investments to get an update on your 401(K) plan, not only can you check your balance, you can explore your portfolio, move it to different funds, or extract money, all with a touch of the keypad.

- When you walk into Sukara Sushi (a local sushi bar), everyone behind the sushi counter greets you in both Japanese and English, and most of them know your name. When you sit down, they ask you if you want to start with the usual. Even if you've been there only a couple of times, they seem to know "your usual." They also take the time during each visit to recommend something new that they believe you'll like. Fairly "low-tech," but effective.

Customer Knowledge Currency is the basic Customer Relationship Currency behind CRM because identifying customer needs is its target focus. Customer Trust Currency is the customer relationship currency behind customer delight because its primary focus is the customer. *The transition in focus from customer needs to the customer themselves is the ultimate reason for Customer Knowledge Currency transforming into Customer Trust Currency.*

Some organizations deploy CRM technologies without a strong CRM process supporting the technology. These organizations can find themselves becoming customer-manipulative if they focus only on improving response rates at all costs. For example…

- Sign up for a credit card, and you'll find that within a couple of weeks you'll start receiving solicitations from multiple departments within the credit card company as well as all the so-called "partners" to whom they have sold your name. Such bombardment, even though they've tried to personalize the messages, becomes negative and irritating.

- Try to get your name removed from a mailing list. It just goes onto another list you haven't asked to have it removed from. Have you ever had the feeling you can't ever get off the list, even when you call and threaten management with a lawsuit?

- A local grocery chain wants you to use something called the "value card." You must keep it on your key chain if you don't want to pay a percentage higher than any of their competitors for the same item. The scanning of your card allows them to continue profiling your buying habits while you're trying to figure out how to avoid going to their stores.

The key to beginning the transition from a Customer Knowledge Currency to a Customer Trust Currency rests in whether your organization is customer-focused or customer-manipulative. Both customer-focused and customer-manipulative organizations can use Customer Knowledge Currency. Only customer-focused organizations will be able to develop a Customer Trust Currency on their way to transforming to an experience-based organization. This is because Customer Trust Currency requires an emotional trust bond to form between the organization and the customer. Customer knowledge alone cannot build this bond – and if you're not sure whether your organization is customer-focused, chances are you're not. This makes developing Customer Trust Currency quite difficult.

Customer Knowledge Currency transitions to Customer Trust Currency when the organization's focus shifts from the customer's needs to the customer.

A considerable amount of technology has been deployed in the practice of CRM with the purpose of accumulating, tracking, and presenting customer knowledge. The knowledge of the customer is more often used to advance the relationship by presenting the customer with more precise and tailored offerings that meet the customer's needs. The motive and value behind those offerings determine the outcome of the trust-building exercise.

To this point, an article entitled, "Getting Your Arms Around Customer Relationship Management (CRM)" included the following comments by Steve Diorio, President, IMT Strategies, and author of *Beyond e: 12 Ways Technology Is Transforming Sales & Marketing Strategy*. We found his remarks quite relevant. Steve says…

> As companies move forward with CRM projects, there are four critical issues to keep in mind. The first is, what value does the

organization place on customer information? This question is critical to determining spending on analytical CRM, which is chiefly concerned with collecting and analyzing customer data.

Organizations currently have a difficult time placing a value on customer information and, consequently, tend to undervalue customer information assets. Therefore, operational CRM deployments have exceeded analytical investments. Business-to-consumer firms, specifically banks and telecom companies, placed the highest value on customer information and, as a result, had the broadest analytical CRM portfolios in place. The value of customer information is growing among insurance and high technology firms, as indicated by increasing analytical CRM investments, but business-to-business firms will continue to lag, according to the report.

Secondly, companies need to define customer patterns so that they can use the customer as the design point for the CRM process, with the ultimate goal being complete customer lifecycle management. Customer lifecycle management will encompass the entire spectrum of customer interactions.

The third issue is the need to balance the CRM technology infrastructure. The report predicts that many companies will need to spend as much as $250 million over the next two to three years on CRM investments.

Finally, companies need to develop hybrid-selling systems, which involve significant process change. An interesting channel finding in the study is that 96 percent or above of all revenues still come from traditional channels. The average organization uses 2.75 channels and plans to automate one or more of these.

In a research article by Accenture entitled, "How Much are Customer Relationship Management Capabilities Really Worth? What Every CEO Should Know," their research noted:

A typical U.S.$1 billion business unit could add U.S.$40 million in profit by enhancing customer-focused capabilities by 10 percent. If that same business were able to ramp up its performance by 30 percent, propelling itself from average to high performance in such customer capabilities, it could improve pretax profit by as much as U.S.$120 million. In the new economy, organizations have the ability to take an overwhelming amount of transaction data and other information about customers and transform it into real customer insight.

The highest-performing companies give their frontline employees quick, easy access to critical data on purchases, contact history, and product inquiries, as well as demographic and lifestyle data. For example, using a Siebel CRM system...Telenor Mobile, Norway's largest wireless provider, has armed every member of its sales organization with all the information needed to manage a customer's complete sales lifecycle. Both sales and margins are increasing as Telenor is targeting the right customers with the right products and services.

Customer knowledge is power. The more knowledge an organization has about an individual customer, the more powerful it becomes in its potential interaction with that customer. Knowledge about the individual customer goes well beyond just knowing your audience, because the audience can become *an audience of one*. Our research shows that such automobile companies as Mercedes-Benz, Toyota, Audi, Lexus, and BMW have fully embraced the customer knowledge concept. Their challenge is to take the next step in transitioning their Customer Relationship Currency from Customer Knowledge Currency to Customer Trust Currency. This shift in Customer Relationship Currency will take time and dedication. People still have strong filters against the image of the used-car salesperson. These companies need to create and deliver a series of Totally Awesome Customer Experiences to create that emotional trust bond to transform them to the next Customer Relationship Currency level.

A typical U.S.$1 billion business unit could add U.S.$40 million in profit by enhancing customer-focused capabilities by 10 percent.

Marriott, the hospitality company, has implemented programs with the intent to leverage their knowledge of the individual customer to create and deliver Totally Awesome Customer Experiences. This excerpt is from an article called "Customer satisfaction: the fundamental basis of business survival."

Marriott has developed a program called Personal Planning Service, which allows Marriott to create personalized vacation itineraries for guests at seven of its resorts well in advance of arrival. When a customer calls and makes a reservation for one of these resorts, the organization starts building an itinerary based on the customer's requests and stored preferences. When the customer arrives at the hotel three weeks later, tee times have already been scheduled, dinner reservations arranged, and recreation itineraries created. Marriott has found that guests who participate in the program show noticeably higher guest satisfaction scores and spend an average of U.S.$100 more per day on services beyond the room rate. They're also more likely to generate repeat business because they have had a great experience.

Marriott is not just satisfying its customers here. Rather, Marriott has consciously organized their organization to delight their customers because customer delight is the fundamental basis of business survival. Marriott is trying to use its Customer Knowledge Currency to provide the customer with experience offerings to help transform that Customer Knowledge Currency into Customer Trust Currency, resulting in customer delight and customer loyalty. Marriott wants its customers to tell everyone about their delightful experiences. Customers just don't tell people an experience was satisfying.

DATA MINING OF CUSTOMER INFORMATION

Data mining is the science of using customer transactions to understand the behavior of a customer. Data mining uses statistical algorithms to determine patterns in that transactional data and convert the transactional data (Customer Information Currency) into Customer Knowledge Currency.

For example, in an article titled "Knowing Your Customers," Martin LaMonica tells us:

> As First Union Bank, in Charlotte, N.C., is finding out, data mining will let companies, particularly those in banking and finance, build an accurate customer profile based on consumer behavior. The key is transactional data.

> "Actually, we're trying to sift out customer behavior, which is really hard to do with ad-hoc query tools. Those get us in the ballpark, then we use true data-mining tools to find what factors cause one behavior or another, particularly who might leave," explains Jeff Headley, First Union Bank's system vice president of knowledge-based marketing.

> "The organization is shifting analysis away from products and predictive models to determine who might buy a product in the future, based on who bought the product in the past. Now it analyzes consumer's transaction patterns at an automated teller machine (ATM), for example, so it can offer the customer products better suited for their needs and preferences.

> The big thing now is customer focus. Let's look at each customer and take each product we have and rate them according to what products customers are likely to buy. We're drawing data from an IBM SP2 massively parallel processor running Informix, so we have all the transactional data.

> For example, if a customer uses ATMs more often than going to a bank and doing transactions with a teller, the bank may offer

this customer more ATM services or offer incentives to use the bank's online service.

When people think of data mining and finding that gold they're talking about, it's really finding clusters of customers that have a behavior pattern they never knew was there. There's probably some segment of the population they've been ignoring," Headley says.

Here's another example of how organizations are using data mining from an article called "Users Find Tangible Rewards Digging Into Data Mines" by Steve Alexander:

> "Fingerhut, which has 9,500 employees and mails 130 different catalogs each year, is among the true believers in data mining. All catalog mailings, credit-granting decisions, and inventory-stocking decisions are based on it," says Andy Johnson, Fingerhut's Senior Vice President of Marketing.

> "Fingerhut wants to find out which customers they can profitably mail catalogs to for future business. It recently used data mining to study past purchases of customers who had changed residences to see if they had preferences. Data mining showed those customers were three times more likely to buy items such as tables, fax machines, phones, and decorative products, but that they were not more likely to purchase high-end consumer electronics," Johnson says. Fingerhut used that information to create a special catalog that it mailed only to those customers who had recently moved.

> Johnson's only caveat: "You need good data that has been properly prepared in order to make money using data mining. People who cannot see the value in data mining as a concept either don't have the data or don't have data with integrity. We've spent a lot of time, money, and energy getting those two things."

> "Although Fingerhut has used statistical modeling for about 20 years, new data-mining software allows the organization to look at a broader range of information and larger databases," says Bill Flach, Fingerhut's Director of Marketing Analysis and Research. "For example, before data mining Fingerhut's statistical analysis was limited to taking samples of 10 percent to 20 percent of its customers. With data mining, it can examine 300 specific characteristics of each of the 10 million to 12 million customers in a much more focused way."

A drawback to data mining is its complexity. Nevertheless, the science of data mining will continue to advance as new technology becomes more feasible for linking together all disparate databases into a single customer-keyed database. Access to all customer knowledge from one central location will be the goal. This capability could significantly help an organization with its Customer Experience Mapping. That's because coordination and consistency of Experience Touch Points is fundamental to accomplishing Experience Response Points and to avoiding Experience Voting Points.

CUSTOMER EXPERIENCE MAPPING USING CUSTOMER KNOWLEDGE

In Chapter 4, we discussed the process of creating and delivering Totally Awesome Customer Experiences. In "Step One – Visualize the Experience," we point out that audience definition is critical. Totally Awesome Customer Experiences need to be audience-specific. It's critical to know how all of your Experience Touch Points will apply to your audience.

Don Pepper and Martha Rogers were among the first true pioneers in this area of audience definition that defines the ideal customer audience as an "audience of one." They say in their book *The One-to-One Future*:

> You will not be trying to sell a single product to as many customers as possible. Instead, you'll be trying to sell a single customer as many products as possible – over a long period of time, and across different product lines. To do this, you will need to concentrate on building unique relationships with individual customer on a 1:1 basis. Some relationships will be more valuable than others. Your best relationships, and your most profitable business, will define your best customers...the nature of your relationship with each of your customers in this new environment will be collaborative. Instead of having to be "sold to"[Customer-Manipulative], your customers increasingly will "sell themselves"[Customer-Focused with Customer Trust Currency], stepping hand in hand with you through the complicated information exchanges that will more and more, accompany individual product sales.

An audience of one means that with the customer's help, you identify the perfect Experience Response Point for meeting that customer's specific needs and can tailor your Experience Touch Points to consistently deliver the right offerings and experiences.

The more you know about each individual customer, the more effectively you can create and deliver Totally Awesome Customer Experiences for that customer, deepening your relationship. The more trust you build with your customers, the greater chance you have to accomplish a 1:1 reality. Customer Experience Mapping for an *audience of one* means that with the customer's help, you identify the perfect Experience Response Point for meeting that customer's specific needs and can tailor your Experience Touch Points to consistently deliver the right offerings and experiences.

CUSTOMER KNOWLEDGE INVESTMENT AND CUSTOMER RESPONSE RATES

When it comes to making offers to your customers, customer response rates are king. All of us want to receive the highest possible customer response rates to our Experience Touch Points and achieve as many Experience Response Points as possible. Research has shown a direct correlation between higher customer response rates from product or service offerings created with higher levels of customer knowledge, customer audience identification and customer needs identification. **The Customer Response Pyramid** graphically depicts this relationship.

From an aerial view of the pyramid, you can see the four sides of the pyramid. The Customer Knowledge side of the pyramid shows how it feeds into the creation of customer audience and customer need identification. The customer audience and customer needs identification then combine into creating the specific customer response rate.

The greater your level of customer knowledge, customer audience identification, and customer need identification, the greater the customer response rate will be to your offers. This is why so many companies are interested in making the investment in improving their customer knowledge through processes and systems like CRM, data mining, and customer profiling initiatives.

The decision to migrate to higher levels of customer knowledge in an attempt to increase your customer response rates is not as simple as you might think. You may want to consider several key factors in making your decision:

1. Return on Investment (ROI). Does migrating make economic sense?

2. Susceptibility to Customer Loss – Will migrating to higher levels of personalization reduce the risk of competitive raids on your customer base because you can achieve deeper customer relationships?

3. Knowledge Attainment – Can the customer knowledge you really need be feasibly and economically acquired?

Assuming that you decide to press on with the science of acquiring higher levels of customer knowledge, you will quickly find out that knowing when to use customer knowledge and how much to use is an art. Skill is required for the preparation of more segmented and personalized offers that allow you to take advantage of your acquired knowledge. If you don't use enough customer knowledge, the customer might feel like just another number. If

The greater your customer knowledge, the more effective your Experience Touch Points can be in reaching your desired Experience Response Point. The true leverage of customer knowledge comes in transforming your Customer Relationship Currency into Customer Trust Currency. This Customer Currency level makes your offerings and experiences welcome, rather than intrusive or annoying. Customer Trust Currency increases customer response rates and deepens customer relationships.

If you don't use enough customer knowledge, the customer might feel like just another number. If you use too much customer knowledge, however, the customer might feel that you're intruding.

The Customer Response Pyramid

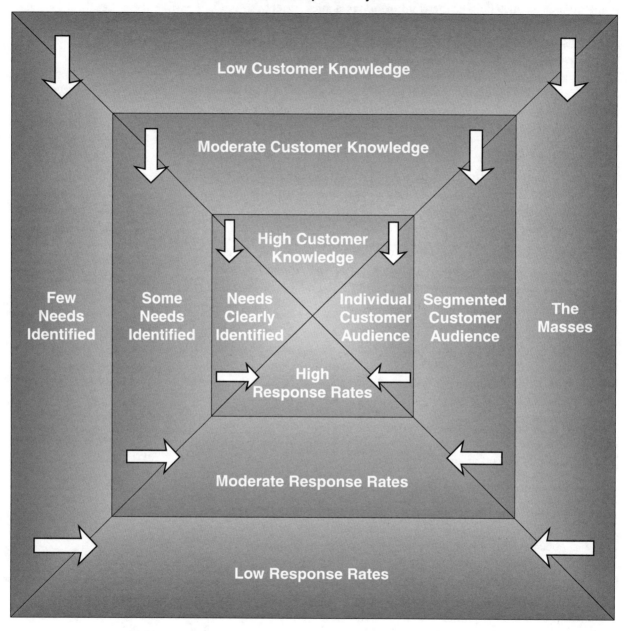

you use too much customer knowledge, however, the customer might feel that you're intruding. The objective of customer audience and customer-need identification is to create experiences and offers to the customer that convey trust without jeopardizing the customer's privacy and evoking an Experience Voting Point. Only then will customer response rates increase. That's why the transformation from Customer Knowledge Currency to Customer Trust Currency plays such a vital role in moving to higher levels of customer knowledge. Customer Trust Currency significantly reduces the risk of triggering an Experience Voting Point. When you carry out your Experience Touch Points designed using Customer Trust Currency, customer response rates are almost always significantly higher.

These three tips will help you keep the offers you present to your customers through your Experience Touch Points from failing:

1. Customers must know you or of you and have some significant level of trust to let you through their primary thought and feeling filters.

2. The customer knowledge used in your Experience Touch Points must be relevant enough to enable you to construct an offer that coincides with their needs and the level of the customer relationship they have with you.

3. Build your Customer Experience Map with successive and progressive Experience Touch Points so the application of customer knowledge through each Experience Touch Point appears continuous and relationship-building-oriented.

Now that you understand the process side of the Customer Response Pyramid, let's examine the human side of the pyramid. The human side to the pyramid requires that you give equal attention to a customer's feelings. This means that if you want to move to the highest level of the Customer Response Pyramid, you must achieve customer delight. It means that you need to use Customer Trust Currency in order to form that emotional trust bond with the customer. If this bonding does not take place, you will only capture your customers' minds, but not their hearts – and the heart is the place from which the Delight Vote emanates. As seen in the Customer Relationship Currency model, winning only the customers' minds limits your highest possible outcome to mere customer satisfaction. This position leaves you vulnerable to competitors who create their strategy to win the customers' hearts as well. Your experiences and offers must be designed to do both.

The Customer Response Pyramid also demonstrates that the only true investment that achieves customer responses is an investment in the customer. The old notion of investing in markets or market segments is com-

Investing in your customers rather than in your markets can greatly insulate your organization from the impact of constantly changing markets, products, and a dozen other competitive factors.

plete nonsense. Customers govern markets; markets don't govern customers. More and more studies are showing that once-touted market segment boundaries are misleading in today's new customer economy. These old ways of viewing "target markets" (hate that word) lack vision. The true nature of segmentation is based completely on the customer – not on the industry, the environment, or a number of other meaningless market attributes.

If you want to achieve higher customer response rates, look for the specific customers you want to do business with, regardless of the market in which you find them. Then invest directly into those customers. They will become your most profitable customers. This change in the nature of investing in your customers rather than in your markets can greatly insulate your organization from the impact of constantly changing markets, products, and a dozen other competitive factors. It also reinforces the fact that measuring customer delight is extremely important. Measuring customer delight is the true measurement of your investment in your most valuable assets – your customers – rather than in your operations or the ever-changing marketplace.

ECONOMICS OF ACQUIRING CUSTOMER KNOWLEDGE

Acquiring customer knowledge often requires a significant investment cost in technology, people, and process. The risk you take in investing in customer knowledge acquisition lies in whether or not additional customer knowledge will facilitate a successful migration in customer needs and identification levels. If it does, then you'll most likely increase your customer response rates and achieve faster attainment of your Experience Response Points. You can calculate the Return on Investment (ROI) on customer knowledge acquisition by measuring the incremental increase in profit derived from increases in customer responses and speed of Experience Response Point attainment, divided by the cost of the investment to acquire that customer knowledge.

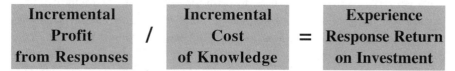

| **Incremental Profit from Responses** | **/** | **Incremental Cost of Knowledge** | **=** | **Experience Response Return on Investment** |

Evaluating the impact of CRM, data mining, and customer profiling is just another reason for measuring Experience Response Point achievement.

Knowing the scope of your customer knowledge requirements reduces your overall costs of gathering information. This is because a Customer Experience Map calls out all resource requirements needed in executing the required Experience Touch Points. Knowing all of the Experience Touch

Points provides an inventory of what customer knowledge is necessary and most valuable. It also eliminates superfluous customer information and unneeded data analysis. A Customer Experience Map provides you with the blueprint for customer knowledge acquisition. It helps you call out the specific customer knowledge variables necessary to collect the right information for building more effective Experience Touch Points – and more effective Experience Touch Points will lead directly to higher Experience Response Point achievement.

ROI on customer knowledge acquisition can be computed on the decision to migrate to higher levels of customer needs and audience identification. In this example, we migrate from The Masses to the Segmented Level in audience identification to achieve higher customer response rates.

The Masses Level – The customer response rate from a direct spam e-mail campaign sent to 100,000 potential customers was one percent. This means that 1,000 customers responded to the offering. If the revenue value of the offering was $500, the offering had a revenue response of $500,000. The cost of the campaign was $200,000, leaving a gross profit of $300,000.

The Segmented Level – The population of 100,000 was divided into groups of 5,000. Each of the 20 different groups was sent a very tailored and specific direct e-mail. The customer response rate from a direct, segmented e-mail campaign was four percent. This means that 4,000 customers responded to the various offerings. If the revenue value of the offering was still $500, the offering had a revenue response of $2,000,000. The cost of the campaign was $800,000, leaving a gross profit of $1,200,000.

The return on knowledge for this campaign would be 150 percent (incremental profit of $900,000 ($1,200,000–$300,000) divided by incremental investment of $600,000 ($800,000–$200,000).

In this particular case, you would proceed with the investment in moving to a more segmented campaign because the costs appear to justify the return.

Acquiring customer knowledge can be tricky. It's sometimes difficult to evaluate whether certain pieces of customer information will ever transform into customer knowledge. If you've already built a Customer Experience Map, it provides almost a "collection grid" that spells out which customer information you want to collect and turn into customer knowledge. The key here is that not all customer information will turn into customer knowledge. Having your Customer Experience Maps in place will help you discern this very quickly.

What another great place to apply the "So What? Test"!

Unless you're using Customer Trust Currency, your attempts to use customer knowledge to tip-toe around the significant issue of customer privacy will be inherently clumsy.

The line is thin between using customer knowledge to provide personalized or segmented offerings, and violating a customer's privacy.

CUSTOMER PRIVACY

Privacy and Knowledge

Unless you're using Customer Trust Currency, your attempts to use customer knowledge to tip-toe around the significant issue of customer privacy will be inherently clumsy. And then even using such tools as CRM, data mining, and customer profiling will not make it any less clumsy.

The technology of collecting and storing massive amounts of information about individuals will continue to increase with sophistication and speed. The line is thin between using customer knowledge to provide personalized or segmented offerings, and violating a customer's privacy. Direct e-mail messaging companies can now track every message sent, every reply made, and every link touched. Internet service providers can track activities on every site visited and the software downloaded. Websites use "cookies," bits of data that can be stored in PCs, to keep a record of who is visiting in order to welcome them back and gather more information. Software now exists that plants itself in a hard drive and then starts digging up information about your net activities, such as monitoring the advertisements you click on, the documents you open, and the transactional patterns of your work. It goes on and on.

Commerce, whether on-line or off-line, is the driving force. The success of an organization's offering is measured by its speed, efficiency, cost, and customer response rate. All of these success variables help determine the increase in profitability. The methods used by organizations to achieve success, however, often erode privacy and put the customer and vendor at odds, escalating a customer's combative response to future offerings presented by that organization.

Customer data abuse threatens to disrupt and handicap the development of customer knowledge as our newest opportunity to increase commerce. The escalation of privacy issues will continue to drive the importance of converting your Customer Relationship Currency from Customer Knowledge Currency to Customer Trust Currency.

If you transform to Customer Trust Currency, the path to overcoming customer privacy issues will become easier and much less expensive.

If you transform to Customer Trust Currency, the path to overcoming customer privacy issues will become easier and much less expensive. Trust gives you the credible authority to directly ask customers what they want. It also places customers in the natural position to honestly answer you. This is far less time-consuming, costly, and risky than obtaining information second-hand, then performing the analysis and making assumptions on the information's relevancy and value. The more your customers participate in providing you information, the less risk you take of breaching their privacy. Currently, the number of privacy breaches continues to escalate. Continued escalation will drive the need for privacy technology, legislation, and more governmental control. For example, the on-line world is already becoming more complex as a result of organizations violating customers' privacy.

Privacy and Mediums

Perceived customer privacy issues vary, based on the communication medium used to address the customer. Certain mediums, such as the phone and e-mail, are considered highly private, while your mailbox and radio are perceived as less private. The personal trust and value a customer places on a medium are the primary factors in determining how the customer ranks the need for privacy within that medium.

For instance, let's take the case of two similar communication mediums: e-mail in the on-line world and direct mail in the off-line world. In study after study, perceived e-mail privacy abuse considerably outweighs direct mail privacy abuse. Why? The answer is twofold. First, a customer's e-mail box is deemed more valuable than his or her mailbox. Second, your e-mail box is more personal and specific to you. You might retrieve your mail once a day, but your e-mail has become like your phone. It's always on.

The Internet is a relatively new medium. It seems that when a new medium appears, many customer-manipulative organizations quickly move in to exploit it until something catastrophic happens that tightens the controls and lessens the effectiveness of that new medium. The Internet was once the most trusted medium of communication among researchers. Now it hovers near dead last in people's perception of a trusted medium. How ironic and disappointing.

The key to understanding customer privacy is to understand respect. Customer privacy isn't tricky; it just takes being customer-focused, using Customer Trust Currency when handling your customers' knowledge.

Respecting a customer's privacy does not mean you stop learning about, communicating with, or providing offers to your customers. It means you learn about them, understand them, then demonstrate that you can be trusted with that knowledge to help them.

Make the Quantum Leap

"Great ideas need landing gear as well as wings."

C.O. Jackson

Chapter 10 has you ready to make the leap off the Olympic ski jump. It's time for you to take off and perform your own perfect landing. This chapter deals briefly with setting the right expectations for both your customers and your employees. We then discuss how to create, assess, and measure experience performance standards that really work. The chapter finishes with additional tips that might help you as you go through your own implementation.

READY, SET, GO!

In ski-jumping, the takeoff might be the cause of the problem, but the landing causes injuries. Landings are what you have to master in spite of any issues you have with your takeoffs. If you've ever wanted to learn to ski-jump, now is your chance. It's time for you to start down the takeoff ramp, *take the quantum leap*, and "get some superior air." We hope we've given you enough concepts, processes, and tools to confidently do a graceful ten-point landing all the way through your rollout.

At the end of the day, it's all about delighting your customers in a language they all understand...the language of experiences.

Before you start down the ramp, there are three last things we want to throw at you that can help you make a spectacular landing...

- Set proper customer experience expectations. It's vital that you and your customer know what it will take to delight them. Only then can you create customer delight and receive the customer's Delight Vote

- Set employee expectations and performance standards to ensure that they deliver your Experience Touch Points as designed.

- Use the additional tips at the end of this chapter to avoid some bumps on your takeoff and landing. In some circles, these tips might be referred to as "comfort foods."

In a recent *The Wall Street Journal* article, Estee Lauder president and COO Fred Langhammer said:

> When disposable income is tight, consumers gravitate towards brands to which they can feel an emotional connection. How many more neckties or lipsticks does anyone need? We're sat-

urated with consumer goods; it becomes very important to have brands that provide an exciting experience as well as excellent products...when you read your 401(K) printout these days, you want something that makes you feel good.

SETTING CUSTOMER EXPECTATIONS

Remember when we talked about the Zions National Bank Gold Service Club? Like so many other potentially great programs, it needs to set more clearly defined customer expectations. The program left the setting of expectations in the hands of the individual customers. Letting customers set their own expectations adds uncontrollable variables to the experience, making it difficult to consistently receive the Delight Vote.

Remember the Rivers case study in Chapter 3? One of the first questions we asked the owner Brent was, "How do you set the expectations for a delightful dining experience with your customer?" The answer was that they didn't. Once again, setting the expectations for the experience was left up to the customer.

Take a moment and think how many times you've had an experience where the setting of expectations for that experience was left up to you. It's alarming how many times this happens!

If the Awesome Customer Challenge is to stop merely satisfying your customers and start delighting them, you'll need to set expectations with your customers. Then when those expectations are accomplished, you'll be able to receive the Delight Vote.

If you want to delight your customers, don't be afraid to ask them what it's going to take to do it! Customers love to participate and have control in their own experiences. Setting experience expectations helps customers become participants.

By not setting customer experience expectations, you never transfer any of the ownership of the experience to the customer. The lack of ownership will guarantee you inconsistent results. If you and your customers never set experience expectations, your customers can change their expectations at any time during an experience without ever telling you. Not setting experience expectations places the customer in the position of being an experience observer rather than an experience participant. Having set no expectations for what a delightful computer ownership experience will be makes it almost impossible for Dell to deliver a delightful computer ownership experience.

Paint-your-own ceramics studios provide a great example of how properly setting customer experience expectations leads directly to the receipt of the Delight Vote. Color Me Mine is a chain of paint-your-own ceramics studios. These studios give their customers the ability to choose from hundreds of unfinished bisque (pottery) shapes, like pots, animals, plates, and so on and paint them their own way. The painted bisque is then glazed, fired, and returned to the customer in about two days.

While some of the customer painting is absolutely brilliant, even the not-so-brilliant painting is still valued by customers. Why? Because they painted it themselves. When seven-year-old Tommy gives Grandma a plate he painted, the plate is no longer just a plate. It transforms itself into a priceless experience for both Tommy and Grandma. The value is in the experience, not in the product. In a paint-your-own ceramics studio, the expectations are set with the customer at the beginning of the session and almost always achieved. If the studio works steadily with its customers during the session, only breakage, poor glazing, and other operational issues generally affect the customer's Delight Vote.

Remember the rules about giving a speech? First, tell your audience what you're going to tell them. Then tell them. Then tell them what you just told them. The same rules apply to setting customer experience expectations. Tell your customers that your job is to delight them, ask them what it takes to delight them, and then show them that you did what they asked. You'll get the Delight Vote.

There are many ways to set expectations with customers. The best way is to directly ask them what you need to do to delight them. Another method is to publish your expectations for delighting customers, and ask them if they agree.

Vagueness has no place in creating and delivering Totally Awesome Customer Experiences. Trust in relationships isn't built from vagueness.

One company we came across found a clever way to set expectations. The company placed excerpts from feedback letters of delighted customers under the glass on top of the wood tables in their reception area. This display helped convey a level of expectations to customers who might not have already set theirs. This particular method helped them set the expectations for many of their customers and brought quick attention to required variations.

As an Experience Artist, you can come up with your own style and special methods. It's critical to set customer expectations at the beginning of a Totally Awesome Customer Experience and have everyone know what those expectations are.

SETTING EMPLOYEE EXPECTATIONS

One of the most significant benefits to becoming experience-based is the authority and empowerment it provides your employees to delight the customer. Being experience-based gives your organization the opportunity to shift its employee performance standards, evaluation, and reward system, from measuring and rewarding operational activities to measuring and rewarding the success of delighting customers and achieving Experience Response Points.

From the employees' point of view, experience-based empowerment is infectious for a number of reasons.

- Employees are rewarded for being customer-focused.

- Employees are empowered to delight customers.

- Customer-focused employees have a stronger belief in and loyalty to the organization.

- Employees feel more responsible because they're now directly connected to the customers and their experiences.

- Feedback is customer experience-oriented and more personal.

- All employees can share in a success.

- It's a lot more fun!

In reality, empowering your employees to delight the customer adds value and depth to your organization's culture. It also improves morale, camaraderie, and employee loyalty, not to mention the deeper relationship your employees form with your customers.

Employee expectations and performance standards come directly from your Customer Experience Maps. As you construct Customer Experience Maps for a Totally Awesome Customer Experience, you likewise define and create the Experience Response Points and Experience Touch Points. Your Experience Response and Touch Points define the strategy and tactics (standards) of what every person in the organization needs to do in order to properly execute a Customer Experience Map. These activities will lead to the customer's Delight Vote.

Sue Mackey, of the Mackey Group, provided us with her expert list of the elements necessary to effectively assess and measure your standards as to employee performance in terms of customer delight...

- Employee competency – Your employees must have the basic skill sets and training to competently execute the proper Experience Touch Points.

- Competency criteria – You must outline the skill sets and training that determine employee competency

- Measurement and Assessment Against Standards – The standards must call out what is to be measured and how it will be measured.

- Employee Capabilities – Identify the strengths and weaknesses of each person in the delivery process. Identify what specific training is needed and where training should be created and administered.

- Profile Customer Delivery – Whenever possible, select the best delivery method to enhance experience acceptability.

- Means to Troubleshoot – You must have a method for quickly isolating and trouble-shooting specific problems.

- Customer-Driven Assessment – It's important to remember that the focus of measurement is the experiences, not the operations.

- Feedback – Feedback is necessary to facilitate accuracy, efficiency, and success as knowledge circulates to improve the process.

Another major benefit to using Customer Experience Mapping is that it naturally creates a *Customer Experience Employee Training Manual*. You can use this manual for employee training, along with integrating the operational activities required to support the experiences being delivered. This combination of both experience-based activities and operational-based activities gives a much broader and deeper perspective to every employee in the organization.

We discovered one other important aspect during the case studies. It had to do with employee-hiring criteria. We noted that the hiring criteria of an experience-based organization become significantly different from the hiring criteria of an operational-based organization. Different employee characteristics are more valuable to an experience-based organization than to an operational-based organization. This discovery about hiring criteria has far-reaching implications for restructuring and for responding to the challenges of being successful in the new customer economy. You want your personnel to reflect your organization's customer-focused philosophy and culture.

WE LEAVE YOU WITH SOME TIPS

Doing our research, working on the case studies, building the charts, and seeing a myriad of experience applications has provided us a rich education in the world of customer experiences. This education has provided us with an excellent blend of theory and practice, seeing how each contributes to customer delight.

As Harvey Mackay, author of *Swim with the Sharks*, says, "Ideas without actions are worthless." With that said, it's time for implementation!

Gary's Relationship Tips...

☐ Always err in favor of building your relationship, even if it means not accomplishing the specific Experience Response Point you set out to accomplish. Solid relationships allow for additional Experience Touch Points to happen, whereas failed relationships allow for the search of another customer. (And allow your customers to go looking for your competitors?)

☐ It's extremely important to convey to your customers that you respect them. However, conveyance of trust comes only through your consistent and repeated actions that garner those feelings of trust from the customer.

☐ The feeling side of a relationship is what directs the action side of a relationship. It's easy to get those reversed when looking at customers as "targets" or "marks", or any other term that fails to acknowledge their humanity and individual identity. Always be cautious in how you see and make your customers feel, because they have strong filters that are not always logical.

☐ When in doubt, always ask your customers and tell them why you're asking. It's okay to admit you don't know the answer to something. Such willingness on your part to inquire will continue to build trust.

☐ Give your employees the power to point out anything in your organization that doesn't have its roots based in delighting the customer. Your support of this one employee initiative will help dissolve all the entrenched political/operational strongholds, free up other employees with genuine customer delight talents, and create tremendous cost savings.

☐ It's never the customer's fault. You may have just selected the wrong customers or don't know yet what it takes to delight them. It's within your power to respond to both of these issues.

(continued)

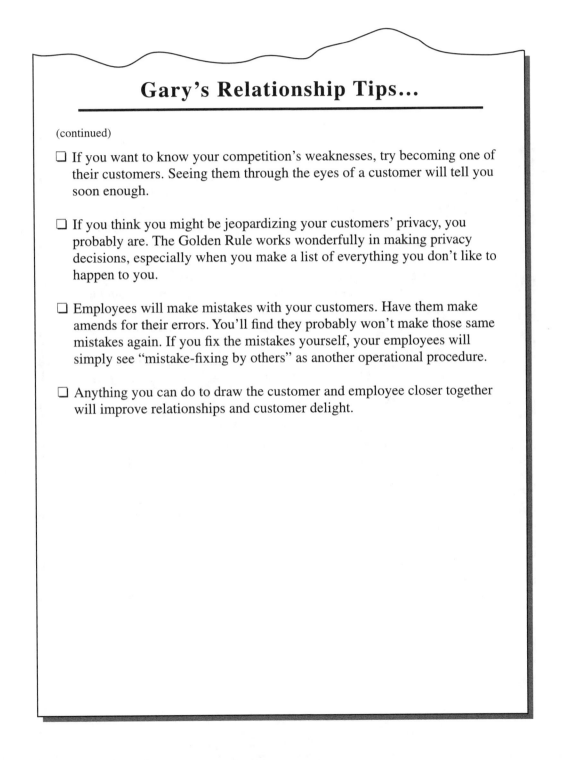

Gary's Relationship Tips...

(continued)

❑ If you want to know your competition's weaknesses, try becoming one of their customers. Seeing them through the eyes of a customer will tell you soon enough.

❑ If you think you might be jeopardizing your customers' privacy, you probably are. The Golden Rule works wonderfully in making privacy decisions, especially when you make a list of everything you don't like to happen to you.

❑ Employees will make mistakes with your customers. Have them make amends for their errors. You'll find they probably won't make those same mistakes again. If you fix the mistakes yourself, your employees will simply see "mistake-fixing by others" as another operational procedure.

❑ Anything you can do to draw the customer and employee closer together will improve relationships and customer delight.

Gary's ImplementationTips...

❑ I can't overemphasize the value of spending as much quality time as you need on the Initial Transaction Assessment. Getting the experience-based transactions separated from the operational-based transactions is extremely eye-opening. It sets the tone for everything else you do.

❑ Adopt the customer experience language in your organization. We've deliberately overemphasized the customer experience language to stress how important it is to talk in the customer's language. There's a huge difference between saying, "I had a satisfying experience" and saying, "I had a delightful experience."

❑ When building your vision, stay at the 40,000-foot level as long as you can. Visualize what a Totally Awesome Customer Experience should look and feel like. There's always time for the minutia, so don't get dragged down into it before you're ready. It will cause you to lose focus.

❑ Use both sides of your brain. Customer Experience Mapping is both a science and an art, and both are necessary to make it work effectively.

❑ Don't let people tell you they can do this all in their heads. Documentation is critical to making it work. When we say build a Customer Experience Map, we mean a literal map on paper. Here's the overriding rule: "If it isn't written, it doesn't exist." You'll thank me later on this one.

❑ Don't be afraid to use the "So What? Test" and use it often. It gets rid of the politics and game-playing quickly. It's great for the customer.

❑ Practice discerning Experience Touch Points. When you have an experience, quickly classify it as to which kind, category, and type it is. Doing so will help you to learn the best flow when it comes to designing and implementing your own.

Gary's ImplementationTips...

(continued)

❏ Have fun creating and delivering totally awesome Customer Experiences. Make sure you have the chance to observe experiences in action. Watch your customers to see how they respond. It will be quite rewarding.

❏ Ensure that the employees who touch the customers are empowered to delight them.

❏ Watch for signs of delight in both your customers and employees. It's a great sign of validation that you're on the right road.

❏ Never be afraid to walk in your customers' shoes!

Blaine's Tips...

❑ This is not customer satisfaction! It's customer delight!

❑ It's imperative that you do your Initial Transaction Assessment before determining your strategic direction. Otherwise, you'll fall victim to creating a strategy in a vacuum, barren of customer focus.

❑ Using Customer Experience Mapping to create the experiences you want for your customers actually feeds your operational and business processes—not the other way around.

❑ Customers are everything. Everything else only matters after your customers are delighted.

❑ Customer delight is a continuous process, not a checkbox on a project work plan you can check off and then move on to the next item.

❑ Commitment, commitment, commitment by everyone is vital. That includes the CEO and executive management team.

❑ Some people can't change. Let them leave and move on. Too much time can cost you too many customers and a whole lot of dollars.

❑ Speed wins! If you're first, you have a huge advantage. Consider Peter Drucker's remark: "Latecomers must be ten times better than what they replace."

❑ Have fun with creating and delivering Totally Awesome Customer Experiences, or it won't be fun for your customers.

❑ Be careful. Once you start thinking in the world of "experiences," you can't ever go back. You'll constantly be judging people and organizations in a whole new light.

Brent's Tips...

❑ Try to imagine what your customers' expectations are all the time. Then build your customer experience maps to meet them.

❑ You must be clever enough to build a series of Customer Experience Maps, each creating a delightful experience. They must then all be seamlessly connected to form a totally delightful, grand experience.

❑ Implementation is the difficult task. Turning your staff from being operational-based to experience-based is often frustrating and disheartening. However, if you start at the top and convince your people of its power and what it can do for them, it will begin filtering down through all of your employees. It definitely helps me think about the criteria on which I want to hire employees in the future.

❑ All managers want to focus on operations. They see their role as ensuring that all operational procedures are being followed. It gives them a feeling of security and they believe it makes their job easier. If this is how they measure their success, then they're successful. But if delighted customers are what you want, then they've failed. No customer cares about how well your business operations are working. The customer only cares about how important and delighted you make him or her feel. It doesn't really matter if all our silverware is sorted in all the right drawers.

❑ When listening to my employees talk about their jobs, I try to point out all the subjects they talk about that are operational in nature versus experiential in nature. I then explain to them that the customer doesn't see or care about the operational things. I try to encourage employees to talk about our customers' experiences and how we can help improve them, and then how operations need to support those experiences.

❑ Employees always look for ways to make their jobs easier. All of their focus is on operational procedures that make their job less difficult. If they spent as much time thinking about what the customer needs to make their experiences less difficult, everybody's job would be easier.

(continued)

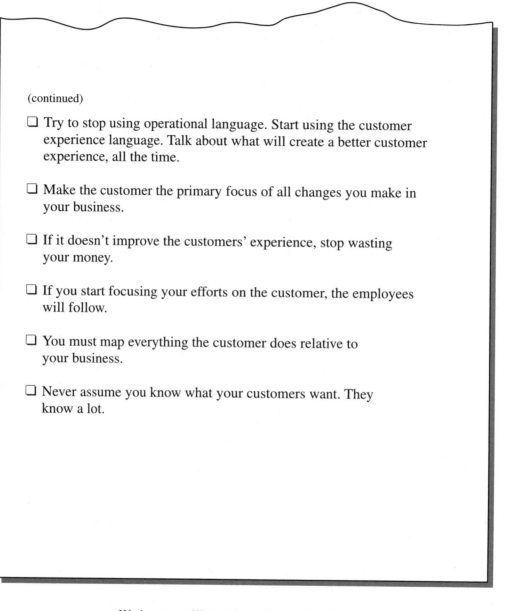

(continued)

❏ Try to stop using operational language. Start using the customer experience language. Talk about what will create a better customer experience, all the time.

❏ Make the customer the primary focus of all changes you make in your business.

❏ If it doesn't improve the customers' experience, stop wasting your money.

❏ If you start focusing your efforts on the customer, the employees will follow.

❏ You must map everything the customer does relative to your business.

❏ Never assume you know what your customers want. They know a lot.

We hope you'll use these tips and make a great start in your path to creating and delivering Totally Awesome Customer Experiences. We appreciate the opportunity to help you delight your customers.

One for the Road

*"Customers have taken control of our companies' destinies. Customers
are transforming our industries. And customers' loyalty – or lack thereof –
has become increasingly important to executives and investors alike."*

Patricia Seybold,
author of The Customer Revolution

Customer attitudes are changing. The day of the customer is upon us. We
need to pay attention to what people think, feel, and care about. Doing so
will open a whole new world for organizations that become experience-
based and really care about people.

We had no greater evidence of this fact than during the terrorist attacks of
September 11, 2001. Amidst all the tragedy, pain, suffering, and loss of life
and property, there emerged those miraculous moments that moved and
strengthened us all – simple stories of people caring, sharing, trusting, and
helping each other. It was overwhelming! This tragic event may have ushered in a new era of people realizing how dependent we all are on one another, and how vital a role trust plays in everything we do.

We wish we could gather everyone who reads this book into one giant hall.
Imagine the richness of all of those "experience experts" sharing their
knowledge, thoughts, and feelings on creating and delivering Totally
Awesome Experiences! It would be incredible.

Nearly every person to whom we mention the title of our book had responded, "Boy, the world can sure use a lot more of those out there."

Customer service continues to erode. Customer loyalty and brand equity are
at an all-time low. Customers are becoming less and less willing to just sit
back and accept whatever an organization chooses to sell. Customers are
demanding experiences that delight them – and they're willing to migrate
quickly to organizations that provide them those experiences and show them
they care. In return, those customers are willing to become passionate advocates. Customers want to feel good and build emotional trust bonds with
organizations they can trust and who respect their privacy.

Our Awesome Customer Challenge is creating and delivering Totally Awesome Customer Experiences that will stop merely satisfying customers and
start delighting them. It's time to don our artist smocks, load up our palettes

and begin painting a new picture in which customer loyalty and trust mean something, and customer-manipulative organizations are simply painted out of the picture. It's time to exhibit our new customer economy, where caring about each other goes both ways and is reflected in the deeper, richer relationships that form between customers and organizations.

The day has arrived for customers to join with customer-focused organizations in controlling and sharing experiences that build trust. It's a new customer frontier. We hope our insights, concepts, processes, and tools will help you leverage your courage, skills, and commitment to staying focused on your most valuable assets – your customers.

It's our vision that everyone who reads this book will be delighted and become a proactive, vocal advocate for creating and delivering Totally Awesome Customer Experiences. In fact, if you're reading this as an e-book, just click this link **http://www.customerexperiencesinc.com/ACC.html** and we'll send a copy of the Awesome Customer Challenge to any of your associates and friends on your behalf.

Thanks so much for sharing some of your precious time with us. We'd love to hear about your experience while reading this book, and what you did to begin your journey to meet the Awesome Customer Challenge. Please let us know at **http://www.customerexperiencesinc.com/myexperiences.html**. We'd also love to continually hear about your most memorable Totally Awesome Customer Experiences, and in turn share our knowledge with you.

Warmest regards,

Gary Millet

Blaine Millet

The Customer Experience Language

Audience Audit

A tool to help refine the profiles of selected audiences by demographics, psychographics, and feelings in creating effective and delightful Experience Touch Points.

Awesome Customer Challenge

To stop merely satisfying your customers and build a consistent and repeatable process to start delighting them. Delighting customers will fulfill the dream of creating a new customer-experience economy in which you can achieve customer loyalty, deepened customer relationships, stronger brand, and solid differentiation. Anything less will leave you vulnerable to your competitors.

Brand Erosion

The decrease in an organization's brand equity as a result of conflicting brand promises, deliveries, or both to a customer.

Brand Word Association

The attributes of a word or phrase that associates itself directly to the brand of an organization, whether negatively or positively.

Category of Experience Touch Point

This governs the source of content creation of an Experience Touch Point.

Combative Response

A spontaneous fight-or-flight reaction to an Experience Touch Point, causing the customer to either say nothing or criticize the organization openly, inevitably terminating the experience. That customer has become your opponent.

Customer Delight

Customer delight is the realization a customer has when stepping beyond being merely satisfied, to mentally and emotionally bonding with your organization and developing trust and passion in the process, because both physical and emotional expectations have been exceeded.

Customer Experience

The active participation of a customer in any event or activity initiated by an organization that elicits either positive or negative thoughts or emotions.

Customer Experience Language

A specific framework of language used inside your organization to describe the terms and measurements surrounding customer experiences. You use it to enhance your discussions, speed up your implementation, and make it easier for your employees to learn the process of creating and delivering Totally Awesome Customer Experiences.

Customer Experience Map

The strategic plan for identifying the Experience Touch Points that will lead to positive votes at Experience Voting Points, resulting in the accomplishment of the Experience Response Point – producing a consistent and predictable action from the customer, evoking positive memories and feelings that would be described as "delight." It is the fundamental building block of a Totally Awesome Customer Experience.

Customer Experience Map Pool

The entire collection of Customer Experience Maps required for a Totally Awesome Customer Experience

Customer Experience Mapping

The process of building a Customer Experience Map through selecting the specific audience, Experience Response Point, and Experience Touch Points; identifying the potential Experience Voting Points; and setting up a means to measure the results of the map's execution.

Customer Experience Vision

A vision focused on customer delight. It is prepared to deliver relevant offerings to your customers that fulfill their physical, emotional, and psychological needs beyond the point of making them merely satisfied.

Customer-Focused

Starting with the customers' needs and a genuine desire to create and deliver Totally Awesome Customer Experiences around the fulfillment of those needs.

Customer-Focused Reality

The consistent creation and delivery of Totally Awesome Customer Experiences for the purpose of delighting customers.

Customer Information Currency

The business currency where customer information is collected and used solely to deliver the organization's product and service offerings to the customer.

Customer Knowledge Currency

The business currency where an organization accumulates customer knowledge in order to create and deliver more tailored product and service offerings that have higher acceptance rates.

Customer Loyalty
The steadfast allegiance to an organization brought on by the creation of an emotional trust bond, with its strength coming with time and the experiences each customer has with the organization.

Customer-Manipulative
Starting with the products and services an organization has to offer, and then trying to build experiences around what they think it will take to get the customer to buy those products and services.

Customer Privacy
The right your customers have to be sure that you protect from unsanctioned intrusion any information they give you about their habits, thoughts, feelings, and lifestyles.

Customer Relationship Currency
The level of knowledge you have about your customers in which to conduct business with them.

Customer Response Rate
The percentage of your offers accepted by the audience to whom they were presented or intended.

Customer Satisfaction Continuum
The varying degrees of customer attitude towards their feeling of satisfaction when responding to certain "thought and feeling" attributes describing what a customer "feels, does, wants, and is."

Customer Trust Currency
The customer has formed an emotional trust bond with the organization so that the customer knows that the organization will use all the knowledge an organization has collected to consistently create and deliver Totally Awesome Customer Experiences.

Customer Vote
The vote cast by a customer during a Touch Point Experience as to whether to continue interacting with the organization.

Delight Vote
The vote cast at the end of a customer's experience that goes beyond mere satisfaction to build a customer's loyalty, emotional trust bond, and willingness to spread the "good word" about your organization to others.

Demographics
Information about your customers such as their age, height, weight, race, hair color, sex, family status (dad, mom, kids), income, education level, occupation, locality, and so forth.

Emotional Trust Bond

The bond in a relationship whose primary strength is derived from the knowledge and feelings of trust and security.

Experience-Based

An organization in which the operations, infrastructure, and resources are acquired and deployed to support the experiences and offerings that will delight their customers, form an emotional trust bond, and earn their loyalty.

Experience-Based Transaction

A transaction that contains some level of customer interactivity. These transactions govern customer product and service offerings and revenue production.

Experience Cost

Experience Costs are derived from all the costs of creating and delivering the Experience Touch Points that deliver your Totally Awesome Customer Experience.

Experience Lapse

A condition when an Experience Touch Point is executed so poorly that it triggers an Experience Voting Point.

Experience Noise

A condition when two or more Experience Touch Points contradict each other in a Customer Experience Map. The conflict may or may not trigger an Experience Voting Point. For example, your frequent flyer program treats a new passenger who flies 100,000 miles in the first year better than the frequent flyer who only flew 50,000 miles last year, but has flown over 3 million miles on your airline.

Experience Plan

The creation of plan to deliver a customer experience based on the appropriate assembly of Customer Experience Maps specific to the right customer audiences.

Experience Profit

The difference between your Experience Revenues and your Experience Costs.

Experience Response Point

Defines the desired response expectations or actions from a customer as a result of delivering the appropriate Experience Touch Points for a Customer Experience Map. The key measurement indicator as to the success or failure of that Customer Experience Map.

Experience Return on Investment

The result of incremental Experience Profit divided by Incremental Experience Cost.

Experience Revenue

Experience Revenues are derived from the products and services your organization sells to its customers as a result of accomplishing any of the Experience Response Points in a Totally Awesome Customer Experience.

Experience Token

A condition when the customer forgives the organization for an Experience Lapse.

Experience Touch Point

Any point of interaction between the customer and the organization. An Experience Touch Point is where the organization tactically delivers the experience to the customer.

Experience Variables

The variables that impact the effectiveness of accomplishing Experience Response Points in a Totally Awesome Customer Experience

Experience Voting Point

An area of potential conflict of Experience Touch Points with a customer's acceptability filters, triggering a conscious or unconscious vote to either stay engaged with or reject an Experience. These conflicts can be in the form of questions, doubts, or feelings of combativeness within your customer. An Experience Voting Point can come as a result of interacting with single or multiple Experience Touch Points.

Experience Voting Point Response Spectrum

It describes the potential responses that can take place when an Experience Touch Point is delivered to a customer. Underneath each point on the spectrum are four response aspects denoting "customer reaction," "what they do," "what they become" and "what they need."

Feeling Response

A feeling of anxiety where the customer expresses doubts regarding the value of continuing with an experience.

Feelings

Information pertaining to the emotive side of fulfilling a customer's needs.

Five-Step Process

The process of creating and delivering a Totally Awesome Customer Experiences, namely 1) Visualize the Experience, 2) Translate the Vision,

Build Customer Experience Maps, and Train Employees, 3) Assemble the Experience Plan, 4) Interact with the Customer, 5) Measure Customer Delight.

Initial Transaction Assessment
A tool for identifying all of the organization's transactions in relationship to their value to the customer and the organization.

Kind of Experience Touch Point
This governs the delivery of an Experience Touch Point

Map Gap
The "void" between two Customer Experience Maps in a Totally Awesome Customer Experience where the customer experience is not contiguous.

Operational-Based Transaction
A transaction that supports experience-based transactions. It does not contain any direct customer interactivity. Its purpose is to internally perform work to provide support for delivering goods and services to the your customers, both internal and external. Operational transactions represent cost to your organization.

Operational-Based
An organization is in which the operations, infrastructure, and resources are acquired and deployed to support the financial and operational objectives of the organization. Their belief is that customers will become satisfied through the continuous improvement of their operational efficiencies.

Psychographics
Information pertaining to the pattern of behavior or lifestyle of a customer such as "how you recreate," "how you shop," "how you dress," "how you take care of yourself," "how you handle your spiritual needs," "what your sexual practices are," and so forth.

"So What? Test"
A powerful tool to help Experience Touch Point artists stay focused on the real purpose behind their Experience Touch Points.

Success Measurement Standard
A measurement standard in which a Customer Experience Map can be evaluated.

Thinking Response
A state where the customer expresses the need for further information to assess the value of continuing with an experience.

Totally Awesome Customer Experience
The successful accomplishment of Experience Response Points (the desired response expectations from the customer) from one or more Customer Experience Maps; it evokes desired positive actions, thoughts, and feelings by the customer toward the organization that can only be characterized as "delight."

Touch Point Palette
Describes the selection of possible Experience Touch Points that can be used to help accomplish an Experience Response Point. The palette exhibits the combined array of Experience Touch Points made from Kind, Category, and Type.

Touch Point Ten
This is a tool containing a checklist of ten excellent rules for creating effective and valuable Experience Touch Points.

Trust
A state where two or more people engage in a transaction or experience whereby outcomes are highly likely and very predictable. Let us also make the point that trust is not gained by any one-time event.

Trustability
The reliability, dependability, and competence of the offers and experiences themselves.

Trustworthiness
Sincerity and honesty in the nature of the organization's offers and experiences themselves.

Type of Experience Touch Point
This governs the acceptability of an Experience Touch Point.

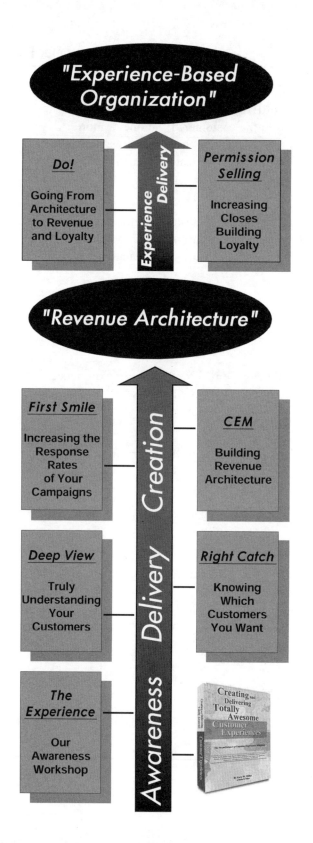

THE PATH TO SUCCESS

CEI offers a series of powerful products to help build effective Revenue Architectures. Our full range of products span from Awareness to Experience Delivery in helping you build and execute your Revenue Architecture.

Awareness

Creating and Delivering Totally Awesome Customer Experiences

Our book describes the concepts, processes and tools to build the totally awesome customer experiences—the cornerstone for all effective revenue architectures.

The Experience™

This workshop is an energizing and motivational way to learn how customer experiences lead directly to increasing revenues and building customer loyalty through a solid Revenue Architecture.

Discovery

Deep View™

Knowing what your customers truly think and feel provides the necessary foundation and "experiential starting point" to building a successful Revenue Architecture and a catalyst for positive, lasting change.

Right Catch™

Knowing the customers you should be investing your resources to acquire, retain and motivate is golden...knowing your "Super Catch" customers from your "Throwbacks," provides the "financial starting point" in a successful revenue architecture.

Creation

First Smile™

First Smile is a "slice" of revenue architecture for any company wanting to increase customer response rates in their sales and marketing campaigns. First Smile is also a perfect Pilot to see exactly how the entire Customer Experience Mapping process brings powerful revenue and loyalty results.

CEM™

CEM is the full implementation of the art and science of building a complete revenue architecture throughout an organization. CEM solidifies, in very quantifiable and experience-based terms all the elements within a revenue architecture.

Experience Delivery

Permission Selling™

Your Close Ratio is king! Permission Selling teaches our book's principles and techniques of Acceptability, Relevance, and Value in helping sales professionals guide a prospect from first contact to final close.

Do!™

"We don't just pontificate and propose, we do!" CEI can help in the creation and delivery of the experiences you want to provide your customers...because no one knows better than us what needs to be achieved for your Revenue Architecture to be successful – and what you need to become an experience-based organization.

For further information on Gary Millet's activities and CEI services either drop him an email or visit the CEI website at gmillet@ceinc.info and customerexperiencesinc.com

Our Address is: Customer Experiences Inc
                  7810 S. Prospector Dr.
                  Salt Lake City, Utah, USA
                  84121
                  Tel: 1.801.943.7342
                  Fax: 1.801.943.6914

A Book Order Form in on the last page of the book

Share the Experience of this Book with Others...

To order copies of the Book:

• Visit our website:
  www.customerexperiencesinc.com

• Fax or Mail us the order form below:

ORDER FORM

Yes, please send me _____ copies of the book *Creating and Delivering...Totally Awesome Customer Experiences* at $24.95 USD/ $38.95 Can. for each copy. Postage & handling: US/Can. $4.95 for one book, $1.50 for each add'l book; Int'l $8.95 for one book and $2.50 for each add'l book. We accept Visa, MC, AMEX, checks and money orders. No Cash/COD. Mail or Fax your orders to:

Customer Experiences Inc.
7810 S. Prospector Drive
Salt Lake City, UT, 84121 USA
Fax #: 1.801.943.6914

Bill my
credit card #_____
___Visa ___MC ___AMEX
Signature: _____

Ship to:
Name   _____
Phone # _____
Address _____
         _____
City   _____State _____ ZIP_____

Book Total $_____

Sales Tax (6.6%)* $_____

Postage & Handling $_____

Total Order Amount $_____

* Utah Residents Only

Please allow 2-4 weeks delivery. Can/Int'l orders please allow 5-6 weeks.
This offer is subject to change without notice.

Index